CORE FOCUS

GRADE 6

TEST PRACTICE
for Common Core

Christine R. Gray, M.Ed.

and

Carrie Meyers-Herron, M.S.

BARRON'S

About the Authors

Christine Gray has been a middle school English teacher in Revere, Massachusetts, for ten years. She is passionate about providing students access to relevant, high-interest novels. Currently pursuing a Certificate of Advanced Graduate Studies as a Reading Specialist, she has also presented at the 2013 National Council of Teachers of English conference. Christine is a Great Schools Partnership trained Professional Learning Group facilitator and organizes PLG meetings for her department colleagues. She has been trained in Universal Design for Learning (UDL) by the Center for Applied Special Technology (CAST), attended the 2014 UDL Summer Institute at the Harvard Graduate School of Education, and regularly presents professional development workshops for colleagues.

Carrie Meyers-Herron has been teaching math to students from kindergarten through college for more than 18 years. Through most of her career, Carrie has excited and educated middle-level adolescents by integrating science and other real-life applications into her math classes. She has also worked with NASA on writing curriculum and as an education specialist for the New York State Education Department on high school Regents exams. Carrie has also presented at state conferences to provide quality professional development to other educators on how to integrate the Common Core Standards into other content areas.

Copyright © 2015 by Barron's Educational Series, Inc.

All rights reserved.
No part of this publication may be reproduced or distributed in any form or by any means without the written permission of the copyright owner.

All inquiries should be addressed to:
Barron's Educational Series, Inc.
250 Wireless Boulevard
Hauppauge, New York 11788
www.barronseduc.com

ISBN: 978-1-4380-0592-8

Library of Congress Control Number: 2014950556

Manufactured by: B11R11
Date of Manufacture: March 2015

PRINTED IN THE UNITED STATES OF AMERICA
9 8 7 6 5 4 3 2

CONTENTS

ENGLISH LANGUAGE ARTS

Language

Reading: Literature

Reading: Informational Text

Writing

MATH

Ratios and Proportional Relationships

Expressions and Equations

The Number System

Geometry

Statistics and Probability

NOTE TO PARENTS AND EDUCATORS

About Barron's Common Core Focus Workbooks

Barron's recognizes the urgent need to create products to help students navigate the Common Core State Standards being implemented in schools across America. To meet this need, we have created these grade-specific workbooks that bring the Common Core standards to life and ensure that students are prepared for these recently implemented national assessments and expectations in learning. It is our hope that students can work through these books either independently or with the guidance of a parent or teacher.

Barron's Core Focus workbooks are meant to supplement the Common Core teaching that students are receiving in their classroom or other learning environment. These workbooks, all created by dedicated educators, provide specific practice on the Common Core standards through a variety of exercises and question types, including multiple-choice, short-answer, and extended-response. The questions are organized to build on each other, increasing student understanding from one standard to the next, one step at a time, and they challenge students to apply the standards in different formats. The English Language Arts (ELA) and Math sections of the books each end with a review test—a great way to sum up what the student has learned and reviewed from the exercises throughout.

What Is Common Core?

"The standards are designed to be robust and relevant to the real world, reflecting the knowledge and skills that our young people need for success in college and careers."

(2012 Common Core State Standards Initiative)

Simply put, the Common Core is a series of standards that spells out exactly what students are expected to learn in English Language Arts and Mathematics throughout their years in school. These standards are fairly consistent across all grades and are designed so that students, teachers, and parents can understand what students should be learning and achieving at each grade level. Standards are organized to provide a clear understanding of the core concepts and procedures that students should master at each step of the way through school.

Unlike previous standards that were created by individual states, the Common Core is meant to be consistent throughout the country, providing all students with an equal and fair opportunity to learn ELA and Math. These Standards are also designed to teach students how to apply this knowledge to their everyday lives and experiences.

By sharing the same standards, states can more accurately gauge and compare students' progress and the quality of education received. The ultimate goal of the Common Core is to ensure that all students, no matter which state or part of the country they are from, will be equally ready and prepared for college and the workforce.

What Is a Standard?

A standard is a skill that should be learned by a student. Standards are organized by *domains*, which are larger groupings of related standards. For instance, in Grade 6 Math, there are five domains: "Ratios and Proportional Relationships," "The Number System," "Expressions and Equations," "Statistics and Probability," and "Geometry."

Under the domain "Statistics and Probability," there are five individual standards which highlight a specific skill or understanding that a student should gain. One standard, **6.SP.B.5**, has 4 sub-standards that range from understanding how to report the number of observations in data sets to calculating mean absolute deviation.

ENGLISH LANGUAGE ARTS

English Language Arts standards are separated into different strands. The grades 6–8 standards are comprehensive and are divided into the following areas: Reading, Writing, Speaking and Listening, and Language. The Common Core has designated separate reading standards for both fiction and nonfiction texts. These standards are identified as Reading: Literature and Reading: Informational Text. Most important, the reading standards emphasize engaging all students in the reading process. To meet the standards, students are expected to read multiple forms of texts, which will provide deeper literary experiences for all students. The Common Core also emphasizes the importance of text complexity. "Through extensive reading of stories, dramas, poems, and myths from diverse cultures and different time periods, students gain literary and cultural knowledge as well as familiarity with various text structures and elements." (2012 Common Core State Standards Initiative)

Each of the grades 6–8 strands is arranged within a College and Career Readiness Anchor Standard. The Anchor Standards are the overarching goals of a K–12 curriculum. These standards remain constant in all grades. Each grade level's strands are built as scaffolds in order to achieve "official" College and Career Readiness Anchor Standards by the end of the twelfth grade. The College and Career Readiness Anchor Standards for Reading Literature and Informational Text focus on identifying key ideas and details, craft and structure, and the integration of knowledge and ideas. To meet the Common Core reading standards, students are expected to read, respond to, and interact with an array of text types of varying complexities. Text types will consist of print and non-print texts, including images and videos. The College and Career Readiness Anchor Standards for Writing focus on text types and purposes, production and distribution of writing, and research to build and present knowledge. To meet the Common Core writing standards, students are expected to write persuasive, narrative, and informational text. The College and Career Readiness Anchor Standards for Speaking and Listening focus on comprehension, collaboration, and presentation of knowledge and ideas. The speaking and listening standards focus heavily on students' ability to actively participate in groups, engage with others, and present academic information in multiple settings. The College and Career Readiness Anchor Standards for Language focus on the conventions of standard English, vocabulary acquisition, and knowledge of language.

The Common Core standards are also designed to help students create digital literature and use technology to communicate ideas and knowledge. The ELA standards are a vision of what it means to be literate in the twenty-first century. These standards foster imperative learning experiences for the twenty-first century learner. "The skills and knowledge captured in the ELA/literacy standards are designed to prepare students for life outside the classroom. They include critical-thinking skills and the ability to closely and attentively read texts in a way that will help them understand and enjoy complex works of literature." (2012 Common Core Initiative)

MATH

The Common Core mathematics standards were developed as a connected progression of learning throughout grades K–12. Ideally, this will enable teachers to close achievement gaps and give students the foundational skills necessary to continue in their learning. The Common Core provides teachers with an opportunity to build a deep and rich understanding of mathematical concepts. Instruction of Common Core mathematics standards encompasses the Mathematical Practices as well. These practices include skills that math students in every grade are expected to master. The Mathematical Practices bring rigor and rich learning opportunities to the classroom.

In grade 6, students focus on how ratio and rates relate to whole-number multiplication and division and to fractions. New to students will be the system of rational numbers, which includes negative numbers, and they will further their algebraic skills by writing, interpreting, and using expressions and equations. They will also develop an understanding of statistics.

The Common Core standards are related across grade levels as well as across the domains. For example, Geometry standards share a number of common relationships with the Operations and Algebra standards. This connectedness helps students prepare for the real world—remember, we don't use just one skill to balance our checkbook or determine the amount of paint for a room in our home. We have to apply a variety of skills every day, and a goal of the Common Core math standards is to help prepare students for this real-life use of math. The Common Core also supports mathematical understanding of concepts that are developmentally appropriate for students. These standards allow students to build strong number sense in the early grades as they learn to count, to order numbers, and to compare numbers to help them think about numbers flexibly and to understand the relationships between numbers as they move into the higher grades.

This workbook focuses on the mathematical practices that help students develop a deeper mathematical thinking process. The practices include making sense of problems and persevering in solving them, reasoning abstractly and quantitatively, constructing viable arguments, and critiquing the reasoning of others. Students also will focus on modeling with mathematics, using appropriate tools, attending to precision, making use of structure, and looking for repeated reasoning.

HOW TO USE THIS BOOK

This test practice workbook is organized by standard—one step at a time—in the order students will likely see the concepts in the classroom or other learning environment. Each standard is organized in an easy-to-navigate spread(s), providing exposure to the Common Core in the simplest way possible.

In this book, students will be able to build skills in multiple formats by answering multiple-choice, short-answer, and extended-response questions. Answers and explanations are included at the end of each section so students, parents, and teachers can easily assess the student's response. These explanations are an important part of the learning process, as they provide information on the understanding needed to answer each question, common misconceptions students might have, and an explanation of how students might best approach and respond to the question. These explanations will help students not only to check the accuracy of their responses but also to learn how they can improve their responses. Students using Barron's Core Focus workbooks will practice each of the specific content standards as they learn them, and also have the opportunity to review *all* of the concepts in Math or English Language Arts through the cumulative assessments.

> A complete listing of all the English Language Arts and Math Common Core Standards can be found at the end of this book in Appendices A and B.

In addition to the practice spreads covering specific standards, each section ends with a comprehensive practice test that allows students to monitor their general progress in either English Language Arts or Math. Answers and explanations provide additional guidance and instruction.

FEATURES AND BENEFITS

Barron's Core Focus workbooks provide educators, parents, and students with an opportunity to enhance their knowledge and practice grade-level expectations within the Common Core English Language Arts and Math standards. Each workbook in this series provides questions that specifically correlate to each standard. Every answer explanation provides helpful insight into a student's understanding, identifying common misconceptions, and then providing multiple strategies. The books also provide a cumulative assessment for each content area in Math and English Language Arts. Throughout the books, there are "TIP" boxes that contain a variety of information and expose students to vocabulary, tips, and strategies.

- Parents can use this book to encourage learning at home. This book can be used as guided practice or extra exposure to concepts students may be struggling to master in school.

- Educators can use the workbooks in their classrooms to identify how to assess each standard. These books give teachers insight into what students should be able to do independently in order to master the standard. The detailed answer explanations provide opportunities for teachers to recognize misconceptions students may have about specific standards and how to successfully approach questions applicable to each standard.

- Students can use these workbooks at home to build their knowledge of English Language Arts and Math content. They can practice the content they have learned, are learning, or are going to learn. The workbooks can help prepare students for what's to come and/or as remedial practice for concepts they find challenging. The explanations in the books are extremely valuable to students as they work independently, increasing their awareness of concepts and improving their confidence as they work through each question.

The benefits that **Barron's Core Focus** workbooks will provide students, parents, and educators are endless as the Common Core is implemented in schools across America.

> **Common Core State Standards Initiative**
> *http://www.corestandards.org/*
>
> **PARCC**
> *http://www.parcconline.org/*
>
> **Smarter Balance Assessment Consortium**
> *www.smarterbalanced.org*

ENGLISH LANGUAGE ARTS

The English Language Arts Standards are separated into five strands. The grades 6 through 8 standards are comprehensive and divided into the following areas: Reading: Literature, Reading: Informational Text, Writing, Language, and Speaking and Listening. The standards from grades 6 through 8 are similar and gradually build on the foundation set by the previous grade's work. In this section, students will practice skills covering a variety of standards. Each section covers a specific standard covered in grade 6 and provides the student with practice through multiple-choice, short answer, and longer written pieces.

USING PRONOUNS APPROPRIATELY

Directions: Circle the appropriate pronoun to be used in each sentence. Read each sentence aloud to help you determine the correct pronoun.

1. Myra hoped the sincerity of the apology would convince Jonathan to finally forgive (she/her).

> **Who** vs. **Whom**. In cases where you would use **he or she** use **who**. In cases where you would use **him or her** use **whom**.

2. After months of considering all options, Mark's mother finally said (he/him) must decide which high school (he/him) will attend in the fall.

3. (Who/Whom) should Jenna ask about registering for swimming lessons at the youth center?

4. The students decided that (they/them) should be able to use (its/their) lockers in between each class to avoid carrying heavy backpacks.

5. Please give (he/him) your number so that (he/him) may be in contact with you.

Directions: Rewrite the following sentences, replacing the underlined words with the appropriate pronoun.

6. When Marie's cell phone suddenly stopped working after two weeks, <u>Marie</u> took the phone to the store and asked <u>the store employees</u> for help.

    _____

    _____

    _____

7. Martin and Julie froze in fear as the fur on top of Remy's head bristled as <u>Remy</u> barked furiously, warning the trespassers that the yard was <u>Remy's yard</u> not <u>Martin and Julie's yard</u>.

    _____

    _____

    _____

8. Ms. McLaughlin informed the incoming students that <u>kids</u> are allowed to borrow books from <u>Ms. McLaughlin's</u> office at any time, but asked that students please return <u>the books</u> when finished.

    _____

    _____

    _____

(Answers are on page 91.)

GRAMMAR CONVENTIONS

L.6.1 Demonstrate command of the conventions of standard English grammar and usage when writing or speaking.

L.6.1.D Recognize and correct vague pronouns (i.e., with unclear or ambiguous antecedents).

L.6.1.E Recognize variations from standard English in their own and other's writing and speaking, and identify and use strategies to improve expression in conventional language.

Directions: Read the sentences below. Rewrite each sentence(s) to create a *clear* antecedent. Circle the pronoun and underline the antecedent to ensure clarity.

1. Simone's mother is always talking to her in the car and she becomes frustrated when she doesn't listen!

   _____

2. Little League tryouts take place this Saturday morning, so David's father said he should be at the field first thing in the morning.

   _____

3. Mike and his brother John went camping together, and he became extremely angry when his GPS broke.

   _____

Directions: Proofread a letter your friend is writing to a local politician. Underline the sentences that need corrections and write your corrections above the sentence. Explain your corrections.

April 3, 2015

Dear State Representative Burke,

My name is Jennifer and I attend Apple Valley Middle School. The students at my school is worried about our music department. We were told their may not be enough money left in the budget to maintain our current music courses. Eliminating music class would be a terrible loss. We are writing to u to let u know how important music education is to our school careers. Please help us keep music alive?

Sincerely,

Jennifer Walsh

4. **Explanation:** _____

    _____

5. **Explanation:** _____

    _____

6. **Explanation:** _____

    _____

7. **Explanation:** _____

    _____

(Answers are on page 91.)

COMMAS, DASHES, AND PARENTHESES

> **L.6.2** Demonstrate command of the conventions of standard English capitalization, punctuation, and spelling in writing.
> **L.6.2.A** Use punctuation (commas, parentheses, dashes) to set off nonrestrictive/parenthetical elements.
> **L.6.2.B** Spell correctly.

Directions: Read the following sentences. Add commas where necessary.

1. Baseball like other team sports requires communication and camaraderie among teammates for success.

> **Appositive Phrases** offer more description about a noun and must be set off by commas.

2. Isaac Asimov a well-known science fiction writer began his career by submitting funny stories to magazines.

3. Choose the sentence that shows correct use of commas.
   Ⓐ Dr. Madden winner of the, Dental Excellence, award has been my dentist for years.
   Ⓑ Dr. Madden, winner of the Dental Excellence award has been my dentist for years.
   Ⓒ Dr. Madden, winner of the Dental Excellence award, has been my dentist for years.
   Ⓓ Dr. Madden, winner, of the Dental Excellence award has been my dentist for years.

Directions: Read the following sentences and place a dash (or dashes) where necessary.

Example: When he slipped and fell in the cafeteria, Jeff was lucky he only wounded one thing—his pride.

4. In preparation for her son's birthday party, Alice picked up the favors, the balloons, the ice cream, and a gift, only to realize she forgot the most important thing the cake.

5. Zeus managed to save his siblings who had been swallowed by their own father and to defeat Cronus and the Titans.

6. Select the sentence that shows correct use of parentheses.
    Ⓐ Add applesauce butter alternative to the brownie mix to create a (lower fat treat).
    Ⓑ Add applesauce butter (alternative to the brownie mix) to create a lower fat treat.
    Ⓒ Add applesauce butter alternative to the (brownie) mix to create a lower fat treat.
    Ⓓ Add applesauce (butter alternative) to the brownie mix to create a lower fat treat.

Directions: Complete each sentence by filling in the accurately spelled word.

7. After moving away to college, Jonathan loved to _____ mail from his family
    Ⓐ recieve
    Ⓑ receeve
    Ⓒ receive

8. Of all the _____ Jimmy has had over the years, Coach Murphy is by far the most inspiring.
    Ⓐ coach's
    Ⓑ coaches
    Ⓒ coachs

(Answers are on page 92.)

SENTENCE VARIETY AND CONSISTENCY IN TONE

L.6.3 Use knowledge of language and its conventions when writing, speaking, reading, or listening.
L.6.3.A Vary sentence patterns for meaning, reader/listener interest, and style.
L.6.3.B Maintain consistency in style and tone.

Directions: Rewrite these sentences to include more variety in sentence structure.

1. We went to a baseball game on Saturday afternoon. We went to watch my cousin Brian and our friend Dave. We had a good time but their team lost.

   _____

   _____

   _____

2. Music is important to a lot of people. It can help relax some people. It can also make people feel excited or happy. Music can stir up memories. Many people like to dance when a favorite song comes on. Some people sing, too.

   _____

   _____

   _____

> Audience plays a big role in maintaining consistency in your style and tone. Always remember to whom you are writing and the purpose of your writing.

3. Due to the risk of getting sunburned, the parents asked the girls to take a break in the shade of their umbrella before swimming in the ocean. After they had rested for a little while, the girls raced down to the water's edge. Because the baby was napping, the mom stayed to watch him.

   _____

   _____

   _____

Directions: Read each example sentence below. Circle the letter of the sentence that maintains the same style and tone of the example sentence.

4. *Letting their children use the Internet can be a frightening experience for some parents because of all the online predators who exist.*
   - Ⓐ Online predators can harm people, especially children, which makes parents guarded when it comes to Internet usage.
   - Ⓑ The Internet is a wicked scary place because so many sickos are out to get you.
   - Ⓒ Parents must restrict their children from using the Internet for any reason whatsoever because they will be kidnapped.
   - Ⓓ Children are very irresponsible when using the Internet.

5. *I have no idea what you are talking about.*
   - Ⓐ You're like the hardest person to understand!
   - Ⓑ I am utterly baffled by the meaning of her comments.
   - Ⓒ I really don't understand what you are saying.
   - Ⓓ What is going on?

6. *Due to budgetary cutbacks, the library will be closing one hour earlier each day. Sorry for the inconvenience.*
   - Ⓐ The library isn't open as late as it used to be. Too bad—we don't have the money.
   - Ⓑ Accept our apologies, but the library will be reducing its hours for financial reasons.
   - Ⓒ Sorry, but it ran out of cash, so the library can't stay open for the normal hours.
   - Ⓓ Come back during regular library hours.

(Answers are on page 92.)

DEFINING VOCABULARY
IN CONTEXT

L.6.4 Demonstrate or clarify the meaning of unknown and multiple-meaning words and phrases based on grade 6 reading and content, choosing flexibly from a range of strategies.

L.6.4.A Use context (e.g., the overall meaning of a sentence or paragraph; a word's position or function) as a clue to the meaning of a word or phrase.

L.6.4.B Use common, grade-appropriate Greek or Latin affixes and roots as clues to the meaning of a word (e.g., audience, auditory, audible).

Directions: Determine the meaning of the root word provided. Read the following sentences paying close attention to the underlined word.

1. Margaret's <u>benevolent</u> nature is evident in all the work she does with her church and the local soup kitchen. <u>Benevolent</u> most likely means
   - (A) Unfriendly
   - (B) Silly
   - (C) Kind
   - (D) Violent

   > When answering vocabulary multiple-choice questions, it is helpful to determine whether the word seems negative or positive so you can eliminate choices with different connotations.

2. Judge Whitman convicted the criminal to life in prison for his unspeakable crimes and <u>malicious</u> behavior. <u>Malicious</u> most likely means
   - (A) Kind
   - (B) Cruel
   - (C) Helpful
   - (D) Sad

Directions: Select the best definition for the underlined words. Underline the context clues (words or phrases) that helped you determine the word's meaning.

3. Peter, a retired professional football player in top physical condition, had not yet become accustomed to his <u>feeble</u> and age-ridden body. <u>Feeble</u> most likely means
   - (A) Strong
   - (B) Unhappy
   - (C) Overweight
   - (D) Weak

4. After his terrible ordeal with the wild and aggressive elephant, the zookeeper was happy to receive a new elephant that seemed much more <u>docile</u>. <u>Docile</u> most likely means
   - (A) Wild
   - (B) Obedient
   - (C) Cute
   - (D) Angry

5. Despite the salesman's expensive suit, polite manners, and soft spoken speech, I had a gut feeling that behind his seemingly trusting smile, he was **deceiving** me about his product's quality. List two possible synonyms for **deceiving**:

    1. _____

    2. _____

6. Danny, a once fun-loving and carefree teenager, has never recovered from the **anguish** of surviving the car crash that left him paralyzed. List two possible synonyms for **anguish**:

    1. _____

    2. _____

(Answers are on page 93.)

INTERPRETING FIGURES OF SPEECH

L.6.5 Demonstrate understanding of figurative language, word relationships, and nuances in word meanings.

L.6.5.A Interpret figures of speech in context.

L.6.5.B Use the relationships between particular words to better understand each of the words.

L.6.5.C Distinguish among the connotations (associations) of words with similar denotations (definitions).

Directions: Read each sentence to determine the figure of speech of the underlined phrase. Explain the meaning of the figure of speech.

Figurative Language Options
Idiom   Simile   Metaphor   Hyperbole   Personification

1. David's <u>confidence slipped out the backdoor</u> the minute he stepped on stage to give his speech.

    _____

    _____

2. Nichole had tried to stop eating junk food late at night but she couldn't seem to <u>get the monkey off her back</u>.

    _____

    _____

3. No matter the situation, time and time again, Diana has proven that <u>she is her sister's rock</u>.

    _____

    _____

4. The <u>clouds began to weep</u> down onto the mourners gathered at the cemetery.

    _____

    _____

> **Similes** and **metaphors** both show comparisons between two things, but **similes** use the words **like** or **as** in their comparisons and metaphors do not.

Directions: Complete each analogy below to show how the words are related or connected.

5. Chapter: Novel: :Scene: _____
   - Ⓐ Clip
   - Ⓑ Film
   - Ⓒ Song
   - Ⓓ Actor

6. Influenza: Disease: :Jazz: _____
   - Ⓐ Trumpets
   - Ⓑ Blues
   - Ⓒ Music
   - Ⓓ Excited

7. Organize the synonyms from *least intense* to *most intense* in connotation.

Gorgeous	Pretty	Attractive

1. _____   **Less Intense**

2. _____   ↓

3. _____   **More Intense**

8. Organize the synonyms from *least intense* to *most intense* in connotation.

Indifferent	Hostile	Unfriendly

1. _____   **Less Intense**

2. _____   ↓

3. _____   **More Intense**

(Answers are on page 93.)

CITING TEXTUAL EVIDENCE IN LITERATURE

RL.6.1 Cite textual evidence to support analysis of what the text says explicitly as well as inferences drawn from the text.

Directions: Look closely at the image.

1. Which of the following is an inference you might draw from this image?
    Ⓐ The woman is wearing running sneakers.
    Ⓑ There are no other runners on the road.
    Ⓒ The woman is dedicated to staying healthy.
    Ⓓ The weather is beautiful.

Evidence: Circle two details from the picture to support the inference you selected.

Directions: Read the following excerpt from *Firegirl* by Tony Abbott.

1   Jeff hadn't been on the bus that morning, but he was already sitting in his seat next to me at the head of row two.

2   He didn't say anything when I said "Hey." He just sat there quietly and chewed his fingernails, which he did a lot, without thinking. I guessed his mother had driven him because he missed the bus. She probably wasn't happy about it and so they probably had a fight. Jeff seemed to get mad a lot more since his father went away. Usually, I just left him alone, and pretty soon he'd be okay.

3   Right now his head was bent to the side, and he was turning his fingertips in his teeth. His tie was loose around his neck, and his top shirt button was undone. I remember thinking that his mother must have washed his shirt over the weekend, or it was an extra one because there were no spots on it. Maybe they had a fight about a shirt, too.

4   His legs dangled out into the teacher's area at the front of the classroom. Mrs. Tracy had asked him a couple of times already that year to reel his legs back in under his desk. He was stretching them out when she came in just then.

5   "Scoot your legs in, Jeff. Your slouching will curve your spine," she said. "You'll be a stooped-over old man by the time you're thirty."

6   She walked past and set down a pile of papers on the middle of her desk.

7   "Thirty *is* an old man!" said Jeff, taking his fingers out of his teeth and half looking around and laughing.

8   I snickered when I saw him joking. Maybe he was okay again.

2. Choose the quote that best supports the following statement:

The narrator is a good friend.

Ⓐ   "….mad a lot more since his father went away."
Ⓑ   "I remember thinking that his mother must have washed his shirt…"
Ⓒ   "…I just left him alone, and pretty soon he'd be okay."
Ⓓ   "I snickered when I saw him joking."

3. Which stereotypical role do you think Jeff plays in the classroom?

- The jock (athlete)
- The bookworm
- The class clown

Use **textual evidence** to support your choice.

_____

_____

(Answers are on page 94.)

FINDING THE
CENTRAL IDEA AND THEME

RL.6.2 Determine a theme or central idea of a text and how it is conveyed through particular details; provide a summary of the text distinct from personal opinions or judgment.

Directions: Read this excerpt from Mark Twain's *The Adventures of Tom Sawyer.*

1   Saturday morning was come, and all the summer world was bright and fresh, and brimming with life. There was a song in every heart; and if the heart was young the music issued at the lips. There was cheer in every face and a spring in every step. The locust-trees were in bloom and the fragrance of the blossoms filled the air. Cardiff Hill, beyond the village and above it, was green with vegetation and it lay just far enough away to seem a Delectable Land, dreamy, reposeful, and inviting.

2   Tom appeared on the sidewalk with a bucket of whitewash and a long-handled brush. He surveyed the fence, and all gladness left him and a deep melancholy settled down upon his spirit. Thirty yards of board fence nine feet high. Life to him seemed hollow, and existence but a burden. Sighing, he dipped his brush and passed it along the topmost plank; repeated the operation; did it again; compared the insignificant whitewashed streak with the far-reaching continent of unwhitewashed fence, and sat down on a tree-box discouraged. Jim came skipping out at the gate with a tin pail, and singing Buffalo Gals. Bringing water from the town pump had always been hateful work in Tom's eyes, before, but now it did not strike him so. He remembered that there was company at the pump.

1. Which of the following best summarizes **paragraph 1**?
   Ⓐ Saturdays are the best days to sing songs out in nature.
   Ⓑ Everyone is happy in the summer time.
   Ⓒ It was a nice Saturday morning and everyone and everything
       appeared happy.
   Ⓓ There were a lot of flowers blooming.

2. Choose two pieces of evidence from **paragraph 1** to support your summary.

   1. _____

   2. _____

3. Write a one sentence summary of **paragraph 2** (no more than 10 words).

   _____

   _____

4. Choose two pieces of evidence from **paragraph 2** that support your summary.

   1. _____

   2. _____

5. How does Jim's appearance at the end of **paragraph 2** contribute to the paragraph's
   central idea?
   Ⓐ Tom is waiting for Jim to return with the water before he can paint.
   Ⓑ Tom thinks Jim has a better chore to do than he has.
   Ⓒ Jim is supposed to help Tom but was called to go get water instead.
   Ⓓ Tom is angry that Jim has such a terrible chore to do as well.

(Answers are on page 94.)

PLOT AND CHARACTER DEVELOPMENT

RL.6.3 Describe how a particular story's or drama's plot unfolds in a series of episodes as well as how the characters respond or change as the plot moves toward a resolution.

Directions: Read the following excerpt from *Esperanza Rising* by Pam Munoz Ryan.

1   Since Miguel was a young boy, Papa had taken him to parts of the property that even Esperanza and Mama had never seen.

2   When she was younger, Esperanza used to complain, "Why does he always get to go and not me?"

3   Papa would say, "Because he knows how to fix things and he is learning his job."

4   Miguel would look at her and before riding off with Papa he would give her a taunting smile. But what Papa said was true, too. Miguel had patience and quiet strength and could figure out how to fix anything: plows and tractors, especially anything with a motor.

5   Several years ago, when Esperanza was still a young girl, Mama and Papa had been discussing boys from "good families" whom Esperanza should meet someday. She couldn't imagine being matched with someone she had never met. So she announced, "I am going to marry Miguel!"

6   Mama had laughed at her and said, "You will feel differently as you get older."

7   "No, I won't," Esperanza had said stubbornly.

8   But now that she was a young woman, she understood that Miguel was the housekeeper's son and she was the ranch owner's daughter and between them ran a deep river. Esperanza stood on one side and Miguel stood on the other and the river could never be crossed. In a moment of self-importance, Esperanza had told all of this to Miguel. Since then, he had spoken only a few words to her. When their paths crossed, he nodded and said politely, "*Mi reina*, my queen," but added nothing more. There was no teasing or laughing or talking about every little thing. Esperanza pretended not to care, though she secretly wished she had never told Miguel about the river.

1. Which quote from the passage best shows Esperanza's attitude toward Papa's time with Miguel?

   Ⓐ "I am going to marry Miguel!"

   Ⓑ "Because he knows how to fix things and he is learning his job."

   Ⓒ "Why does he always get to go and not me?"

   Ⓓ "No, I won't."

2. Which word best describes Miguel's tone when he calls Esperanza "mi reina"?

   Ⓐ Affectionate

   Ⓑ Sarcastic

   Ⓒ Angry

   Ⓓ Respectful

3. Which sentence below best describes Papa's character?

   Ⓐ He is kind because he helps prepare Miguel for the future.

   Ⓑ He is strict because he forces Miguel to work even as a child.

   Ⓒ He is judgmental because he only wants Esperanza to marry a rich boy.

   Ⓓ He is silly because he sticks his tongue out at Esperanza.

4. Explain what causes Esperanza's feelings toward Miguel to *change* as the passage progresses. Use textual evidence to support your answer.

   _____

   _____

   _____

   _____

(Answers are on page 95.)

EFFECT OF WORD CHOICE

RL.6.4 Determine the meaning of words and phrases as they are in a text, including figurative and connotative meanings; analyze the impact of a specific word choice on meaning and tone.

Directions: Read the following excerpt from *Mockingjay* by Suzanne Collins.

Is there any point in doing anything at all? My mother, my sister, and Gale's family are finally safe. As for the rest of 12, people are either dead, which is irreversible, or protected in 13. That leaves the rebels in the district. Of course, I hate the Capitol, but I have no confidence that my being the Mockingjay will benefit those who are trying to bring it down. How can I help the districts when every time I make a move, it results in suffering and loss of life? The old man shot in District 11 for whistling. The crackdown in 12 after I intervened in Gale's whipping. My stylist, Cinna being dragged, bloody and unconscious, from the Launch Room before the Games. Plutarch's sources believe he was killed during the interrogation. Brilliant, enigmatic, lovely Cinna is dead because of me. I push the thought away because it's too impossibly painful to dwell on without losing my fragile hold on the situation entirely.

1. Which word is the best synonym for the word intervened as it is used in the passage?
   - Ⓐ Interviewed
   - Ⓒ Participated
   - Ⓑ Involved
   - Ⓓ Interfered

2. What effect does the word dragged have on the sentence?
   - Ⓐ It downplays the seriousness of his death.
   - Ⓑ It emphasizes the brutality with which he was killed.
   - Ⓒ It clarifies that it was a normal part of the Games.
   - Ⓓ It conveys a feeling of boredom.

3. What does it mean to "push the thought away"?
   - (A) To shove the person who is speaking
   - (B) To refuse to admit something
   - (C) To avoid thinking about something
   - (D) To become violent

4. Reread the last sentence of the paragraph. Explain what the word <u>fragile</u> suggests about the narrator's situation.

   _____

   _____

   _____

   _____

   _____

5. Read the following sentence, "Brilliant, enigmatic, lovely Cinna is dead because of me." Identify what *emotion* these words bring forth for the reader and explain your answer with evidence.

   _____

   _____

   _____

   _____

   _____

(Answers are on page 95.)

PLOT DEVELOPMENT

RL.6.5 Analyze how a particular sentence, chapter, scene, or stanza fits into the overall structure of a text and contributes to the development of the theme, setting, or plot.

Directions: Read the short story "The Curse of the Amulet" by Ann McLaughlin.

1   With his fingers crushing the weight of the amulet into the hand behind his back, Henry's eyes darted around the excavation site: Farid, his guide and tutor, stood off to the side, speaking softly with Dr. Richard Braxton, Henry's father.

2   In Egypt since his mother's death, Henry felt the burden he was to his famous archaeologist father. In the three years his father had been working towards discovering the lost tomb of Antony and Cleopatra, he had often mentioned that his dig sites were no place for children.

3   Now, with no other family to speak of, Henry's father was forced to allow his fourteen-year-old son to join the dig. It had been so long since the father and son had seen each other in person that the reunion was awkward and slow-going.

4   Henry had left his mother's comfortable and stylish Massachusetts home to live in a virtual tent city in the middle of a desert. His father's team paid him little attention—especially since they'd begun discovering some artifacts.

5   Thus far, most of the artifacts seemed to be common household items, not necessarily fit for a king or a queen: some broken bowls, part of a comb, and what may have been a bracelet had so far been found in the ancient soil.

6   However, today, while taking a break from his lessons with Farid, Henry had felt compelled to head toward the dig site. As if drawn by a magnet, Henry moved toward the northeast corner of the site, a spot where so far, nothing had been found. He caught a glimpse of something just beneath the dirt—it looked like a piece of small rope.

7   Scanning the area, assured no one could see him, Henry jumped into the hole and brushed some dirt off the object. Suddenly, a gemstone gleamed in the desert sun. Shocked by this find, Henry's thoughts immediately went to his father: "Maybe now he'll stop being such a bear and let me in. Maybe now, he'll let me help him. Maybe now, he'll be like a dad."

8   The second he palmed the gem, which was attached to a small leather strap like a necklace, an unfamiliar feeling washed over Henry. His emotions instantly settled, like a pond after a storm. He realized he didn't need his father's approval, nor did he need his help. Wasn't it Henry who'd found this buried amulet? "The great Dr. Richard Braxton, in three years, has only found common items, while I, Henry Braxton, have made a valuable discovery. I will be famous. I will be in history books. I will find the tomb of Antony and Cleopatra. I am greater than my father. . ."

1. What is the purpose of the flashback used in **paragraphs 2–5**?
   - (A) To show the close relationship between Henry and Richard
   - (B) To prove how unsuccessful Richard's work has been
   - (C) To describe the strained relationship between father and son
   - (D) To explain how Henry ended up in Egypt

2. Which phrase from **paragraph 1** best indicates Henry's struggle?
   - (A) "stood off to the side…"
   - (B) "eyes darted around…"
   - (C) "speaking softly…"
   - (D) "his guide and tutor"

3. Which word(s) in the following sentence best reveals Richard's feelings?

   "Now, with no other family to speak of, Henry's father was forced to allow his fourteen-year-old son to join the dig."

   _____

(Answers are on page 96.)

POINT OF VIEW

> **RL.6.6** Explain how an author develops the point of view of the narrator or speaker in a text.

Directions: Read the paragraph below about a girl named Amber.

Paragraph 1

Amber is the most popular girl in the 12th grade, the whole school even! She was named captain of the cheerleading squad for the second year in a row. All the other girls on the squad envy Amber and wish they could be more like her. Amber and her boyfriend, Danny, are definitely going to win cutest couple of the year!

> A 1st person narrator uses the pronoun *I* to tell the story. **I and 1** look alike. When you see the pronoun *I think* **1** for 1st person narrator.
>
> A 3rd person narrator uses pronouns such as he, she, or they.

1. From what perspective is this story narrated?
   Circle the correct choice.

   1st person   *or*   **3rd person**

2. Explain how you know which type of narrator is telling the story.

   _____

   _____

   _____

3. Which sentence best represents the reader's overall opinion of Amber after reading this paragraph?
   - (A) Amber is a well-liked and talented girl.
   - (B) Amber is on the cheerleading squad.
   - (C) Amber is in love.
   - (D) Amber is unfriendly.

Directions: Read the paragraph below. Think about its similarities to the paragraph about Amber.

Paragraph 2

I am the most popular girl in the 12th grade, the whole school even! I was named captain of the cheerleading squad for the second year in a row. All the other girls on the squad envy me and wish they could be more like me. My boyfriend, Danny, and I are definitely going to win cutest couple of the year!

4. From what perspective is this story narrated? Circle the correct choice.

   1st person   or   **3rd person**

5. Explain how you know which type of narrator is telling the story.

   _____

   _____

   _____

6. Which sentence might best represent the reader's overall opinion of the narrator after reading this paragraph?
   Ⓐ   She is a well-liked and talented girl.
   Ⓑ   She is athletic.
   Ⓒ   She is too full of herself.
   Ⓓ   She is Danny's girlfriend.

(Answers are on page 96.)

COMPARING TEXTS ACROSS GENRES

RL.6.9 Compare and contrast texts in different forms or genres (e.g., stories and poems; historical novels and fantasy stories) in terms of their approaches to similar themes and topics.

Directions: Read the following excerpt from "Saving the Sound" from *Spill! The Story of the Exxon Valdez* by Terry Carr. This article is about an oil spill that took place in Alaska in 1989.

1　　All this time, the oil continued to spread. It reached into every corner of some islands. It washed up hundreds of miles of shoreline. It turned beaches black with slippery slime. Each high tide laid on a new layer of muck.

2　　The tide also washed up a more terrible toll: dead birds and sea otters. Within a week after the spill, thousands of dead murres, loons, and other birds littered the beaches. One island had 500 dead birds on a 4-mile (6.4-km) stretch of shore. Oil had turned the dead birds into a stiff, black mass.

3　　Some of the birds had drowned. Once the heavy oil got onto their feathers, they could not float. Other birds died from the cold, because feathers contaminated with oil lose their shape and thus their ability to insulate. This left the birds vulnerable to the deadly cold of the Sound's waters. Yet more birds were poisoned when they ate plants that had oil on them. The toxic chemicals in the oil destroys the birds' internal organs or poisons their blood, causing them to weaken and die.

1. Read **paragraph 2**. How does the author **most effectively** show the result of the spill?
   - Ⓐ He says it was terrible.
   - Ⓑ He adds a story about what he personally saw.
   - Ⓒ He uses facts and numbers that will shock the reader.
   - Ⓓ He talks about birds that will be familiar to the reader.

2. Which words in **paragraph 1** most help the reader visualize the spill?
   - Ⓐ "oil continued to spread"
   - Ⓑ "washed up"
   - Ⓒ "dead birds"
   - Ⓓ "black with slippery slime"

3. Why does the author explain all the specific ways the birds died?
  (A) to emphasize the far reaching effects of the spill
  (B) to provide a gruesome picture for the reader
  (C) to show his anger at those who spilled the oil
  (D) to maintain the reader's interest by exaggerating

Directions: Read the **poem** inspired by the oil spill in Alaska.

Soaring above the sparkling waters,
I heard the chirps and trills,
And barks and calls,
Of those who call this island home.

Serene songs become desperate cries.

Swooping down I see the intruder—dark as night.
He oozes through the waters chasing his prey,
Slithers through the long reeds,
Creeps into the grain at the water's edge,
Burrows himself into the sandy shore.

I land atop the water's surface,
"Get out!" I squawk.
The others too, cry out, begging him to leave.
He does not listen.

Flapping in outrage,
I remember what it was like to be a baby in my mother's nest,
Struggling to take flight.
The intruder tugs at me—refusing to release.
My body is an anchor, mooring me to this spot.

Down,
        He pulls.
                Further down.
                        Further,
                            D
                                o
                                    w
                                        n

4. How does the speaker describe the oil?
   - Ⓐ As a bird
   - Ⓑ As a burden
   - Ⓒ As an intruder
   - Ⓓ As a nest

5. What image do the words "ooze," "slither," and "creep" raise for the reader?
   - Ⓐ A peaceful environment filled with wildlife.
   - Ⓑ A predator who seeks out and sneaks up on victims.
   - Ⓒ A typical beach on a summer's day.
   - Ⓓ A bird competing for the same prey.

6. Identify what the author means by "My body is an anchor."

   _____

   _____

   _____

   _____

   _____

Directions: Use **both** the **article** and the **poem** to answer questions 7 and 8.

7. Explain the **central idea** conveyed by **both** pieces of writing.

_____

_____

_____

_____

_____

8. Describe the major difference in the language used by the first author from the language used by the second author. Use textual evidence from both to support your answer.

_____

_____

_____

_____

(Answers are on page 96.)

CITING EVIDENCE IN INFORMATIONAL TEXTS

RI.6.1 Cite textual evidence to support analysis of what the text says explicitly as well as inferences drawn from the text.

Directions: Read the following excerpt from *I Am a SEAL Team Six Warrior: Memoirs of an American Soldier* by Howard E. Wasdin and Stephen Templin.

1   When the U.S. Navy sends their elite, they send the SEALs. When the SEALs send their elite, they send SEAL Team Six. It's the navy's equivalent to the army's Delta Force. Its job is to fight terrorism and armed rebellion, often secretly.

2   I was a sniper for SEAL Team Six.

3   This is the first time a SEAL Team Six sniper's story has been told. My story.

4   In the morning darkness of September 18, 1993, in Mogadishu, Somalia, another SEAL and I crept over a wall and up to the top of a six-story tower. Below us, people were waking up. Men, women, and children relieved themselves in the streets. I smelled the morning fires, fueled by dried animal dung. The fires heated the little food the Somalis had. The warlord who rules this part of the city, Mohamed Farah Aidid, controlled the population by controlling the food supply. Every time I saw a starving child, I blamed Aidid.

5   Although the middle of a city may not seem the logical place for navy commandos, SEALs are trained to fight anywhere. That's where the name comes from: SEa, Air, and Land. On many operations, we were in all three: We'd parachute in, complete our task on land, and make our way back on water.

> Some answers can be found directly in the text. Be sure to read carefully and go back to the text to look. Other questions require you to think for yourself.

1. What can you infer about the Delta Force?
   - Ⓐ They are inferior to the SEALs.
   - Ⓑ They are used in minor operations.
   - Ⓒ They are also an exclusive division.
   - Ⓓ They are the female version of SEALs.

2. Find a quote from the text to support this inference:

   Navy SEALs must be physically fit.

   Evidence: _____

   _____

3. Based on the text, why do you think this is the first SEAL story to be told?
   - Ⓐ Their work is generally confidential.
   - Ⓑ They are not usually well-spoken.
   - Ⓒ They cannot remember their experiences
   - Ⓓ They never make it out alive.

4. When does this story take place?
   - Ⓐ 1995
   - Ⓑ 1990
   - Ⓒ 1993
   - Ⓓ 2012

5. Provide two pieces of textual evidence from the excerpt that indicate the standard of living in Mogadishu. Explain what each quote tells you about life in Somalia.

   1. _____

   2. _____

(Answers are on page 97.)

FINDING THE CENTRAL IDEA

RI.6.2 Determine a central idea of a text and how it is conveyed through particular details; provide a summary of the text distinct from personal opinion or judgments.

Directions: Read the following passage from *World History: Ancient Civilizations* by McDougal Littell.

Early Humans on the Move

1   Hunter-gatherers were **nomads**, people who move from place to place. Movement often was limited. Groups returned to the same places with the changes of seasons. At certain times of the year, these early bands joined together, forming larger communities. There was probably time for storytelling, meeting friends, and finding marriage partners.

2   Early humans also moved to new and distant lands. The act of moving from one place to settle in another is called **migration**. Migrations may have been the result of people's following animals to hunt. By around 15,000 B.C., hunter-gatherers had migrated throughout much of the world. They even traveled across a land bridge connecting Siberia and Alaska. In this way, they entered the Americas.

3   The arrival of migrating groups in the territory of another people could lead to both good and bad outcomes. Everyone benefited when knowledge and tools were shared. However, people sometimes turned violent when they felt threatened by newcomers. They feared that the newcomers might try to take their territory. Sometimes they may have feared them just because they were different.

1. Which of the following best indicates the central idea of **paragraph 1**?
   - Ⓐ Moving is a lot of work when done seasonally.
   - Ⓑ Nomads are groups that travel depending on available resources.
   - Ⓒ Nomads like to communicate with each other.
   - Ⓓ Sometimes traveling caused violence.

2. What is the main purpose of **paragraph 2**?
   - Ⓐ to show the great distance people traveled
   - Ⓑ to give background information about Alaska
   - Ⓒ to indicate a specific date
   - Ⓓ to explain how America was discovered

3. Which statement below best explains why nomads began to migrate?
   - Ⓐ They became bored living in one place.
   - Ⓑ They were forced to move due to weather problems.
   - Ⓒ They were pursuing sources of food.
   - Ⓓ They moved to avoid encountering enemy groups.

4. Reread **paragraph 3**. Give the paragraph a heading title that reflects its central idea.

   Heading title: _____

(Answers are on page 97.)

DEVELOPMENT OF
KEY IDEAS AND DETAILS

RI.6.3 Analyze in detail how a key individual, event, or idea is introduced, illustrated, and elaborated in a text (e.g., through examples or anecdotes).

Directions: Read the following excerpt from *Warriors Don't Cry* by Melba Pattillo Beals.

1   I couldn't imagine they would ever change their minds and allow their children to go to school with me, no matter what laws those men on the Supreme Court made. But on May 24, 1955, the newspapers said the Little Rock school board had adopted a plan to limit integration to Central High School. They weren't going to allow it to actually begin, however, for two years—not till September 1957.

2   When my teacher asked if anyone who lived within the Central High School district wanted to attend school with white people, I raised my hand. As I signed my name on the paper they passed around, I thought about all those times I'd gone past Central High, wanting to see inside. I was certain it would take a miracle to integrate Little Rock's schools. But I reasoned that if schools were open to my people, I would get access to other opportunities I had been denied, like going to shows at Robinson Auditorium, or sitting on the first floor of the movie theater.

3   By December 1, 1955, I began to realize that Grandma was right. Our people were stretching out to knock down the fences against segregation. I read in the newspaper that one of our people, a woman named Rosa Parks, had refused to give up her seat to a white man on an Alabaman bus. Her willingness to be arrested rather than give in one more time led to the Montgomery, Alabama, bus boycott. I felt such a surge of pride when I thought how many people had banded together to force a little change. It gave me hope that things in Little Rock could change.

1. What changes from the *beginning* of **paragraph 1** to the *end*?
   - Ⓐ The school board agrees to integration and then revokes the decision.
   - Ⓑ Integration goes from unimaginable to a real possibility.
   - Ⓒ The narrator loses hope of integration occurring.
   - Ⓓ The season changes.

2. What causes the narrator to raise her hand in **paragraph 2**?
   - Ⓐ She is scared to go against the teacher.
   - Ⓑ She sees all her friends volunteering.
   - Ⓒ She is hoping to be afforded more prospects.
   - Ⓓ She knows it will make her family proud.

3. What is the purpose of mentioning the Rosa Parks incident?
   - Ⓐ To show the unrest around the whole country
   - Ⓑ To show the positive effect on the narrator's attitude
   - Ⓒ To explain some of the crimes committed against white people
   - Ⓓ To present a commonly known event for readers

4. Which quote **best** describes the narrator's overall attitude?
   - Ⓐ "It gave me hope that things in Little Rock could change."
   - Ⓑ "I began to realize that Grandma was right."
   - Ⓒ "I thought about all those times I'd gone past Central High, wanting to see inside."
   - Ⓓ "I couldn't imagine they would ever change their minds and allow their children to go to school with me…"

(Answers are on page 97.)

WORD MEANING AND FIGURATIVE LANGUAGE IN CONTEXT

RI.6.4 Determine the meaning of words and phrases as they are used in a text, including figurative, connotative, and technical meanings.

Directions: Read the following excerpt from "A Symbol of Alabama's Part, Indelible to Black and White," by Rick Bragg, in *The New York Times,* September 15, 1998, Dateline: Birmingham, Ala.

1   For 65-year-old James Harper, sitting on his tiny front porch in West Anniston with the day still brand new, the news that George C. Wallace was dead caused in him to lower his eyes and catch his breath for a second, as if some last, dying chorus of "Dixie" had <u>lodged</u> in his throat.

2   "I didn't know," he said. "You were here to talk about him? Sit down. I voted for him. Every time. I *like* him standing up there in that school door, by God," he said, referring to Governor Wallace's <u>positioning</u> himself at the entrance to the University of Alabama on June 11, 1963, to <u>prevent</u> <u>integration</u> there.

3   "And the Federals had to move him," said Mr. Harper, who is white, and then he grinned.

4   "He was a man, by God. He wasn't no boy."

5   But when he was asked if he still respected the former Governor after a would-be-<u>assassin</u>'s bullet crippled him in 1972, after old age and history had mellowed him and even made him say he was sorry, Mr. Harper seemed not to hear.

6   "I loved that man," he said.

1. What is the best synonym for the word <u>lodged</u> as it is used in **paragraph 1**?
   - (A) a place where people gather for social events
   - (B) to spend the night at a place other than home, e.g., in a cabin
   - (C) to be stuck and blocking something off
   - (D) to throw lightly or to toss

2. What is most likely the definition of <u>integration</u> as it is used in **paragraph 2**?
   - (A) The act of segregating
   - (B) The act of keeping things the same
   - (C) The act of going to school
   - (D) combining two different groups of people

3. What part of speech is <u>positioning</u> as used in **paragraph 2?**
   - (A) Verb
   - (B) Adverb
   - (C) Noun
   - (D) Preposition

4. What is the most likely definition of the word <u>assassin</u> in **paragraph 5**?
   - (A) Someone who murders another person
   - (B) A dear friend
   - (C) A person who is in a powerful political position
   - (D) A famous celebrity

5. Explain what the author means by the phrase "would-be-assassin" as used in **paragraph 5**?

   _____

   _____

   _____

6. Which word could be used as a synonym for the word <u>prevent</u> as used in **paragraph 2**?
   - (A) Prepare
   - (B) Help
   - (C) Stop
   - (D) Cause

(Answers are on page 98.)

TEXT STRUCTURE

> **RI.6.5** Analyze how a particular sentence, paragraph, chapter, or section fits into the overall structure of a text and contributes to the development of the ideas.

Directions: Read the excerpt from *Warriors Don't Cry* by Melba Pattillo Beals.

1   Three thirty-nine, that was the number of the homeroom on my card; I was assigned to the third floor. We quickly compared notes. Each of us was assigned to a different homeroom.

2   "Why can't any of us be in the same homeroom or take classes together?" I asked. From behind the long desk, a man spoke in an unkind booming voice. "You wanted integration . . . you got integration."

3   I turned to see the hallway swallow up my friends. None of us had an opportunity to say a real good-bye or make plans to meet. I was alone, in a daze, following a muscular, stocky white woman with closely cropped straight black hair. Up the stairs I went, squeezing my way past those who first blocked my path and then shouted hurtful words at me. "Frightened" did not describe my state; I had moved on to terrified. My body was numb. I was only aware of my head and thoughts and visions.

4   I had <u>fantasized</u> about how wonderful it would be to get inside the huge beautiful castle I knew as Central High School. But the reality was so much bigger, darker, and more treacherous than I had imagined. I could easily get lost among its spiral staircases. The angry voices shouting at me made it all the more difficult to find my way through these unfamiliar surroundings. I was panic-stricken at the thought of losing sight of my guide. I ran to keep up with her.

5   "Move it, girlie," she called back at me.

6   "Pheeew!" one boy said, backing away from me. Others stopped and joined in his ridicule. For an instant I stood <u>paralyzed</u>.

7   **"Don't stop!" the woman commanded**. Her words snapped me into action. I scuffed to move behind her. Suddenly I felt it—the sting of a hand slapping the side of my cheek, and then warm, slimy saliva on my face, dropping to the collar of my blouse.

1. What does the sentence "We quickly compared notes" tell you?
    - (A) They were nervous about being separated.
    - (B) They were hoping to be in different classes.
    - (C) They were angry at the teachers they received.
    - (D) They were good students.

2. Why is it significant that the author uses the word <u>fantasized</u> in **paragraph 4**?
    - (A) Because she had been thinking about it for a long time.
    - (B) Because her fantasy was fulfilled.
    - (C) Because fairytales do not usually come true.
    - (D) Because she is not paying attention to where her guide is going.

3. Explain how the opening sentence of **paragraph 3** relates to the overall passage.

    _____

    _____

    _____

4. Reread the exchange that takes place in **paragraph 2**. What does the man's reply help the reader understand?
    - (A) How welcomed the students were by the staff and students
    - (B) How confusing it can be in a new school
    - (C) How dissatisfied this man is with his job
    - (D) How terribly the students were treated by the entire school

5. Which of the following sentences provides a summary of **paragraph 7**?
    - (A) The narrator is assaulted in the hallway.
    - (B) The narrator is separated from her guide.
    - (C) The narrator is verbally assaulted by her guide.
    - (D) The narrator is running down the hallway.

6. What is the significance of explaining that she felt <u>paralyzed</u> in **paragraph 6**?
Ⓐ It shows how badly she's been abused.
Ⓑ It shows that being stopped leaves her vulnerable.
Ⓒ It shows how slowly she was moving.
Ⓓ It shows she is in good physical condition.

Mood is how *you* feel when you're reading something.

Tone is how the *author* feels about the subject.

Remember: **M**ood = **M**e
Tone = **T**hem (Author)

7. Which of the words from **paragraph 4** best indicates the overall *mood* of the paragraph?
Ⓐ Beautiful
Ⓑ Unfamiliar
Ⓒ Darker
Ⓓ Panic-stricken

8. Why does the author call Central High a castle?
Ⓐ To contrast the imagined with reality
Ⓑ To inform the reader about the school's history
Ⓒ To compare the quality of the school with a castle
Ⓓ To describe the new setting

9. How does the last sentence of the excerpt fit in with the rest of the excerpt?

Ⓐ It allows the reader to see that things weren't as bad as they seemed.

Ⓑ It helps the reader understand why the narrator was frightened throughout.

Ⓒ It proves that people can be unfriendly.

Ⓓ It provides a big picture of what school life was like.

10. Explain why you think the author chose to describe the spitting incident with such vivid language instead of directly stating, "I was spit on." What effect does the description have on the reader? Use textual evidence to support your answer.

_____

_____

_____

_____

_____

_____

(Answers are on page 98.)

AUTHOR'S POINT OF VIEW

RI.6.6 Determine an author's point of view or purpose in a text and explain how it is conveyed in the text.

Directions: Read this article from a government website dealing with girls' health.

Peer Pressure

1   There are two kinds of peer pressure: **positive** peer pressure and **negative** peer pressure. Peer pressure is when you try something because "everyone else is doing it."

2   Positive peer pressure is when you act a certain way because your friends are acting that way, but it is for a good reason. For example, if your friends talk you into joining the soccer team, and you end up really liking soccer, that's positive peer pressure. Or, if your friend volunteers to tutor younger kids, and you decide you would like to do the same, that's another example of positive peer pressure.

3   Negative peer pressure is when you feel you have to act a certain way because everyone else is, but the end result is bad. If your friends are mean to the new girl at school and so you treat her badly, too, then that is an example of negative peer pressure.

4   So why do some girls follow their friends, even when it's not a good idea? Girls may worry about what their friends will think, not know how to say no, or fear being left out. Some friends may pressure you to do something because "everyone else does it," such as making fun of someone, using alcohol or drugs, or smoking. The best thing to do is say, "No, thanks" or "I don't want to." Keep in mind, you are always in charge of what you do and don't do. It can help to talk with your parents or guardians about how to handle pressures that may come up.

Popularity

5   There are lots of things that you and your friends may do to fit in. It may be having the right clothes or being friends with the cool kids. It is normal to want to be liked by others, but it is more important to focus on what matters to YOU. Having lots of friends and dressing like everyone else may seem important right now, but try to focus on being yourself and having real friends who care about you.

Here are 7 ways to know if your friends really care about you:

- They want you to be happy.
- They listen and care about what you have to say.
- They are happy for you when you do well.
- They say they are sorry when they make a mistake.
- They don't expect you to be perfect.
- They give you advice in a caring way.
- They keep personal things between the two of you.

Cliques

6   A clique is a small group of friends that is very picky about who can and cannot join the group. While it's nice to have a close group of friends, being on the outside of a clique may not be fun! Girls in cliques often leave out other girls on purpose. They may bully girls who are not "cool enough." If you are being picked on, try to make friends with new people who care about YOU. Keep in mind, it is the quality or value of the friendship that counts, not how many friends you have. And, if you are leaving someone else out, think about how you would feel if you were the one being left out. If you are having a hard time with moving, read about dealing with The Moving Blues.

7   There can be a lot of peer pressure in cliques. You may feel like you need to do things like drink or do drugs to be part of the gang. Keep in mind, you always have the right to say no! Real friends will respect that. You also have the right to make new friends.

1. Which of the following might be a good title for this article?
   - Ⓐ Making Friendships That Last
   - Ⓑ Friends Who Pressure You
   - Ⓒ Cruel Cliques
   - Ⓓ Friends: Who Needs Them?

2. What does the author do to help readers understand topics covered in the article?
   - Ⓐ He breaks it into paragraphs.
   - Ⓑ He uses bolded headings.
   - Ⓒ He uses direct quotes from teens.
   - Ⓓ He uses bullet points.

3. Check off all the places you may find an excerpt such as this one.

   _____ School Guidance Office   _____ Science Textbook

   _____ Teen Magazine   _____ Health Class Textbook

   _____ Historical Fiction Novel   _____ Manual

4. Which statement would the author likely agree with? Circle the correct statement.

   Cliques are beneficial.   *or*   **Cliques are harmful.**

5. Provide one line from the excerpt that supports your answer to **question 4** and explain.

   _____

   _____

   _____

6. In **paragraph 4**, the author places the phrase "everyone else does it" in quotes. What is the author's purpose in putting this phrase in quotes?

_____

_____

_____

_____

_____

7. What is the author's main purpose in writing this text?
   Ⓐ To Entertain
   Ⓑ To Persuade
   Ⓒ To Inform
   Ⓓ To Question

8. Reread **paragraph 7**. Why does the author use an exclamation point in this paragraph?
   Ⓐ To show he is excited about the topic
   Ⓑ To emphasize their options
   Ⓒ To display his anger
   Ⓓ It is a mistake

(Answers are on page 99.)

TRACING AND EVALUATING ARGUMENTS

RI.6.8 Trace and evaluate the argument and specific claims in a text, distinguishing claims that are supported by reasons and evidence from claims that are not.

Directions: Read the article "5 Ways to Cut Spending . . . and Still Get to Do and Buy Cool Things" from *Start Smart: Money Management for Teens* (2006), *https://www.fdic.gov/consumers/consumer/news/cnsum06/spending.html.*

Do you want to find ways to stretch your money, so it goes farther and is there when you really need it? Here are some suggestions for knowing how much money you have, how much you need for expenditures, and how to reach your goals by cutting back on what you spend.

1. **Practice self-control.** To avoid making a quick decision to buy something just because you saw it featured on display or on sale:

    - Make a shopping list before you leave home and stick to it.
    - *Before* you go shopping, set a spending limit (say, $5 or $10) for "impulse buys"—items you didn't plan to buy but that got your attention anyway. If you are tempted to spend more than your limit, wait a few hours or a few days and think it over.
    - Limit the amount of cash you take with you. The less cash you carry, the less you can spend and the less you lose if you misplace your wallet.

    For more guidance on spending wisely, see "Do You Really *Need* Those $125 Designer Sneakers?"

2. **Research before you buy.** To be sure you are getting a good value, especially with a big purchase, look into the quality and the reputation of the product or service you're considering. Read "reviews" in magazines or respected Web sites. Talk to knowledgeable people you trust. Check other stores or go online and compare prices. Look at similar items. This is known as "comparison shopping," and it can lead to tremendous savings and better quality purchases. And if you're sure you know what you want, take advantage of store coupons and mail-in "rebates."

3. **Keep track of your spending.** This helps you set and stick to limits, what many people refer to as budgeting. "Maintaining a budget may sound scary or complicated, but it can be as simple as having a notebook and writing down what you buy each month," said Janet Kincaid, FDIC Senior Consumer Affairs Officer. "Any system that helps you know how much you are spending each month is a good thing."

    Also pay attention to small amounts of money you spend. "A snack here and a magazine there can quickly add up," said Paul Horwitz, an FDIC Community Affairs Specialist. He suggested that, for a few weeks, you write down every purchase in a small notebook. "You'll probably be amazed at how much you spend without even thinking."

4. **Think "used" instead of "new."** Borrow things (from the library or friends) that you don't have to own. Pick up used games, DVDs and music at "second-hand" stores around town.

5. **Take good care of what you buy.** It's expensive to replace things. Think about it: Do you really want to buy the same thing twice?

1. What does the author hope to achieve with the opening paragraph's question?

    _____

    _____

    _____

    _____

2. What effect do the numbered suggestions have on the reader?
    Ⓐ They show that the article will be short.
    Ⓑ They show that the author is organized and structured.
    Ⓒ They show that the author is writing about finances.
    Ⓓ They show the author's love for numbers.

3. What does the author do in the **Practice self-control** section that **most** shows his advice is valid?
    Ⓐ He uses specific dollar amounts for spending.
    Ⓑ He uses bullet points under the section.
    Ⓒ He suggests further readings from other sources.
    Ⓓ He tells the reader how to avoid losing a wallet.

4. Reread the **Keep track of your spending** section. Identify **one thing** the author does that effectively proves his point. *(Hint: Look in the first paragraph of the section.)*

    _____

    _____

    _____

    _____

5. Reread the **Keep track of your spending** section. Identify a **second thing** the author does that effectively proves his point. *(Hint: Look in the second paragraph of the section.)*

    _____

    _____

    _____

    _____

6. What is the purpose of the question in the last paragraph of the text?
    Ⓐ To ask readers' opinions about their spending habits
    Ⓑ To ask a commonsense question and make readers think
    Ⓒ To ask the readers about their next steps
    Ⓓ To ask a question he is curious about

7. How does the following statement support the author's claim?

    "The less cash you carry, the less you can spend and the less you lose if you misplace your wallet."

    _____

    _____

    _____

    _____

8. Which of the following could the author have added to the article to strengthen his argument?
    - Ⓐ Included a personal story of someone who followed the tips and saw improvements
    - Ⓑ Included charts about how teenagers are generally irresponsible with their money
    - Ⓒ Included pictures of the two people quoted in the article
    - Ⓓ Included quotes from experts in the field

(Answers are on page 99.)

COMPARING AND CONTRASTING AUTHORS' PRESENTATIONS

RI.6.9 Compare and contrast one author's presentation of events with that of another (e.g., a memoir written by and a biography on the same person).

Text 1

Directions: Read the short biography of Elie Wiesel, from *http://www.nobelprize.org/nobel_prizes/peace/laureates/1986/wiesel-bio.html*.

1   **Elie Wiesel** was born in 1928 in the town of Sighet, now part of Romania. During World War II, he, with his family and other Jews from the area, were deported to the German concentration and extermination camps, where his parents and little sister perished. Wiesel and his two older sisters survived. Liberated from Buchenwald in 1945 by advancing Allied troops, he was taken to Paris where he studied at the Sorbonne and worked as a journalist.

2   In 1958, he published his first book, *La Nuit*, a memoir of his experiences in the concentration camps. He has since authored nearly thirty books, some of which use these events as their basic material. In his many lectures, Wiesel has concerned himself with the situation of the Jews and other groups who have suffered persecution and death because of their religion, race or national origin. He has been outspoken on the plight of Soviet Jewry, on Ethiopian Jewry and on behalf of the State of Israel today.

3.   Wiesel has made his home in New York City, and is now a United States citizen. He has been a visiting scholar at Yale University, a Distinguished Professor of Judaic Studies at the City College of New York, and since 1976 has been Andrew W. Mellon Professor in the Humanities at Boston University where he teaches "*Literature of Memory*." Chairman of the United States Holocaust Memorial Council from 1980–1986, Wiesel serves on numerous boards of trustees and advisors.

1. Fill in the blanks with all that we learn about Wiesel in the **first paragraph**.

   Year of birth: _____

   Ethnicity: _____

   His parents and younger sister _____

   Forced to live in _____

2. Why do you think the author opened with so many important facts about Wiesel's life?
   - Ⓐ To deliver background information before moving on to later parts of Wiesel's life
   - Ⓑ To get the basic information out of the way to move on to more exciting details
   - Ⓒ To help the reader feel close and gain sympathy for Wiesel
   - Ⓓ To establish the focus on Wiesel's early life in World War II

3. Which of the following has the same connotation as the word <u>perished</u>?
   - Ⓐ Executed
   - Ⓑ Killed
   - Ⓒ Murdered
   - Ⓓ Deceased

4. Based on the first sentence in **paragraph 2**, what types of things do you think the reader will learn in Wiesel's book *La Nuit*?

   _____

   _____

   _____

   _____

Text 2

Directions: Read the following excerpt from *Night* by Elie Wiesel (1960).

1   Not far from us there were some prisoners at work. Some were digging holes, others carrying sand. None of them so much glanced at us. We were so many dried-up trees in the heart of a desert. Behind me, some people were talking. I had not the slightest desire to listen to what they were saying, to know who was talking or what they were talking about. No one dared to raise his voice, though there was no supervisor near us. People whispered. Perhaps it was because of the thick smoke which poisoned the air and took one by the throat . . .

2   We were made to go into a new barracks, in the "gypsies' camp." In ranks of five.

3   "And now stay where you are!"

4   There was no floor. A roof and four walls. Our feet sank into the mud.

5   Another spell of waiting began. I went to sleep standing up. I dreamed of a bed, of my mother's caress. And I woke up: I was standing, my feet in the mud. Some people collapsed and lay where they were. Others cried:

6   "Are you mad? We've been told to stay standing. Do you want to bring trouble on us all?"

7   As if all the trouble in the world had not descended already upon our heads! Gradually, we all sat down in the mud. But we had to jump up constantly, every time a Kapo came in to see if anybody had a pair of new shoes. If so, they had to be given up to him. It was no use opposing this: blows rained down and in the final reckoning you had lost your shoes anyway.

8   I had new shoes myself. But as they were coated with a thick layer of mud, no one had noticed them. I thanked God, in an improvised prayer, for having created mud in His infinite and wonderful universe.

9   Suddenly the silence grew oppressive. An SS officer had come in, and with him, the odor of the Angel of Death. We stared fixedly at his fleshy lips. From the middle of the barracks, he harangued us.

5. What does the use of the word <u>prisoners</u> tell you about the treatment of people living in the concentration camp?

_____

_____

_____

_____

6. Why does the narrator say he "thanked God . . . for having created mud"?

_____

_____

_____

_____

7. Read the following sentence from **Text 1 (biography)**: "Wiesel has concerned himself with the situation of the Jews and other groups who have suffered persecution and death because of their religion, race or national origin."

Explain why this has become Wiesel's life work, using textual evidence from *Night*.

_____

_____

_____

_____

8. How do the two authors **differ** in their presentation?
   - Ⓐ The author of Text 1 uses straightforward language, while Wiesel uses descriptive language.
   - Ⓑ The author of Text 1 strikes more of an emotional chord than does Wiesel.
   - Ⓒ The author of Text 1 and Wiesel both affect the reader equally.
   - Ⓓ The author of Text 1 is more authoritative than Wiesel.

(Answers are on page 100.)

ARGUMENT WRITING

W.6.1 Write arguments to support claims with clear reasons and relevant evidence.

1. Although you would like a cell phone for your birthday, your parents think you are too young. Write a letter to your parents convincing them that you need a cell phone.

   _____

   _____

   _____

   _____

   _____

   _____

2. You're running for 6th grade class president, and you must deliver a speech that discusses the two most significant problems in your school. Write a speech to your classmates and teachers that clearly states the school's problems, and be sure to convince your audience that the issues are worth caring about.

   _____

   _____

   _____

   _____

   _____

   _____

Note to Parents and Teachers
The writing prompts presented in this section will likely yield longer responses than the allotted space provides. Please encourage students to use additional paper to ensure their responses are thorough and achieve the standard requirements set forth by the rubric.

3. The school committee has announced it must make drastic budget cuts so there will no longer be _____ classes offered in your school (fill in the blank with one of the following: *art, music, foreign language, drama, computer).* You've created a petition for the students and staff to sign. Write a position statement at the top of the petition that describes your opposition to cutting _____ classes.

_____

_____

_____

_____

_____

_____

_____

Directions: Read the following excerpt from a newspaper article.

State Legislators to Raise Driving Age

Lawmakers who gave serious consideration to the driving age issue and perhaps to the disappointment of teenagers all over the state, decided that the age will increase from sixteen-years-old to eighteen years of age. "Sixteen-year-olds are just not mature enough to handle this kind of responsibility," commented one local parent. "I'm glad my son will have to wait a few more years."

At eighteen years, children are no longer considered children but become adults. "We believe that requiring teenagers to reach adulthood before receiving their license will decrease the number of reckless teen drivers on the road," noted a proponent of the bill. Many politicians cited teen accident statistics as a major factor in moving forward with the bill.

"It's ridiculous," said Jared Smithe, a fifteen-year-old freshman in high school. "I've been looking forward to getting my license next year and now I'll have to wait. There's no real difference between the sixteen-year-olds and the eighteen-year-olds I know."

4. After reading this excerpt, where do you stand on the license issue? Write an argument in favor of or against raising the driving age. Be sure to use original logical reasons and evidence to support your opinion.

_____

_____

_____

_____

_____

_____

5. Read the following statement: Video games are bad influences on young children and have no educational value. Write an argument that **disagrees** with this statement.

_____

_____

_____

_____

_____

_____

6. The cost of college education is becoming increasingly unaffordable for many students. Write why you think college education should be free. Provide at least three reasons to support your argument.

_____

_____

_____

_____

_____

_____

7. Most professional athletes in major sports markets earn massive salaries. Do you think they deserve to make such gigantic salaries? Why or why not? Provide at least three reasons to support your argument.

_____

_____

_____

_____

_____

_____

(Answers are on page 100.)

INFORMATIONAL WRITING

W.6.2 Write informative/explanatory texts to examine a topic and convey ideas, concepts, and information through the selection, organization, and analysis of relevant content.

1. Write an essay that explains how you determine if you are reading a **fiction** or **nonfiction** text. Provide specific characteristics from each genre to explain the differences.

    _____

    _____

    _____

    _____

    _____

    _____

2. Think of your hobbies—sports, music, video games, skateboarding, drawing, and so on. Write an essay that explains your hobby, providing information to people who might be interested in taking up this hobby.

    _____

    _____

    _____

    _____

    _____

3. Explain the process of cooking/making a simple food item that you are able to prepare by yourself. Imagine that your audience has not prepared the food before, so you must use appropriate transition words and include all necessary steps.

    _____

    _____

    _____

    _____

    _____

4. Write an essay that explains the major difference between elementary school and middle school. To stay organized, choose three to four specific aspects of each grade level and compare them.

_____

_____

_____

_____

_____

_____

5. Write an essay that explains how technology has both improved and harmed our society. Use headings to differentiate topics.

_____

_____

_____

_____

_____

_____

6. Explain what the Pledge of Allegiance is and why we recite this as a nation.

_____

_____

_____

_____

_____

(Answers are on page 101.)

NARRATIVE WRITING

W.6.3 Write narratives to develop real or imagined experiences or events using effective technique, relevant descriptive details, and well-structured event sequences.

1. Think back to a memorable holiday you had with your family or friends. Describe a specific moment in the day that made it memorable (in a good or bad way).

> To help your reader visualize your story, remember to use language that appeals to the senses—smell, sight, hearing, touch.

_____

_____

_____

_____

_____

_____

_____

2. The first day of school can be an anxiety-filled day for some kids. Write a short story about a student's terrible first day of middle school.

_____

_____

_____

_____

_____

_____

_____

_____

3. Write a story that describes your encounter with the creature above.

_____

_____

_____

_____

_____

_____

_____

4. Write a story that conveys the following theme: _Being honest is difficult but necessary._

_____

_____

_____

_____

_____

_____

_____

(Answers are on page 102.)

CONSIDERING AUDIENCE AND PURPOSE

> **W.6.4** Produce clear and coherent writing in which the development, organization, and style are appropriate to task, purpose, and audience.

1. Write an e-mail to your teacher asking for an extension on your project. Be sure to consider your purpose and your audience when composing the e-mail.

_____

_____

_____

_____

_____

_____

_____

2. Your grandparents are celebrating their 50th wedding anniversary, and you've decided to write a speech congratulating them. You will read the speech in front of all the guests at the party.

_____

_____

_____

_____

_____

_____

_____

3. Write a letter to your pen pal in Russia explaining what middle school is like in America. Please keep your audience in mind when writing—he or she will know little English.

_____

_____

_____

_____

_____

_____

4. Write a blog entry in your online journal to discuss a serious local or world event happening right now. You may blog about problems in your neighborhood, bullying in schools, environmental issues, or any concerning issues.

_____

_____

_____

_____

_____

_____

5. Create a flyer advertising babysitting services to hang in local establishments. Be mindful of your audience and what they might be looking for.

_____

_____

_____

_____

_____

_____

_____

(Answers are on page 102.)

REVISING AND EDITING

W.6.5 With some guidance and support from peers and adults, develop and strengthen writing as needed by planning, revising, editing, rewriting, or trying a new approach.

Checklist for Argument Writing Standard W.6.1

Textual Feature	Present in Writing	Suggestions for Improvement
Claim and evidence are introduced to reader clearly	Yes or No	
Shows knowledge and understanding of topic	Yes or No	
Evidence is logical/reasonable	Yes or No	
Use transition words when moving between topics	Yes or No	
Writing is formal	Yes or No	
Strong concluding statement (makes an impact on the reader)	Yes or No	

Avoid using the phrase "I think" in your writing. It makes you, as the writer, seem unsure, as if perhaps you believe what you're saying, but maybe not. Just state your opinion firmly.

Checklist for Informational/Explanatory Writing Standard W.6.2

Textual Feature	Present in Writing	Suggestions for Improvement
Topic is introduced clearly	Yes or No	
Uses facts, details, or other info to explain topic	Yes or No	
Helps reader understand the topic using headings, images, definitions of topic-specific words	Yes or No	
Uses transition words when moving between topics	Yes or No	
Writing is formal and uses language specific to the topic	Yes or No	
Strong concluding statement that fits with information provided	Yes or No	

When organizing your informational text, think of questions that readers might have about the topic: **who**, **what**, **where**, **when**, **why**, **how**. These questions can become guides for sections of your writing.

Checklist for Narrative Writing Standard W.6.3

Textual Feature	Present in Writing	Suggestions for Improvement
Pulls the reader in from the beginning	Yes or No	
Has a narrator(s) and character-events that happen in a sensible sequence	Yes or No	
Uses dialogue and descriptions to help reader get to know characters and follow events	Yes or No	
Uses a variety of sentence structures and styles	Yes or No	
Uses sensory language to help readers picture the story	Yes or No	
Has a conclusion that matches the events in the story	Yes or No	

Your introduction is like making a first impression when you meet your readers. You want them to like you and to continue "talking" with you. Think of some novels or short stories you really enjoy. Read the first couple of paragraphs of a few of your favorites. Notice how each paragraph kept your interest and incorporate that into your writing.

Directions:

1. Return to pages 54–57 and review the pieces you wrote. Select **two** pieces of your writing from the Argument Writing section (W.6.1) that you would like to revise.

2. Work with an adult or friend to use the checklist provided to assess your writing.

3. Using the rubric, focus on one of the areas and rewrite the pieces, paying particular attention to that aspect of the writing.

1. **Revised Argument Piece:**

_____

_____

_____

_____

_____

_____

_____

_____

_____

_____

_____

_____

_____

_____

2. **Revised Argument Piece:**

_____

_____

_____

_____

_____

_____

_____

_____

_____

_____

_____

_____

_____

_____

_____

(Answers are on page 103.)

CREDIBLE SOURCES

W.6.8 Gather relevant information from multiple print and digital sources; assess the credibility of each source; and quote or paraphrase the data and conclusions of others while avoiding plagiarism and providing basic bibliographic information for sources.

1. Which of the websites would you be most likely to use to help write your social studies essay about 9/11?

   Ⓐ *http://www.usa.gov/Citizen/Topics/History-American.shtml*

   Ⓑ *http://www.nyblogspot.omg.9/11.com*

2. Explain which features of the address helped you determine the answer to question 1?

   _____

   _____

   _____

3. Which of the websites would you be most likely to use when gaining information for science fair topics/ideas?

   Ⓐ *http://scienceblogs.com/dotphysics/*

   Ⓑ *http://www.edheads.org/*

> **Paraphrasing** means taking the **ideas** presented in a text without quoting directly *or* copying words without using quotes to give credit to the source and saying them in a different way. You may have to read the text a few times before you **understand** the idea enough to put it in **your own words.**

Directions: Read the information presented below from *www.cia.gov.*

Our Mission

1   The employees of the CIA provide intelligence (or information) to the President, the National Security Council, and all other government officials who make and carry out US national security policy.

2   We *do not* make policy or even make policy recommendations. That's the job of the US executive branch, such as the State Department or the Defense Department. We provide these leaders with the best information possible to help them make policy involving other countries.

3   A lot of people still think that our employees lurk around in trench coats, send coded messages, and use exotic equipment like hidden cameras and secret phones to do their job. (You know, all those things you see in the movies or read about in spy novels.) There is a little of that, but that's only part of the story.

4   **We fulfill our mission in two ways:**

- We give accurate and timely **intelligence** on foreign threats to our security.
- We conduct counterintelligence or other special activities relating to foreign intelligence and national security when the president asks us to. (Through counterintelligence, we prevent our opponents from obtaining secret information, and in some cases, we spread disinformation to confuse them.)

4. Choose a quote that explains why the CIA purposely lies.

_____

_____

_____

5. **Paraphrase** the ideas from **paragraph 3**.

_____

_____

_____

Directions: Read the following information below from
http://www.nlm.nih.gov/medlineplus/headache.html

Headache

1   Almost everyone has had a headache. Headache is the most common form of pain. It's a major reason people miss days at work or school or visit the doctor.

2   The most common type of headache is a tension headache. Tension headaches are due to tight muscles in your shoulders, neck, scalp and jaw. They are often related to stress, depression or anxiety. You are more likely to get tension headaches if you work too much, don't get enough sleep, miss meals, or use alcohol.

3   Other common types of headaches include migraines, cluster headaches, and sinus headaches. Most people can feel much better by making lifestyle changes, learning ways to relax and taking pain relievers.

4   Not all headaches require a doctor's attention. But sometimes headaches warn of a more serious disorder. Let your health care provider know if you have sudden, severe headaches. Get medical help right away if you have a headache after a blow to your head, or if you have a headache along with a stiff neck, fever, confusion, loss of consciousness, or pain in the eye or ear.

6. Provide textual evidence from the excerpt that cites the *behaviors* that are likely to cause tension headaches.

_____

_____

_____

_____

_____

7. **Paraphrase** the ideas in **paragraph 3**.

_____

_____

_____

_____

_____

8. Read the following *paraphrase* below that a student included in her essay.
   Explain why it is incorrect.

   Get medical help immediately if you have a headache after a hit to your head, or
   if you get a headache and a stiff neck, fever, confusion, become unconscious,
   or have pain in your eye or ear.

   _____

   _____

   _____

   _____

   _____

   _____

   _____

   _____

(Answers are on page 103.)

DRAWING EVIDENCE TO SUPPORT ANALYSIS

W.6.9 Draw evidence from literary or informational texts to support analysis, reflection, and research.

Directions: Read this excerpt from an article titled "Tried by Deadly Tornado, An Anchor of Faith Holds" *New York Times,* April 3, 1994, Dateline: Piedmont, Ala, April 2.

1   This is a place where grandmothers hold babies on their laps under the stars and whisper in their ears that the lights in the sky are holes in the floor of heaven. This is a place where the song "Jesus Loves Me" has rocked generations to sleep, and heaven is not a concept, but a destination.

2   Yet in this place where many things, even storms, are viewed as God's will, people strong in their faith and their children have died in, of all places, a church.

3   "We are trained from birth not to question God," said 23-year-old Robyn Tucker King of Piedmont, where 20 people, including six children, where killed when a tornado tore through the Goshen United Methodist Church on Palm Sunday.

4   "But why?" she said. "Why a church? Why those little children? Why? Why? Why?"

5   The destruction of this little country church and the deaths, including the pastor's vivacious 4-year-old daughter, have shaken the faith of many people who live in this deeply religious corner of Alabama, about 80 miles northeast of Birmingham.

6   It is not that it has turned them against God. But it has hurt them in a place usually safe from hurt, like a bruise on the soul.

7   They saw friends and family crushed in what they believed to be the safest place on earth, then carried away on makeshift stretchers of splintered church pews. They saw two other nearby churches destroyed, those congregations somehow spared while funerals for Goshen went on all week and the obituaries filled an entire page in the local paper.

8   But more troubling than anything, said the people who lost friends and family in the Goshen church, were the tiny patent-leather children's shoes scattered in the ruin. They were new Easter shoes, bought especially for church.

9   "If that don't shake your faith," said Michael Spears, who works at Lively's Food Market in downtown Piedmont, "nothing will."

10 The minister of the Goshen church, the Rev. Kelly Clem, her face covered with bruises from the fallen roof, buried her daughter Hannah on Wednesday. Of all people, she understands how hurtful it is to have the walls of the church broken down.

11 "This might shake people's faith for a long time," said Mrs. Clem, who led a congregation of 140 on the day of the storm. "I think that is normal. But having your faith shaken is not the same as losing it."

12 Ministers here believe that the churches will be more crowded than usual on Easter Sunday. Some will come for blessings, but others expect answers.

1. Reread **paragraph 1**. **Based on this paragraph alone**, what would you think the article might be about?
   - Ⓐ A deadly tornado
   - Ⓑ A peaceful little town
   - Ⓒ A noisy city street
   - Ⓓ The constellation

2. Explain the **irony** (the opposite of what is expected) the author points out in **paragraph 2**.

   _____

   _____

   _____

   _____

   _____

3. Read the quote from **paragraph 11,** "But having your faith shaken is not the same as losing it." What does the minister mean by this—what is the difference between the two? Use textual evidence from the article to support your answer.

   _____

   _____

   _____

   _____

   _____

4. Reread **paragraph 8**. After reading the entire excerpt, do you agree that this is the most "troubling" thing? Explain why or why not. Use **textual evidence** to support your opinion.

_____

_____

_____

_____

_____

Directions: Look closely at the image below, which depicts the aftermath of a tornado.

5. Which word **best** conveys the same mood as the picture above?
   - Ⓐ Depressing
   - Ⓑ Joyous
   - Ⓒ Filthy
   - Ⓓ Angry

6. Use visual evidence from the image to support your answer to question 5.

7. Do these two texts (the article and the image) convey similar messages about faith? Use textual evidence to support your answer.

_____

_____

_____

_____

_____

8. Which of the two texts do you feel delivers a more powerful version of this message? Use textual evidence to support your answer.

_____

_____

_____

_____

_____

(Answers are on page 103.)

ENGLISH LANGUAGE ARTS PRACTICE TEST

My Name: _____

Today's Date: _____

Directions: Read the following poem and answer the questions that follow.

Dusting

Julia Alvarez

Each morning I wrote my name
on the dusty cabinet, then crossed
the dining room table in script, scrawled
in capitals on the backs of chairs,
5   practicing signatures like scales
while Mother followed, squirting
linseed from a burping can
into a crumpled-up flannel.

She erased my fingerprints
10   from the bookshelf and rocker,
polished mirrors on the desk
scribbled with my alphabets.
My name was swallowed in the towel
with which she jeweled the table tops.
15   The grain surfaced in the oak
and the pine grew luminous.
But I refused with every mark
to be like her, anonymous.

https://teacherweb.com/MA/DrKevinMHurleyMiddleSchool/dsturner/poemdustinjuliaalvarez.pdf

1. Reread **line 6**. How does this line contribute to your understanding of the mother's character?
   - Ⓐ It shows that the mother values cleanliness above all else.
   - Ⓑ It shows that the mother is content with others taking the lead.
   - Ⓒ It shows that the mother is unhappy in her life.
   - Ⓓ It shows that the daughter enjoys helping her mother clean.

76

2. Reread **line 13**. Identify the figurative language and explain the literal meanings of the phrase "My name was swallowed in the towel."

   _____

   _____

3. Using context clues, what is most likely the meaning of the word **linseed** as used in **line 7**?

   Ⓐ water   Ⓒ cleaner
   Ⓑ plant   Ⓓ dust

4. Rewrite the following sentence correctly.

   The speaker in the poem continues to write their name on every surface despite the fact that her mother insists on making them disappear.

   _____

   _____

5. What part of speech is the word **polished** as used in stanza 2?

   Ⓐ Noun   Ⓒ Adverb
   Ⓑ Verb   Ⓓ Adjective

6. Write one **word** that conveys the **theme** of this poem.

   _____

7. In her poem "Dusting," Julia Alvarez portrays a relationship between a mother and daughter in which the daughter desires a very different life from her mother's. Look at the actions of both the mother and the daughter in the poem.

   Write an original story from the mother's point of view in response to "Dusting." In your story, be sure to use what you have learned about the mother and the daughter to help develop the mother's perspective.

   _____

   _____

   _____

   _____

   _____

   _____

Directions: Read the article below about Ellis Island and answer the questions that follow.

Ellis Island

Oysters, Pirates and Ammunition: The Early Days of Ellis Island

1   Native Americans, pirates, settlers, and explosives: Ellis Island had a colorful history even before it became the busiest point of entry for immigrants to the United States.

2   Ellis Island is famous as the place where most immigrants entered the country in the late 19th and early 20th centuries. It is believed that 100 million Americans have ancestors who were admitted through Ellis Island. Maybe you are one of them.

3   Did you know that this famous island started out as just three acres of sand in New York Harbor, south of Manhattan? The Native Americans who lived nearby, the Mohegan tribe, named it *Kioshk*, which means "Gull Island." In the 1630s, Dutch settlers called it "Oyster Island" because it had rich oyster beds and good fishing. The British took over the area in 1664. At first, they named it "Gull Island," but that soon changed. The island was used as a place to hang pirates, and so it was soon called "Gibbet Island" because "gibbet" is another word for "gallows." Samuel Ellis bought the island in the 1770s, around the time of the Revolutionary War. By then, it had had at least six different names.

4   Samuel Ellis turned his island into a picnic spot. In 1785 he tried to sell it again, but could not find a buyer. New York bought it in 1807, after Samuel Ellis had died. The United States government bought it from New York in 1808 for $10,000. Over time, the island grew from its original size of just over three acres to 27.5 acres because soil, rocks and other debris were dumped there.

5   In the years leading up to the War of 1812, the United States government built defenses on islands in the area. During that war, Fort Gibson was built on the island to hold prisoners. Later, during the Civil War, the island was used as a munitions arsenal for the Union Army. "Ellis Island" became the island's official name in 1861.

6   Before 1890, individual states were responsible for regulating immigration. The Castle Garden immigration facility, located on the southern tip of Manhattan, was the New York State immigration station from 1855 to 1890. Eight million people entered the United States through Castle Garden. Most came from Northern and Western Europe. The federal government took over the job of regulating immigration in 1890, and Castle Garden closed on April 18, 1890. As a second wave of immigration lasting from 1890 to 1924 began to reach the United States, the federal government built a new federal immigration station on Ellis Island to process the large number of immigrants arriving in New York.

7   The Ellis Island immigration facility opened on January 1, 1892. A fifteen-year-old Irish girl named Annie Moore was the first of more than twelve million people who would ultimately pass through the Ellis Island facilities on their way into the United States.

http://www.abcteach.com/free/17333.pdf © 2005–2010 abcteach.com

8. Which quotation from the article best explains why the government began to use Ellis Island?

   Ⓐ "Before 1890, individual states were responsible for regulating immigration."

   Ⓑ "The United States government bought it from New York in 1808 for $10,000."

   Ⓒ "The Castle Garden immigration facility, located on the southern tip of Manhattan, was the New York State immigration station from 1855 to 1890."

   Ⓓ "As a second wave of immigration lasting from 1890 to 1924 began to reach the United States . . . ."

9. Write a one sentence summary of this article.

   _____

10. How many Americans have ancestors who passed through Ellis Island?

    Ⓐ Twelve million people   Ⓒ 27.5 people

    Ⓑ 100 million people   Ⓓ 1865 people

11. What is the best synonym for the word **debris** as used in paragraph 4?

    Ⓐ Boats   Ⓒ Immigrants

    Ⓑ Land   Ⓓ Wreckage

12. What is the author's purpose in this article?

    Ⓐ to entertain   Ⓒ to persuade

    Ⓑ to inform   Ⓓ to question

13. If you wanted to do more research on Ellis Island, which of the following resources would you use?

    Ⓐ www.my familyhistoryellisisland.com

    Ⓑ www.ellisislandtimeline.org

    Ⓒ www.cooltourismspotsny.inc

    Ⓓ www.immigrationissues.blogspot

14. Explain the author's purpose in beginning his article with the following list:
    "Native Americans, pirates, settlers, and explosives."

    _____

    _____

    _____

15. Ellis Island is one of the most important places in our country's history. Write an essay that supports this claim. (You may use textual evidence.)

_____

_____

_____

_____

Directions: Read the following story about a young girl's eleventh birthday. Answer the questions that follow, referring back to the text as needed.

Eleven
by Sandra Cisneros

1   What they don't understand about birthdays and what they never tell you is that when you're eleven, you're also ten, and nine, and eight, and seven, and six, and five, and four, and three, and two, and one. And when you wake up on your eleventh birthday you expect to feel eleven, but you don't. You open your eyes and everything's just like yesterday, only it's today. And you don't feel eleven at all. You feel like you're still ten. And you are—underneath the year that makes you eleven.

2   Like some days you might say something stupid, and that's the part of you that's still ten. Or maybe some days you might need to sit on your mama's lap because you're scared, and that's the part of you that's five. And maybe one day when you're all grown up maybe you will need to cry like if you're three, and that's okay. That's what I tell Mama when she's sad and needs to cry. Maybe she's feeling three.

3   Because the way you grow old is kind of like an onion or like the rings inside a tree trunk or like my little wooden dolls that fit one inside the other, each year inside the next one. That's how being eleven years old is.

4   You don't feel eleven. Not right away. It takes a few days, weeks even, sometimes even months before you say Eleven when they ask you. And you don't feel smart eleven, not until you're almost twelve. That's the way it is.

5   Only today I wish I didn't have only eleven years rattling inside me like pennies in a tin Band-Aid box. Today I wish I was one hundred and two instead of eleven because if I was one hundred and two I'd have known what to say when Mrs. Price put the red sweater on my desk. I would've known how to tell her it wasn't mine instead of just sitting there with that look on my face and nothing coming out of my mouth.

6   "Whose is this?" Mrs. Price says, and she holds the red sweater up in the air for all the class to see.   "Whose? It's been sitting in the coatroom for a month."

7   "Not mine," says everybody. "Not me."

8   "It has to belong to somebody," Mrs. Price keeps saying, but nobody can remember. It's an ugly sweater with red plastic buttons and a collar and sleeves all

stretched out like you could use it for a jump rope. It's maybe a thousand years old and even if it belonged to me I wouldn't say so.

9   Maybe because I'm skinny, maybe because she doesn't like me, that stupid Sylvia Saldivar says, "I think it belongs to Rachel." An ugly sweater like that, all raggedy and old, but Mrs. Price believes her. Mrs. Price takes the sweater and puts it right on my desk, but when I open my mouth nothing comes out.

10   "That's not, I don't, you're not . . . Not mine," I finally say in a little voice that was maybe me when I was four.

11   "Of course it's yours," Mrs. Price says, "I remember you wearing it once." Because she's older and the teacher, she's right and I'm not.

12   Not mine, not mine, not mine, but Mrs. Price is already turning to page thirty-two, and math problem number four. I don't know why but all of a sudden I'm feeling sick inside, like the part of me that's three wants to come out of my eyes, only I squeeze them shut tight and bite down on my teeth real hard and try to remember today I am eleven, eleven. Mama is making a cake for me for tonight, and when Papa comes home everybody will sing Happy birthday, happy birthday to you.

13   But when the sick feeling goes away and I open my eyes, the red sweater's still sitting there like a big red mountain. I move the red sweater to the corner of my desk with my ruler. I move my pencil and books and eraser as far from it as possible. I even move my chair a little to the right. Not mine, not mine, not mine.

14   In my head I'm thinking how long till lunchtime, how long till I can take the red sweater and throw it over the schoolyard fence, or leave it hanging on a parking meter, or bunch it up into a little ball and toss it in the alley. Except when math period ends Mrs. Price says loud and in front of everybody, "Now, Rachel, that's enough," because she sees I've shoved the red sweater to the tippy-tip corner of my desk and it's hanging all over the edge like a waterfall, but I don't care.

15   "Rachel," Mrs. Price says. She says it like she's getting mad. "You put that sweater on right now and no more nonsense."

16   "But it's not—"

17   "Now!" Mrs. Price says.

18   This is when I wish I wasn't eleven, because all the years inside of me—ten, nine, eight, seven, six, five, four, three, two, and one—are pushing at the back of my eyes when I put one arm through one sleeve of the sweater that smells like cottage cheese, and then the other arm through the other and stand there with my arms apart like if the sweater hurts me and it does, all itchy and full of germs that aren't mine.

19   That's when everything I've been holding in since this morning, since when Mrs. Price put the sweater on my desk, finally lets go, and all of a sudden I'm crying in front of everybody. I wish I was invisible but I'm not. I'm eleven and it's my birthday today and I'm crying like I'm three in front of everybody. I put my head down on the desk and bury my face in my stupid clown-sweater arms. My face all hot and spit coming out of my mouth because I can't stop the little animal noises from coming out of me, until there aren't any more tears left in my eyes, and it's just my body shaking like when you have the hiccups, and my whole head hurts like when you drink milk too fast.

20   But the worst part is right before the bell rings for lunch. That stupid Phyllis Lopez, who is even dumber than Sylvia Saldivar, says she remembers the red sweater is hers! I take it off right away and give it to her, only Mrs. Price pretends like everything's okay.

21   Today I'm eleven. There's a cake Mama's making for tonight, and when Papa comes home from work we'll eat it. There'll be candles and presents and everybody will sing Happy birthday, happy birthday to you, Rachel, only it's too late.

22   I'm eleven today. I'm eleven, ten, nine, eight, seven, six, five, four, three, two, and one, but I wish I was one hundred and two. I wish I was anything but eleven, because I want today to be far away already, far away like a runaway balloon, like a tiny o in the sky, so tiny-tiny you have to close your eyes to see it.

16. Provide two pieces of evidence from the story that prove Rachel is having a disappointing birthday.

_____

_____

17. Mrs. Price does not apologize even after she finds out that the sweater does not belong to Rachel. What does this tell you about her character?

Ⓐ She is a distrustful person and does not believe Phyllis.

Ⓑ She does not like to admit her mistakes.

Ⓒ She is a very kind person.

Ⓓ She is an angry person who does not like Rachel.

18. Which of the quotations best supports the **theme** of the story?

Ⓐ "There's a cake Mama's making for tonight, and when Papa comes . . . ."

Ⓑ "It's maybe a thousand years old and even if it belonged to me I wouldn't say so."

Ⓒ "Because the way you grow old is kind of like an onion . . . ."

Ⓓ "That's when everything I've been holding in since this morning . . . ."

19. Read the quote from **paragraph 8**: "It's maybe a thousand years old and even if it belonged to me I wouldn't say so."

Identify what type of figurative language is being used here and the purpose of the literary device.

_____

_____

20. Write one sentence to summarize this story.

_____

_____

21. Write an informational piece explaining what you should do when you feel a teacher is treating you or a classmate unfairly.

_____

_____

_____

_____

Directions: Read the following excerpt from *A Long Way Gone: Memoirs of a Boy Soldier* by Ishmael Beah

1   There were all kind of stories told about the war that made it sound as if it was happening in a faraway land. It wasn't until refugees started passing through our town that we began to see that it was actually taking place in our country. Families who had walked hundreds of miles told how relatives had been killed and their houses burned. Some people felt sorry for them and offered them places to stay, but most of the refugees refused, because they said the war would eventually reach our town. The children of these families wouldn't look at us, and they jumped at the sound of chopping wood or as stones landed on the tin roofs flung by children hunting birds with slingshots. The adults among these children from the war zones would be lost in their thoughts during conversations with the elders of my town. Apart from their fatigue and malnourishment, it was evident they had seen something that plagued their minds, something that we would refuse to accept if they told us all of it. The only wars I knew of were those that I had read about in books or seen in movies such as *Rambo: First Blood,* and the one in neighboring Liberia that I had heard about on the BBC news. My imagination at ten years old didn't have the capacity to grasp what had taken away the happiness of the refugees.

2   The first time that I was touched by war I was twelve. It was in January of 1993. I left home with Junior, my older brother, and our friend Talloi, both a year older than I, to go to the town of Mattru Jong, to participate in our friends' talent show. Mohamed, my best friend, couldn't come because he and his father were renovating their thatched-roof kitchen that day.

3   The four of us had started a rap and dance group when I was eight. We were first introduced to rap music during one of our visits to Mobimbi, a quarter where the foreigners who worked for the same American company as my father lived.

4   We often went to Mobimbi to swim in a pool and watch the huge color television and the white people who crowded the visitors' recreational area. One evening a music video that consisted of a bunch of young black fellows talking really fast came on the television. The four of us sat mesmerized by the song, trying to understand what the black fellows were saying.

5   At the end of the video, some letters came up at the bottom of the screen. They read "Sugarhill Gang, 'Rapper's Delight.'" Junior quickly wrote it down on a piece of paper. After that, we came to the quarters every other weekend to study that kind of music on television. We didn't know what is was called then, but I was impressed with the fact that the black fellows knew how to speak English really fast, and to beat.

22. What type of narration is used in this excerpt? Circle the correct narrator.

1st person   *or*   **2nd person**   *or*   **3rd person**

23. What is the most likely definition of **refugee** as used in paragraph 1?
Ⓐ A soldier who fights in a war
Ⓑ A person displaced from his or her home because of violence or danger
Ⓒ A young person living in a village
Ⓓ A singer on the TV

24. Read the following sentence from **paragraph 1**.

"… until refugees started passing through our town that we began to see that **it** was actually taking place in our country."

What word has been replaced with the pronoun "it"? (*Hint: Go back to the paragraph. You may have to read more than just the sentence itself to determine the answer.*)

Word: _____

Explain how you determined your answer:

_____

_____

25. Based on **paragraph 4**, how can you infer the narrator felt about his trips to Mobimbi?

_____

_____

26. Read the sentence from **paragraph 2**.

> "We were first introduced to rap music during one of our visits to Mobimbi, a **quarter** where the foreigners who worked for the same American company as my father lived."

Which of the following sentences uses **quarter** in the same way as this sentence above?
- Ⓐ Did you see that beautiful quarter moon last night?
- Ⓑ After the party, there was a quarter of the birthday cake left.
- Ⓒ I found three quarters under my couch cushions this morning!
- Ⓓ The living quarters at our camp were better than we expected.

27. Explain why it is significant that the narrator has heard stories that make war seem "faraway."

_____

_____

28. What does the word **malnourishment (paragraph 1)** most likely mean?
- Ⓐ Extreme hunger
- Ⓑ Extreme exhaustion
- Ⓒ Extreme excitement
- Ⓓ Extreme pain

29. Explain why the refugees turn down good offers from villagers who will let them stay in their homes.

_____

_____

30. Which of the following best summarizes **paragraph 3**?
- Ⓐ A boy remembers an experience with music that had a profound effect on him.
- Ⓑ A boy shares his favorite rap songs.
- Ⓒ A refugee is treated kindly and taken on a trip to a big hotel.
- Ⓓ A young refugee lodges with friendly villagers.

Directions: Closely study the image below.

31. Which of the following is an inference you might draw from this image?
    Ⓐ The girl is carrying a container.
    Ⓑ The girl is not financially well off.
    Ⓒ The girl is not wearing any shoes on her feet.
    Ⓓ The girl is about to be attacked.

32. Provide two pieces of **textual evidence** to support your **inference** in the previous question.

    1. _____

    2. _____

33. Which of the following might be an appropriate title for this image?
    Ⓐ Vacation to the Big City   Ⓒ   Danger Around Every Corner
    Ⓑ Out for a Stroll Through Town   Ⓓ   Life in the Village

34. **Compare** and **contrast** what you learned from the image with the excerpt from *A Long Way Gone: Memoirs of a Boy Soldier.*

    _____

    _____

    _____

35. Based on the image, write a memoir that tells this girl's story. Use details from the image to help you craft a memoir.

    _____

    _____

    _____

Directions: Read the following poem titled "Faith Free" and answer the questions that follow.

Do I,
in the darkness of this space,
with only whispers shouting in my ears,
between the burning rivers,
5   build a bridge to carry grief,
you ask.

Believe
without seeing,
absent of proof,
10 empty of evidence.
He—
whose word is Word,
whose kingdom knows no address—
invites no visitor to rest, but only a moment
15 whose perfect promises require only faith for follow-through.

In Heaven,
sins undone,
wrongs righted,
lies unspoken,
20 flaws forgiven,
I think.

The incomplete arc of your arm,
Searches for my hand,
Impatient to know.
25 I envelop your hand in mine, and squeeze gently,
(Forgive me),
I nod.

36. How many stanzas are in this poem?
  Ⓐ 27   Ⓒ 4
  Ⓑ 5   Ⓓ 1

37. Explain what question the speaker is being asked.

_____

38. The line *"whose word is Word"* (line 12) is an example of:

(A) Personification   (C) Simile

(B) Alliteration   (D) Idiom

39. What is the significance of the nod at the end of the poem?

_____

40. What part of speech is the word **envelop** as used in line 25?

(A) Adjective   (C) Verb

(B) Noun   (D) Preposition

41. Reread stanza 1. Explain how the phrase "Only whispers shouting in my ears" is an example of personification. What does the speaker mean by this?

_____

_____

42. Gather two sources from the Internet to learn about two **different** religious faiths. Be sure to evaluate the sources for credibility. Write a summary of each faith's main beliefs, paraphrasing and citing when necessary.

_____

_____

Directions: Read each sentence below and circle the appropriate pronoun to be used in each sentence.

43. Craig did not know (who/whom) to ask about the score of the football game because

everywhere (he/him) looked he could only see hockey fans.

44. My sister asked (me/I) to please bring her water bottle with me when I left the house.

She left (it/them) on the kitchen counter.

Directions: Replace the underlined words by writing the correct pronoun above the underlined words.

45. The violent hurricane left the city destroyed after the violent storm tore through the city,

    eating up everything that got in the storm's way.

46. Robert refused to pay a late fee for the books that Robert had borrowed from the library

    because Robert was positive that Robert's wife had returned the books months ago.

Directions: Use a reflexive pronoun to add emphasis to the sentence.

47. Father Bill _____ said that he would be more than happy to volunteer
    his time at the church's food pantry even though he will be preparing for the service
    that afternoon.

48. Despite the desperate pleas from the coach _____, no players
    decided to join the summer league, so she had to forfeit the games.

Directions: Read the sentence and use context clues to define the bolded word.

49. Liz had a scary **premonition** when the mirror fell from her bedroom wall and came
    crashing to the ground. She was nervous about what the night would bring!

    Premonition means _____

    _____

50. Sophia always dreamed that someday a man would sweep her off her feet by **serenading**
    her while playing his guitar in front of a crowd of jealous spectators.

    Serenade means _____

    _____

(Answers are on page 104.)

ENGLISH LANGUAGE ARTS ANSWERS EXPLAINED

LANGUAGE

Using Pronouns Appropriately, page 2

1. **her.** The pronoun is receiving the action of Jonathan's forgiveness. Objective pronouns such as her, him, me, them, and us are used to replace nouns that receive action. When you read the sentence with both options, you will recognize that *her* sounds like a better fit than *she*.

2. **he, he.** The antecedent in this sentence, Mark, is performing the action—he is *deciding* which school to *attend*. Subjective pronouns such as she, he, I, they, and we are used to replace nouns delivering action.

3. **whom.** This pronoun is receiving the action in this sentence and therefore serves as an objective pronoun. If you imagine answering this question, you might say, "Ask him" or "Ask her." Instead of him or her, you should use the pronoun *whom*.

4. **they, their.** The first pronoun replaces *students*, the subject of the sentence and the pronoun performing the actions of *deciding* and *using*. If you read the sentence aloud, you will hear that *they* sounds like the appropriate pronoun. The second pronoun used must show possession of the lockers. *Students* is a plural noun that represents many people.

5. **him, he.**

6. **she, them.** Marie is the subject of this sentence and is performing the action of this sentence. When replacing Marie with a pronoun, you must choose between *her* and *she*. If you read the sentence aloud and fill in both options, you will hear that *she* is the better choice. The store employees represent multiple people so you must use *they* or *them*. The employees are receiving the action of Marie asking for help. You will see you must choose the objective pronoun—*them*.

7. **he, his yard, theirs.** Remy is barking (action), so you must replace Remy with a subjective pronoun.

The second and third pronouns in the sentences both have to show possession. The yard belongs to Remy, so you could replace the phrase *Remy's yard* with a single pronoun that conveys ownership. Martin and Julie require a plural noun because there is more than one person.

8. **they, her, them.** The *kids* are producing action in the sentences so a subjective pronoun is needed to replace this noun. Since *kids* is a plural noun, you must choose between *them* or *they*. If you read the sentence aloud, you will hear that "them are allowed to borrow" does not sound correct. Students recognize that ('s) added to McLaughlin indicates possession. *Her* replaces the antecedent *Ms. McLaughlin's* because it shows ownership of the office. Finally, the *books* refers to the multiple books kids may have borrowed from the office. The books are receiving the action of being returned, so you need an objective pronoun that represents a plural subject.

Grammar Conventions, page 4

1. **Simone's mother is always talking to (her) in the car and she becomes frustrated when Simone doesn't listen!** You should recognize that in the original sentence there were too many pronouns and since both people in the sentence are girls, it becomes confusing. By changing the pronoun to Simone, it is clear that Simone was being talked to by her mother.

2. **Little League tryouts take place this Saturday morning, so David's father told David (he) should be at the field first thing in the morning.** It was unclear to the reader whether David or his father should be at the field. By adding the phrase *told David* in front of the pronoun it helps clarify for the reader that David is the *he* being referred to.

3. **Mike and his brother John went camping together and (Mike or John) became angry when (his) GPS broke.** In the original, you will notice that the pronoun *he* does not refer to a specific noun and could mean either of the men.

By adding the name of one of the brothers (your choice here), the reader has a clearer understanding of whose GPS malfunctioned.

4. **The students at my school is(are) worried about our music department**. The word *is* should be changed to *are*. There are many students in the school so the subject is plural. There must be agreement between the subject of a sentence and the verb—the verb must reflect the singular or plural nature of the noun.

5. **We were told their (there) may not be enough money left in the budget to maintain our current music courses.** There are different uses for the words *there, their, they're,* but *their* indicates ownership of an item, and *they're* is a contraction for they are. There are no issues of ownership here. The proper word is *there*.

6. **We are writing to u(you) to let u(you) know how important music education is to our school careers.** In writing a letter of this nature, you must use standard acceptable language. Although you may shorten words when writing to informal audiences such as friends, or in text messages or blogs, you may not use the informal spelling "u" to replace the formal spelling of *you*. Use formal spelling for formal occasions.

7. **Please help us keep music alive?** This last sentence is not a question, but rather a request. Since the sentence is a statement, a *period* or an *exclamation point* would be more appropriate than a question mark.

Commas, Dashes, and Parentheses, page 6

1. **Baseball, like other team sports, requires communication and camaraderie among teammates for success.** The phrase "like other team sports" is an appositive phrase and not necessary to the overall meaning of the sentence. Appositive phrases add extra detail or information to the sentence and must be set off in commas. When you read the sentence without the phrase, it still forms a complete thought.

2. **Isaac Asimov, a well-known science fiction writer, began his career by submitting funny stories to magazines.** "A well-known science fiction writer" is a description of Asimov. This

information helps the reader learn more about Asimov, but the sentence is complete without this description. This description is not essential to comprehend the sentence; therefore, it should be set off in commas.

3. **(C)** "winner of the Dental Excellence award" is an additional detail about Dr. Madden and is not necessary to understand the sentence. When you remove this descriptive phrase, you will realize that the sentence forms a complete thought.

4. **In preparation for her son's birthday party, Alice picked up the favors, the balloons, the ice cream, and a gift, only to realize she forgot the most important thing—the cake.** Dashes can be used to highlight a word or phrase in a sentence. By setting "the cake" off after the dash, it adds details about which important item she forgot.

5. **Zeus managed to save his siblings—who had been swallowed by their own father—and defeat Cronus and the Titans.** Setting off "who had been swallowed by their own father," emphasizes to the reader what a strong opponent Cronus must have been for Zeus. Without the words inside the dashes, the sentence would still be informative and logical.

6. **(D)** The parentheses are used here to explain the use of applesauce in the recipe. It is unnecessary to the overall sentence for the reader to know that applesauce is used as an alternative. Parentheses can be used to define unfamiliar terms or to add information to the sentence.

7. **(C)** The spelling rule is that *i* generally comes before *e* except when the two letters follow the letter *c*. In this case, you will realize that *i* must follow *e*.

8. **(B)** The word needed to fill the sentence must be a plural noun since Jimmy has had many of these "over the years." To make a noun plural, students know that they must add *es* to words ending in *ch, th,* or *sh*.

Sentence Variety and Consistency in Tone, page 8

1. **We went to the baseball game on Saturday afternoon to watch my cousin Brian and our**

friend Dave. **Even though their team lost, we had a good time.** Beginning each sentence in a paragraph or multiple sentences with the same word can feel repetitive and sound bland. Look to combine sentences where similar ideas can be joined.

2. **Music is important to a lot of people because it can help them relax, feel excited, happy, or even stir up memories. Many people sing or dance when a favorite song comes on.** Paragraphs that contain a lot of simple sentences make the paragraph feel choppy and elementary. Look to vary the lengths of your sentence by combining shorter sentences. Since these are similar points, they should be combined into one sentence.

3. **Due to the risk of getting sunburned, the parents asked the girls to take a break in the shade of their umbrella before swimming in the ocean. The girls raced down to the water's edge after they had rested for a while. The mom had to stay under the umbrella to watch the baby because he was still sleeping.** Each of the sentences starts with a dependent clause followed by a comma and an independent clause, so the style becomes predictable and repetitive when used in so many consecutive sentences. Rearrange the sentence structure to give the paragraph more variety.

4. **(A)** Sentence **B** does not maintain that *formal* tone of the original sentence and must be eliminated. Sentences **C** and **D** do not have the same meaning as the original sentence. Sentence **A** uses formal language and has almost the same meaning as the original sentence. Both sentences discuss the fear of allowing children to use the Internet because of online predators.

5. **(C)** Sentence **C** maintains the informal tone of the original sentence and captures the meaning of the sentence. "No idea" is idiomatic language meaning that you don't know something. Sentence **B** should be ruled out due to the formal language it uses.

6. **(B)** Sentence **B** combines the two original sentences into one, but maintains both the formal style and the meaning. The sentence structure may be rearranged, but the sentence still conveys an apologetic announcement.

Defining Vocabulary in Context, page 10

1. **(C)** The Latin root *bene* means good or well. Combine your knowledge of the root with the context clues about Margaret working in a church and volunteering at a soup kitchen—both of which you recognize as positive or good deeds.

2. **(B)** The root *mal, male* means bad or abnormal. Combine your knowledge of the root with the context clues about a criminal who must spend life in prison—both of which you recognize as negative or bad deeds.

3. **(D)** Use context clues from the sentence to determine its meaning. The appositive phrase about Peter being a retired football player indicates that at one time he must have been a very strong man. This is in contrast to the use of the word *feeble*, which describes Peter's physical condition at present. Additionally, you can use the phrase "age-ridden body" to convey the idea that Peter is now old.

4. **(B)** Use the phrases "terrible ordeal" and "wild and aggressive" as context clues to show the exact opposite of the word *docile*. The sentence describes both a terrible and a happy experience with elephants.

5. **Lying, cheating, swindling, (being) dishonest** The salesman has the appearance of honesty, but the client does not feel convinced that he is trustworthy. If the man appears honest but is not, you will conclude that *to deceive* must mean to be dishonest.

6. **Grief, sorrow, suffering, torture** Use the phrase "left him paralyzed" as a context clue to realize that Danny would be understandably saddened by this event. The context clues that describe Danny's prior personality are used to show that he behaves in an opposite manner after the accident. Danny has been through a severe ordeal, so *anguish* must be an intense sadness.

Interpreting Figures of Speech, page 12

1. **Personification** When using personification, authors give human qualities to inanimate objects. David's **confidence** is being spoken about as if it is a living person that can be scared and physically

run away from a situation. The expression is meant to describe how frightened David was during his onstage moment. Confidence cannot literally run away but you will recognize that the expression emphasizes David's lack of self-assurance at the time.

2. **Idiom** Idioms are common phrases in which the words take on different meanings than what they might literally suggest. There is not a literal monkey on Nichole's back. The "monkey" on her back refers to a bad habit that she is having a difficult time giving up, which is eating junk food.

3. **Metaphor** Metaphors make direct comparisons between two things that seem different. Diana is being compared to a rock. A woman and a rock do not seem to have a lot in common, but a rock is a tough, hard object that provides a foundation and can be difficult to move. The expression here is meant to describe Diana's support and constant role in her sister's life.

4. **Personification** Clouds are not humans and they do not have emotions or the ability to cry as humans do. The expression is meant to describe the rainy scene at the gravesite. The author describes the clouds as crying (or raining as tears) to emphasize how sad all the mourners are.

5. **(B)** A chapter is a small part of an entire novel. Applying this relationship to the second half of the analogy, *scene* must be a portion of something larger. A film is an entire production made up of many scenes. Therefore, *Scene: Film* conveys that same relationship as does *Chapter: Novel.*

6. **(C)** Influenza and disease are related because the flu is one type of disease. Applying this relationship to the second half of the analogy, you will see that *Jazz* must be one type of something else. Jazz is one of many genres of music; therefore, *Music* is the best word to complete the relationship.

7. **Attractive, Pretty, Gorgeous** All three words could be used to describe a person or thing's appearance, and it is clear that they convey varying levels of emotion. *Attractive* is the most neutral of the group so it would be considered the *least intense* of the three words. *Pretty* carries a more positive connotation than *attractive*, but it

is not as charged as *gorgeous*. The most intense word of the group is *gorgeous*. This word is used less commonly than *pretty* and carries the connotation that something is extremely pretty or breathtaking.

8. **Indifferent, Unfriendly, Hostile** All of these words can be used to describe someone's behavior or personality. The most neutral of the group is the word *indifferent*, so it is ranked the *least intense*. Acting *indifferently* means that the person is not showing intense like or dislike of something. Acting *unfriendly* is more intense than acting *indifferently* because acting unfriendly conveys a more negative or unpleasant feeling. Acting *hostile* is the most intense of the actions because it conveys a feeling of aggression or anger.

Citing Textual Evidence in Literature, page 14

1. **(C)** Evidence from the image may include the woman being thin, wearing workout gear, or running alone when it appears to be early in the morning. The sun is rising in the back right section of the image, which tells you that she is serious about staying fit, so she wakes up early to exercise.

2. **(C)** This particular quote describes how the narrator handles his friend Jeff when he is mad or upset about something. Each of the other quotes is an observation, but choice **C** shows that the narrator has patience with his friend and gives him space when he needs it.

3. **Class Clown** When Mrs. Tracy speaks to Jeff about his feet, he is quick to comment back ("Thirty *is* an old man!"). As he says this, Jeff is "half looking around and laughing." This piece of evidence shows you that he is looking for approval from his classmates and is trying to incite laughter. These pieces of evidence support the idea that Jeff is the class clown.

Finding the Central Idea and Theme, page 16

1. **(C)** A summary should be a brief retelling of the main points and should not include opinions or judgments. Also, a summary should not focus on

the small or supporting details, but on the main point of the text. Sentence **C** provides a brief description of the detailed scene described in the paragraph.

2. **"brimming with life," "song in every heart," "cheer in every face and spring in every step"** Any of the details listed above support the idea that all the people and things in the town appear happy on the particular day being described. The smaller details of a paragraph help develop the central idea, which is what each of these details does for paragraph 1.

3. *Tom is upset by the amount of work he has.* Using 10 words or fewer will require you to focus on the most essential parts of the paragraph. You should provide a summary that includes the central point of this paragraph that Tom is very unhappy with his situation.

4. **"all gladness left him and a deep melancholy settled down upon his spirit," "Life to him seemed hollow…" "and sat down on a tree-box discouraged"** Reread paragraph 2 looking for details that show Tom is upset. Negative emotions or words with negative connotations indicate unhappiness. Each of these smaller details is an example of the overall point of the paragraph—Tom's sadness.

5. (B) Jim appears in the last three sentences of the paragraph and seems happy (skipping and singing). Look for Tom's reaction to Jim's entrance since the central idea of the paragraph is about Tom's mood. Tom considers Jim's chore and then his opinion begins to change. The last sentence of the paragraph tells the reader that Tom finds Jim's chore more desirable because at least there is "company" there.

Plot and Character Development, page 18

1. (C) Children can be jealous of time spent with adults, and Esperanza shows this by being upset when she is not allowed to go with her father and Miguel. By asking this question, she shows that she desired to go on the trips and feels left out.

2. (B) Miguel only began calling her this after she had offended him and reminded him of his lower station in life. In the beginning of the passage

Esperanza appears to think of Miguel as an equal. When her attitude toward him changes, Miguel begins calling her "queen" sarcastically.

3. (A) Papa's explanation to Esperanza reveals that he is a kind and thoughtful person. He wants Miguel to be prepared for the future and knowledgeable so that Miguel can be productive when he grows up.

4. **Once Esperanza is older, she realizes the difference between Miguel's family and hers. She realizes now that they are not equals because she comes from a wealthy family and his family serves her.** This realization is hinted at in paragraph 6 when Mama tells her that she will feel differently about marrying him someday. This should help you realize that the difference that prevents marriage is their class.

Effect of Word Choice, page 20

1. (D) The prefix *inter* means between. The narrator interfered in the whipping. You should be familiar with the word *interview* and realize it does not fit in this sentence.

2. (B) Dragged is followed by "bloody and unconscious." This phrase appeals to the senses and helps the reader visualize a gruesome scene as opposed to just saying he was killed. Dragging a person to death is an unusual and brutal act.

3. (C) This is an idiom that does not literally mean to move or shove an object. In the context of the sentence, the narrator is trying not to remember Cinna's death because it makes her too emotional. This will help you realize that she is trying to avoid thoughts by "pushing them away."

4. **It suggests that it could easily be destroyed** The word fragile is often used in relation to glass objects or things that literally shatter. The use of the word fragile here suggests that the narrator is trying to "keep all the pieces" together by avoiding dangerous or painful thoughts.

5. **Sympathy, empathy, sadness, grief** You should use some emotion with a negative emotion because the narrator is expressing her grief over the loss of her friend. She also feels responsible for her friend's death, which could make you feel sympathy for her. The three adjectives used to describe Cinna make him seem like a wonderful

person, which heightens the reader's grief at his death.

Plot Development, page 22

1. **(C)** The father and son have not seen each other in years, which will make their relationship awkward and distant. Richard also mentions that his son does not belong at digs, which readers can conclude would cause resentment on Henry's part.

2. **(B)** To dart around means to move in a very quick motion back and forth or side to side. When people do this with their eyes, they may be on high alert for danger or to see if someone is watching them because they are being secretive or behaving in a way that makes them seem guilty. Henry's behavior shows that he is unsure of what to do.

3. **Forced** Being forced to do something means doing it against your will. It is typical behavior for a father to want to spend time with his son, but in this sentence, Richard reveals his unwillingness in having Henry around: he's doing it only because there is no one else to watch his son.

Point of View, page 24

1. **3rd person** A 3rd person narrator is not part of the story. Using the Tip will help you determine the type of narrator you're reading.

2. **Pronouns and proper nouns** You can determine the narrator by looking at the type of pronouns used in the text. When you see pronouns such as he, she, or they or names (proper nouns) being used, it indicates that an outside person (3rd person) is talking about the characters.

3. **(A)** You have read in the paragraph that Amber is popular and other students like her. You can cite different examples throughout the paragraph that prove Amber is accepted by her classmates, such as being captain of the squad and popular with the student body.

4. **1st person** A 1st person narrator is generally a character in the story who is telling the story. Using the Tip will help you realize that the type of pronouns being used in the paragraph indicate a 1st person point of view.

5. **Personal pronouns** You know that a 1st person narrator is a character in the story and is witness to the events in the story. You should recognize that pronouns such as I, we, our, us, and my indicate a person in the story, or a 1st person narrator.

6. **(C)** You should pick up on the tone change when the narrator changes from 3rd person to 1st person. People don't generally speak so highly of themselves in the way this narrator does because it gives off an air of superiority.

Comparing Texts Across Genres, page 26

1. **(C)** Giving statistics and facts will cause the readers to imagine the severity of the spill. The author does call it "terrible," but this doesn't help the reader visualize what exactly has been affected that makes it terrible. The distance and number of birds affected both help the reader see effects of the spill.

2. **(D)** Black and slippery are descriptive words that appeal to the senses and help the reader form pictures in his or her head about what the spill must have looked like.

3. **(A)** This is a factual account of the spill, so the author would not be exaggerating or making things seem more disgusting than reality. The birds died in many ways because the oil affected many different areas of their environment.

4. **(C)** There is a shift in the poem when the bird goes from soaring peacefully to swooping down. The intruder is described as "dark as night" and entering the environment. This poem is inspired by the oil spill, which helps you determine that the intruder is the oil.

5. **(B)** These words all carry a negative connotation and almost an eerie feeling. An intruder also carries a negative connotation. *Intruder* and *predator* are synonyms.

6. **The comparison is meant to show his struggle at being held down unwillingly.** An anchor is an item used to hold boats in their current position and prevent them from moving. In this metaphor the speaker is using it in a negative way to explain how he feels when he tries to fly away.

7. **They both focus on the oil spill, but specifically the damaging and fatal effects that the spill had on some creatures.** While the article uses statistics and details to describe how birds were affected, the poem uses an imagined version of one bird's experience in the spill.

8. **In the article, the language is straightforward and explains exactly how birds were killed.** "One island had 500 dead birds on a 4-mile (6.4-km) stretch of shore." "Oil had turned the dead birds into a stiff, black mass." "Some of the birds had drowned." "Once the heavy oil got onto their feathers, they could not float." "This left the birds vulnerable to the deadly cold of the Sound's waters." "Yet more birds were poisoned when they ate plants that had oil on them."

In the poem, the language is more sensory and figurative, imagining what the birds must have felt like in the oil. This language is more emotional and less factual. "Serene songs become desperate cries." "'Get out!' I squawk." "I remember what it was like to be a baby in my mother's nest,/Struggling to take flight." "The intruder tugs at me—refusing to release./My body is an anchor, mooring me to this spot."

Citing Evidence in Informational Texts, page 30

1. (C) The first paragraph of the text says that SEALs are elite teams and that Delta and SEALs are *equivalent*. The word equal is in "equivalent," so you should be able to conclude that Delta Force must be of the same elite reputation as SEALs.

2. **"trained to fight anywhere," "SEa, Air, and Land," "on many operations, we were in all three: We'd parachute in, complete our task on land, and make our way back on water."** These quotes show the diverse nature of their job. You recognize that to be competent in all three terrains, a person must be in top physical condition.

3. (A) The narrator tells the reader that SEALs' work is frequently "secret." By knowing that things that are secret are not shared with many people, you will conclude that the secretive or confident nature of their work is what has prevented many SEALs from sharing their stories.

4. (C) To answer an "in the book" question such as this, you must return to the text to check for accuracy. Paragraph 4 provides the reader with both the month and the year in which the story takes place.

5. **"Men, women, and children relieved themselves in the streets." "I smelled the morning fires, fueled by dried animal dung." "The fires heated the little food the Somalis had." "The warlord who rules this part of the city, Mohamed Farah Aidid, controlled the population by controlling the food supply."** Having to urinate in the streets is both unsanitary and humiliating, using animal feces to build fires is unhealthy, and having a scarcity of food supply all indicate a terrible standard of living.

Finding the Central Idea, page 32

1. (B) The main idea can sometimes be found in the opening or closing sentences of a paragraph. In this paragraph, you will reread the first sentence and notice that it contains a definition for nomads, which is the basic gist of the paragraph.

2. (A) Often, the opening sentence of a paragraph introduces the topic of the paragraph. In this paragraph the phrase "new and distant lands" introduces the idea that the nomads traveled to unfamiliar places at great distances.

3. (C) In paragraph 2, which discusses migration, the supporting detail mentions the nomads followed animals, which they killed to provide food for the group. The nomads had been hunting the animals to kill them for food.

4. **Possible Title: Friend or Foe?** This title reflects the idea that when strangers approached the group they were sometimes seen as another person to pool resources or share tools with, but other times they were viewed as a safety threat or an intruder. You find these supporting details throughout paragraph 3.

Development of Key Ideas and Details, page 34

1. (B) The narrator begins the paragraph by saying she could never imagine going to school with white children, but by the end of the paragraph

a law has been passed. Integration hadn't happened yet in the paragraph, but the idea has become a future possibility.

2. **(C)** Reread paragraph 2 and see what is going on internally with the narrator. She recalls seeing the high school and wanting to go in, as well as entertaining the idea of sitting in the front of the movie theater. Each of these thoughts prompts the narrator to think of more opportunities she might encounter if she attended the white school.

3. **(B)** Return to the paragraph and read that upon learning of Rosa Parks' protest, the narrator "felt such a surge of pride" rather than fear or anger. This event helped the narrator see how she might bring change to her community in a powerful but peaceful and positive way.

4. **(A)** Reread the entire passage, focusing on where the quotes appear. B is not the correct answer because it is more about her grandmother than about the narrator. Choice C conveys a feeling of longing for a better chance. The narrator's overall attitude is positive, making **A** the best choice.

Word Meaning and Figurative Language in Context, page 36

1. **(C)** You are looking for a verb, which will eliminate choice A. The phrase "in his throat" following *lodged* indicates that the word must nearly mean something stuck somewhere. Although you may have heard it used as meaning to spend the night, that meaning does not fit the context.

2. **(D)** Use the prefix *in* to help you estimate that it might mean going into or mixing something. This, in combination with the story of Governor Wallace standing at the school door to prohibit something from happening, will help you realize that *integration* means combining different groups of people.

3. **(A)** Verbs indicate action, and in this sentence Governor Wallace is said **to be doing something** against the door. This helps you determine the word is being used as an action word and is therefore a verb.

4. **(A)** You may have heard the word *assassin* through popular video games and have some idea of its meaning. It must be someone negative because whoever it is caused Governor Wallace to become crippled.

5. **An assassin is a murderer, but the author describes the assassin as "would-be," which suggests that the assassination was unsuccessful.** This is further proven when you read that Wallace was still alive years after the attempted murder in 1972.

6. **(C)** To prevent something is to make sure it does not happen. Governor Wallace is trying to prevent integration. Fill in each of the choices and you will find that *stop* is the best fit for the meaning of the sentence.

Text Structure, page 38

1. **(A)** The word *quickly* helps you see that it was done in haste, which indicates nervousness. In the next paragraph the narrator asks why they can't all be together, which shows anxiety about being without her group of friends.

2. **(C)** Fantasy and fairytales are somewhat synonymous. Generally, you will think of young, possibly foolish, girls who play make-believe and pretend to be living the life of royalty. Fantasies or fairytales do not usually come true (as is the case with the narrator).

3. **The author uses personification when she says that the hall swallowed her friends. This gives the reader the image of an animal devouring its prey, which is connected to how she and her friends are treated entirely differently.**

4. **(D)** You will compare and contrast their encounters with staff based on the narrator's experience here. The man is extremely rude to the students, as are others later in the paragraph, so their high school overall treats them cruelly.

5. **(A)** A summary does not give all the supporting details; rather, it just pulls out the most important or central idea. Choice **A** provides a summary of the basic event of paragraph 7 because it describes the narrator being physically attacked.

6. **(B)** A person with paralysis cannot physically move because of the loss of feeling to the limbs. The word shows that the feeling of being paralyzed leaves the narrator feeling unable to move, or weak. The guide yells at her not to stop.

7. **(D)** Reread the paragraph to determine that the mood is a negative one, and eliminate choice A immediately. The dominant feeling is that the narrator's panic is what taints everything and makes the facility look darker and more menacing than it might actually be.

8. **(A)** It is certainly not a castle once the narrator gets inside. The word *castle* is used to explain what she saw as an outsider passing by. This image is shattered when the narrator enters as a student and learns how dark and frightening it can be. Her real experience differs drastically from her fantasies—which shows the author was setting up a contrast between the two.

9. **(B)** From the beginning of the excerpt the narrator was nervous about being in the hallway alone without her friends and about what would happen to her. The last sentence of the excerpt confirms that she was right to be worried throughout the text.

10. Look at the phrase "warm, slimy saliva on my face" to see the vivid language used by the author. You will likely feel disgusted by the descriptions, so you should explain that the author chose to use such graphic language to help the reader visualize the seriousness of the act. The effect on the reader is to feel anger toward the person spitting or to make the reader feel sympathy for the narrator.

Author's Point of View, page 42

1. **(A)** The title of an article indicates what it is mostly about. The textbox helps the reader to realize that the author's main purpose is to talk about lasting friendships.

2. **(B)** You will refer back to the text and notice the words in bold that begin a new topic being covered in the article.

3. **School Guidance Office, Teen Magazine, Health Class Textbook** This article gives advice to adolescents, so you should think about which of the texts in the list are geared toward preteens or teens. The science text and the manual both inform the reader about a specific task rather than offer advice or suggestions.

4. **Cliques are harmful** You will notice right from the first sentence about cliques that the author uses a lot of charged and emotional language to describe cliques, and his stance toward cliques is rather negative.

5. Any of the following quotes: **"very picky about how they hang out with," "often leave other girls out on purpose," or "may bully other girls who are not 'cool enough'"** These quotes from the text show that the author's stance toward cliques is that they cause more damage than they provide benefits.

6. **This phrase is used as a hyperbole.** Everybody is not literally doing the questionable behavior, but this is a phrase used to describe the feeling of peer pressure.

7. **(C)** You will have established in previous questions that the overall point here is how to help adolescents navigate through tough friendships and offer advice. Advising is a form of informing because the author is helping his readers become informed about troublesome friendships.

8. **(B)** The author is neither excited nor angry with his audience. In this particular sentence he is informing his readers that although they may be offered drugs or other inappropriate substances, they always have options. The author uses the exclamation point to emphasize how many options the readers have.

Tracing and Evaluating Arguments, page 46

1. **The author asks a question to make his readers interested in learning the answer.** After the question, the author offers suggestions to the readers, which makes the author appear like an authority on the topic, earning his audience's trust.

2. **(B)** A numbered list conveys a sense of organization and structure. It helps the text be more predictable because the reader knows what to anticipate when reading.

3. **(C)** The author mentions the name and author of another book about money and self-control. This adds validity to the author's argument because

it proves that other people share his opinion and can support his ideas.

4. **The author uses a direct quote from a Consumer Affairs Officer to help strengthen his argument.** One technique of effective writing is to quote experts on the topic to earn the reader's trust.

5. **The author uses a direct quote from a Community Affairs Specialist to help strengthen his argument.** One technique of effective writing is to quote experts on the topic to earn the reader's trust.

6. (B) This a commonsense question because readers do not want to pay for the same thing twice. The rhetorical nature of this question will help you see that the author wants to get readers thinking and start an internal dialogue.

7. **This statement is very logical and true because you cannot lose something you do not have. Readers will see reason in this statement and be more likely to trust that the author is providing sensible advice and making a logical argument.**

8. (A) One effective technique when writing argumentatively is to include personal stories that readers can connect with. Readers like to read things they can relate to, so reading stories about successful teens might encourage readers to take the author's advice.

Comparing and Contrasting Authors' Presentation, page 50

1. **1928, Jewish, died, extermination/concentration camps** Focus closely on these details or descriptions that occur within the first paragraph and that serve as details/facts about Wiesel's life.

2. (A) Although Wiesel is well-known for his survival during the Holocaust, the author here delivers this information quickly to give the reader background or context. The biography focuses on Wiesel's accomplishments and experiences after World War II. The information provided in the first sentence helps readers learn about Wiesel's past, but not all of the information provided in the first sentence is essential to the overall understanding of the text.

3. (D) *Perish* means to die. There are polite (positive connotations) and crude (negative connotations) ways to express that someone has died. *Perished* is a neutral way of saying that someone is no longer living.

4. **The sentence describes the book as a memoir of Wiesel's experiences living in the concentration camps. The book will probably be about day-to-day things of how the concentration camp worked and possibly about how Wiesel and his two older sisters managed to survive while other members of his family did not.**

5. **The word *prisoners* tells the reader that people in the camp were being treated as if they had done something wrong.**

6. **In the previous paragraph, the narrator explains that the officer came searching for people with new shoes. The narrator's shoes happened to be covered in mud, making them look old, which saves them from being seen. For this, he is grateful.**

7. Look at the *Night* excerpt and find any word or phrase that shows the serious suffering Wiesel and the others around him endured as a result of their religion. Possible details might include being poisoned, living in tiny barracks with no floors or ceilings, or standing in mud to the point of falling asleep. Any of this evidence will help explain why Wiesel feels compelled to get involved with others.

8. (A) The language in the *Night* excerpt is much more sensory and figurative than the literal language used in Text 1. The dates and names used in Text 1 are indicators that this author's language is factual and direct, with little to no figurative language.

Argument Writing, page 54

1. A strong argument must contain solid reasons/evidence and clear explanations. The letter should include legitimate reasons why an adolescent might need a cell phone. Possible claims may include **needing the phone for emergency situations, letting parents know of whereabouts, tracking responsible behavior, freeing up the home phone for more use by other family members, or reaching you when at a friend's house.** You should use these legitimate reasons

to explain logical times when a cell phone would come in handy, help you in a dangerous situation, or prevent your parents from worrying. The letter should follow all standard conventions and the friendly letter format.

2. You may write about any two problems that you see in your own school or you might choose hypothetical issues that occur in schools. Possibilities include: **large class sizes, lack of extracurricular activities, bullying, not enough technology, poor lunches in the cafeteria, or an unclean environment.** You must provide a description of the issue and explain how it is problematic to the students and staff. The explanation must provide reasonable and logical examples of the specific ways this issue presents itself in the school. (Example: "The lack of technology prevents teachers from taking students to the lab to work on research projects. Without computers it is hard for us to learn from credible websites and sources because our teachers do not have the resources to let us use the Internet.")

3. You must provide a sound argument for why the school must continue to offer this class. With the school committee as an audience, you should write a defense of this class and all the education benefits resulting from it. To strengthen your argument, you should call on students and teachers who participate in the courses and perhaps include some direct quotes from these people (these can be fictional people to serve the writing task).

4. Clearly state whether you agree or disagree with changing the driving age and provide solid reasons to defend your opinion using some evidence from the excerpt. You must also generate original reasons to support your argument. Possible arguments against raising the age might include teenagers needing a car for transportation to sporting commitments, work responsibilities, or school. Possible arguments in favor of raising the age might include 16 is not a legal adult so 16-year-olds shouldn't be allowed to operate a car without parents, 16-year-olds are easily persuaded by peer pressure and friends, or 16-year-olds do not have enough practice.

5. The prompt asks you to take an oppositional stance, so even if this is not your true opinion, you must be able to produce solid reasons from the opposing side. To strengthen your argument you could mention some of the common complaints adults voice about video games and use your reasons to disprove those complaints.

6. To support your stance that college should be free, you must use evidence to show some of the following: current cost of education is too high; students who may be intelligent but in a lower economic class won't be able to attend college; students have to work too hard during college to pay for school, which could affect their studies; it might take students too long to finish college because they can't afford to pay for it in four years, which might lead to a high drop out rate; students are not guaranteed a job when they graduate college; or too many students or families go into debt paying for college.

7. If you argue that athletes deserve high salaries, you must use clear reasons, such as that athletes are elite and special, they make money for others because the fans pay money to watch the games, they sacrifice time with their families to play sports and entertain, or they risk injury to their health and sometimes life for the game. Each of these reasons must be explained as a justification for being paid large sums of money. If you believe their salaries are too high, you might use reasons such as that the athletes are playing games for a living, the athletes make much more money than the fans who pay to watch the games, there are other jobs that are "more deserving" of higher salaries, and they do not work every day.

Informational Writing, page 58

1. First explain what the word *genre* means and give the reader specific examples that show the differences between fiction and nonfiction. Fiction stories have made-up stories with characters, a conflict, climax, and resolution. Non-fiction includes information and facts about a true story. In your essay, explain to readers that they could use the summary, title, or an excerpt from the text to determine the genre of a text.

2. To describe your hobby you must organize your essay so that even people who do not participate in the hobby can understand it. Describe the

purpose or the objective of your hobby and use specific vocabulary terms relating to your hobby.

3. Whichever process you choose to describe, you must first brainstorm and consider all the steps it takes to successfully complete the process. Rather than using numerical transitions by simply listing the steps first, second, or third, you should use appropriate transitions to help the readers determine how to complete the process. You may use words like *first, after,* or *in a while.*

4. Brainstorm both similarities and differences before writing your essay. You might also describe the general commonalities between the school experiences or use headings to discuss elementary and then middle school or separate your essay into different aspects of the school day (example: lunch, classes, or extracurricular activities.)

5. Your response could include examples of some medical advances made because of technology as a positive but the increasing number of cyberbullying instances as a negative. Your headings should clearly separate the benefits and drawbacks.

6. Your explanation does not need to include the actual pledge itself, just the act of standing to salute the flag. Discuss some instances of where and when we stand to salute the flag. Explain that the pledge is a way to show patriotism and support for the country. You may separate your response into "how" and "why" headings.

Narrative Writing, page 60

1. To describe an event or experience you must use relevant details and organize your thoughts. Include an opening that engages the reader and introduces the reader to the memory. Use transition words (then, next, or after) to clarify time and sequence of events. The writing should have a clear closing that ends the story without being too abrupt.

2. Include an engaging opening that helps the reader visualize the scene on the first day of school. The story should include dialogue to show different types of characters and move the events along. Avoid simply *telling* the events, and use other techniques such as vivid details and dialogue to *show* the events.

3. An alien is a fictional (science fiction) character, so your story must reflect this. Your story may be set on a different planet or in a foreign, unidentified land. Science fiction is often set far into the future, so your story should reflect this. Dialogue in the story may include unintelligible "alien" language.

4. The theme of a story is the meaning or real-world lesson the author intends the readers to learn from the story. A possible story to reflect this theme might be about a person who avoids being honest because he or she thinks being honest will be too difficult. As a result of being dishonest, the character will experience a negative outcome, which will help the character realize that he or she never should have lied. The setting and characters are secondary to the conflict and resolution.

Considering Audience and Purpose, page 62

1. E-mail is simply an electronic letter, so you should treat the e-mail using the "friendly-letter format," in which you address your teacher formally (e.g., Dear Ms. Jones,). Be respectful and use manners to ask rather than demand. Sign your name at the bottom of the e-mail. Include a clear e-mail subject to help the teacher determine the e-mail's purpose.

2. Consider your audiences in two ways—you are writing the speech about your grandparents for them to hear, but all the guests at the party will also hear the speech. Since the speech is for your grandparents, you can mix formal and informal language. The speech should likely include an anecdote (short story) that shows your grandparents' relationship.

3. Your writing should follow the "friendly-letter format," which includes the date and a greeting. Consider that the pen pal speaks only a little English. Also, you must limit your use of idiomatic language.

4. In this format you know that you may use formal or informal language to express your views on an event. If you use informal language, be sure that your point is not lost because of unclear writing. The topic of the blog is serious, so treat it respectfully.

5. Consult posters on the Internet to see common formats. Flyers generally have an attention grabbing heading that pulls people in to read more information. Include only the essential information on the flyer—qualifications, contact information, and possibly rate of pay. Include these as bullet points or each in a separate heading.

Revising and Editing, page 64

1. You should ask a friend or adult to use the checklist to assess your chosen piece. The person editing the piece should be honest—is she or he confused or clear as a reader of this piece of writing? You should take into consideration whether all features are evident in the writing, as well as the suggestions offered.

2. You should ask a friend or adult to use the checklist to assess your chosen piece. The person editing the piece should be honest—is he or she confused or clear as a reader of this piece of writing? You should take into consideration whether all features are evident in the writing, as well as the suggestions offered.

Credible Sources, page 68

1. **(A)** Look at both the title of the website in the address and the domain name. The word *blog* makes you doubt the credibility or unbiased nature of this website.

2. **The "dot com" vs. "dot gov" domain name** When evaluating a website's credibility, look to the domain to see who is producing the information presented on the site. The dot com indicates that the website may be produced by an individual free of cost or by a company for profit; therefore, the information *may* be inaccurate or incomplete in its delivery. A dot gov site generally offers impartial information.

3. **(B)** Look at both the title of the website in the address and the domain name. The word *blog* makes you doubt the credibility or unbiased nature of this website.

4. **"(Through counterintelligence, we prevent our opponents from obtaining secret information, and in some cases, we spread disinformation to confuse them.)"** Reread the entire passage to find the overall purpose of the CIA. To quote a

source, you must copy the words *exactly* as they appear in the original, use the same capitalization and punctuation, and put the entire sentence (or phrase) in quotations.

5. To *paraphrase* means to take the basic ideas of the text but to explain them in your own words. Reread paragraph 3 and see that the paragraph discusses common misconceptions people have about the CIA. A possible paraphrase is: **Despite what people have seen in the media, the CIA does much more than just secret operations.**

6. **"You are more likely to get tension headaches if you work too much, don't get enough sleep, miss meals, or use alcohol."** Cite particular actions that may cause a person to get a tension headache.

7. **People who get migraines frequently might be able to end this pattern by altering some of the health decisions they make.** This paraphrase does not include any of the exact words from the text, but it maintains the overall idea that migraines can be fixed through changing habits.

8. The student has not paraphrased correctly. She has plagiarized. Paraphrasing is taking information or ideas from the original but writing them in a new way in your own words. The student changed a few words in the text but kept the same sentence structure and important words and phrases.

Drawing Evidence to Support Analysis, page 72

1. **(B)** The overall feeling of paragraph 1 is calm and relaxed. Although you know the article is actually about the tornado, the details in the first paragraph alone describe a serene setting.

2. It is **ironic** that church and faith are so strong to the people in this area, yet their church was destroyed by a tornado. Reread paragraph 2 and use the definition of **irony** provided to you to determine what seems strange about this paragraph. If people attend church regularly and believe in God's will, they might not expect that a tornado would destroy this place of safety.

3. Having your faith shaken means to begin questioning things you once thought you knew for certain. Read the line from the first paragraph about heaven being a "destination" to the people

of Piedmont and compare that with the woman who asked "Why? Why? Why?" or the man who said the shoes in the destruction would "shake your faith." Not losing your faith means that you still believe even when you question. Use the last paragraph's details to show that the minister believes the church will have many parishioners and that some will come looking for answers. These behaviors show that people still have some faith.

4. Support your opinion by using other details from the text to show things that are *more* troubling than the shoes or to show why the shoes are the *most* troubling thing. Explain the quotes and details you use and explain clearly how those textual details help support your opinion. You may say the total death toll is more troubling or the fact that some people's faith was shaken, or you may say the loss of such young lives trumps all other effects.

5. (A) *Joyous* can be eliminated immediately because the image does not depict an overly happy scene. *Filthy* conveys a dirty area but does not come close to conveying the demolished and destroyed nature of the picture.

6. Point to details that show destruction and debris—the broken trees, the broken items over the trunk and the car and trailer (to the left in the picture), the pieces of wood everywhere, the small house/living area that is destroyed. These items suggest a depressing mood because they focus on all the negative things easily seen in the picture.

7. Use some of the guiding questions to frame your thinking about the connections between the two texts. Question 3 asks you to think about the idea of shaken versus lost faith, so you will under-stand that by returning to church, the people of Piedmont continue to show their strength and faith in the face of destruction and turmoil. In the image, you must focus on the use of the flag and what it symbolizes to be placed atop the pile of debris. You should realize that the flag symbolizes freedom and patriotism. You may interpret the use of the flag to mean that the people experiencing the devastation will have the fight and pride to get through this tough time.

8. Choose between the article and the image presented to explain which of the two you feel is more powerful. Use evidence from each of the

texts to explain why you are more affected by a certain text.

1. (B) The daughter refuses to be like her mother. The speaker uses the word *anonymous*, and you should understand that she uses it to describe her mother. Because "anonymous" means without being identified or nameless, you can conclude that her mother prefers not to be a leader of any sort. Line 6 helps contribute to this character trait because it describes the mother as following the speaker around cleaning up after her. (RL.6.5)

2. **Personification. The phrase literally means that the mother is erasing the narrator's signature off the surface with a towel.** A towel is an inanimate object, but it is being given humanlike qualities of being able to swallow something. Towels cannot literally swallow, and you may look to line 9, in which the speaker uses the word *erased*. Seeing the familiar word *erased* will help you see that *swallowed* serves as a synonym for *erased*. (L.6.5)

3. (C) Using context clues means returning to the poem and reading the entire line as well as lines before and after the line in question. The word *squirting* in line 6 helps determine that linseed must be a liquid, which helps eliminate some choices. The phrases "burping can" (line 7) and "into a crumpled-up flannel" (line 8) in combination with your knowledge that the mother is erasing the daughter's writing are context clues that will help you recognize that linseed must be a cleaning product of some sort. (RL.6.4)

4. **The speaker in the poem continues to write her name on every surface despite the fact that her mother insists on making it disappear.** The pronoun *their* is a plural pronoun, which represents a group, but the speaker is only one person. (L.6.1)

5. (B) Reread stanza 2. In the first line of the stanza, the mother is erasing, which is an action or a verb. The word *polished* also describes the mother's actions, so it is a verb. (L.6.4)

6. **Potential Answers: Independence, Individuality, Uniqueness, Originality** You should use the last line of the poem to confirm that the narrator of

the poem wants to be anything but anonymous. You know that to be anonymous is to be unknown or unrecognized, and the narrator wants the opposite of this existence. *(RL.6.2)*

7. An original story must have an interesting beginning that draws readers in, as well as a series of events that unfold in a logical order. Using dialogue can help reveal character traits and events. The story should have a conclusion that falls in line with the rest of the story. Also, use the mother's experience from the poem to help shape the story. *(W.6.3)*

8. **(D)** Go back to the passage and read each quote in context. The quotation in choice **D**, explains that the government began to use the island as an "immigration station" to "process the large number of immigrants" entering the country. This evidence supports the explanation of why the federal government took over Ellis Island. Each of the other quotations provides details about the island at different points in its history but before it was officially used as a federal immigration post. *(RI.6.1)*

9. **Possible Answer: Ellis Island has had many uses over the years and has allowed many people to enter the country safely.** To craft a summary of a text, you should use your own words to write a shortened version of what the article is about, including any important details from the text. Although the central idea is evident throughout the article, you can often look at the title, the introductory paragraph, or even the concluding paragraphs to help find the central idea of the text. *(RI.6.1)*

10. **(B)** To answer straightforward questions such as this, you should return to the text and locate the fact that will answer the question. Although all numbers appear in the text, you will find the answer in paragraph 2. *(RI.6.1)*

11. **(D)** Reread paragraph 4 in its entirety. The sentence describes items that are being dumped, such as soil and rocks. Replace each of the four word choices to determine which one fits best. The word *dumped* has a negative connotation, so you know you should choose the word that has the most negative connotation. *(L.6.4)*

12. **(B)** The author uses facts and dates, which provide information to the reader. Also, the author

uses questions such as "Did you know . . .," which further shows that the author is providing information to the reader. *(RI.6.6)*

13. **(B)** Choice A has a dot com, choice C has a dot inc, and choice D has a dot blogspot. All of these addresses indicate that the websites have been created by companies or individuals who may not present all factual information. Choice **B** has a dot org. Organizations are generally more credible sources. *(W.6.8)*

14. Read the entire paragraph to better understand the purpose of the list. The list includes examples of the "colorful history" Ellis Island has. The author's purpose is to provide some exciting, high-interest topics to pull in readers to learn more about the island. *(RI.6.6)*

15. A convincing argument must have clear logic and reason. Use facts and details from the article to support the claim. You could also do your own research and include anecdotes from immigrants who've passed through Ellis Island. *(W.6.2)*

16. *"There'll be candles and presents and everybody will sing Happy birthday, happy birthday to you, Rachel, only it's too late." "That's when everything I've been holding in since this morning, since when Mrs. Price put the sweater on my desk, finally lets go, and all of a sudden I'm crying in front of everybody." "I'm eleven and it's my birthday today and I'm crying like I'm three in front of everybody." "I don't know why but all of a sudden I'm feeling sick inside . . ."* Select any two of the quotes listed above to show that Rachel is having a disappointing birthday. All of the quotes show that Rachel is feeling sick and is emotionally affected by the sweater situation. *(RL.6.1)*

17. **(B)** Refer back to the text to see how Mrs. Price responds when Phyllis admits that the sweater belongs to her. The line ". . . only Mrs. Price pretends like everything's okay" will help you understand Mrs. Price's reaction to the news. Based on the evidence about Mrs. Price pretending that nothing is wrong and that she did not apologize to Rachel, you can conclude that Mrs. Price does not like to acknowledge when she is wrong. *(RL.6.3)*

18. **(C)** The *theme* of a story is the meaning of the author's overall message. The similes in letter **C** help develop the idea that people are made up of all their experiences over the course of their

lives and not simply their age at the moment. This message appears at other points in the story as well, such as when the narrator mentions that she has "years rattling inside me like pennies in a tin Band-Aid box" and when she says, "I'm eleven, ten, nine, eight, seven, six, five, four, three, two, and one . . ." Each of the other answers are too specific to the text and do not stretch beyond the text to send a message to humankind in general. *(RL.6.2)*

19. **Hyperbole** Refer back to paragraph 8 and read the entire paragraph to see that "it" refers to the red sweater. The sweater is clearly not *literally* one thousand years old, so you recognize that the narrator is using an exaggeration to show that the sweater is really old looking. The **purpose** of the hyperbole is to show that the sweater is extremely old and worn looking, making it even more undesirable for any student to claim. The exaggeration is meant to show Rachel's distaste for the sweater and help the reader understand how uncomfortable she will be when she is forced to wear the sweater. *(RL.6.4)*

20. **A young girl's birthday is ruined because of a problem at school.** Summaries should include the important parts of an excerpt without focusing on any details that are too minor. The whole story describes a very short amount of time in one day at school, so you should explain the most important event that happened. *(RL.6.2)*

21. Introduce the topic clearly and organize your writing to make it easy for the reader to understand. You may choose to use headings to indicate the different stages of the experience and how students should react. Remember, you must use formal language in writing such as this. *(W.6.2)*

22. **1st person** 1st person narrator is a person in the story who also tells the story. A 1st person narrator uses the pronoun I, which you see throughout the excerpt. *(RI.6.6)*

23. **(B)** Use context clues to determine the meaning of the word. The second sentence of paragraph 1 describes refugees as traveling through a village telling of a war and searching for a safe place. *(RI.6.4)*

24. **War** In the first sentence, the narrator talks about war and how it seemed like it was happening elsewhere. The second sentence says, "**it** was actu-

ally taking place in our country," which continues the comparison of what the narrator thought about the war to what he realized about it. *(L.6.1)*

25. **Based on the details in the paragraph, you can infer that the narrator enjoyed his trips to Mobimbi.** Some of these details include watching television and swimming in the pool—special privileges that would lead you to infer that the narrator had fun during these trips. *(RI.6.1)*

26. **(D)** The word quarter has multiple meanings, and you must read the sentence carefully to decide which meaning is used in the context. Use the context clue that says that people "lived" there, which will help you determine letter **D** because it uses the word quarters to also mean a place where people live or stay. *(L.6.4)*

27. Read the sentences following the opening sentence to learn that the narrator explains that war came to his town and that he has experiences with war. **This is a significant detail because it shows the reader the narrator's experience of feeling removed from war and then being forced to deal with it.** *(RI.6.5)*

28. **(A)** Use your knowledge of roots to determine that *mal* indicates a negative word. The word *nourishment* may be familiar, and you should understand its relationship to food or being fed. By breaking the word into parts, you should be able to approximate the word's definition. *(L.6.4)*

29. Return to paragraph 1. The refugees **refused good offers because they were worried that if they stayed in this town, the war would come and destroy this town also.** *(RI.6.1)*

30. **(A)** Reread this paragraph and determine that the narrator is describing different memories, but the main portion of the text focuses on his trip to Mobimbi, where he heard the rap song and became mesmerized by the screen. This detail will help you conclude that the paragraph is mostly about the boy's experience with the song. *(RI.6.2)*

31. **(B)** Choices A and C state details from the image but are not inferences. There is no evidence from the image to support choice D, so based on the evidence from the image, choice **B** is your best choice. *(RI.6.1)*

32. **The girl is not wearing any shoes, she is carrying a container, perhaps to carry water;**

she is walking on a dirt road; there are very few "things" in the picture aside from dirt and scrub brush. Any of these details from the image will help you support your inference about the girl's financial situation. To make an inference you must always be able to support it with details from the text. *(RI.6.1)*

33. **(D)** The girl is walking in bare feet and appears to have a destination, so she is not out for a stroll (a walk for fun). There is no evidence of immediate danger in the image, so choice C is not correct. The word "village" should help you determine this is the correct answer because she is on a dirt road surrounded by tall grasses, which you would associate with a village or country setting rather than a city. *(RI.6.2)*

34. **Similarities (compare):** Both the image and the excerpt focus on a young child who lives in a village. In the excerpt, the author talks about his friend fixing his thatched-roof kitchen, and the image shows a dirt path and tall grasses, indicating a setting where you might find such a house. **Differences (contrast):** The excerpt discusses a young boy's life, whereas the image depicts a young girl. The excerpt also discusses TV, movies, swimming pools, hotels, and rap music. None of these luxuries or entertainment items is shown in the image. You will notice that the girl's life in the image seems much more limited than that of the author of the excerpt. *(RI.6.9)*

35. A memoir is a personal account of someone's life, similar to an autobiography. Look closely at the image and imagine what type of experiences the girl in the photo has had. Talk about her trips on the dirt path. Where is she traveling? Did she encounter danger along the way? What is her role in the family? Your memoir should be written in the 1st person and include an imagined story about this girl's life. Use the narrative writing rubric to assess the memoir. *(W.6.3)*

36. **(C)** A stanza is the word used to describe groups of lines in a poem that usually center on the same topic and are separated from each other by white space. In this instance, you can look and see the four distinct groups of lines in this poem. *(RL.6.5)*

37. You should see the line "you ask" at the end of stanza 1. When you continue to the next stanza, you will encounter the word *believe*. **You should**

infer that narrator is being asked if he or she believes in something.** *(RL.6.1)*

38. **(B)** Alliteration is a type of figurative language with repeated consonant sounds at the beginning of words. The author repeated the "w" sound at the beginning of each of the words in the line, creating an alliterative phrase. *(L.6.5)*

39. You have identified that the speaker in this poem is being asked a question, so you might determine that the nod is the speaker's response to this question. **To nod means "yes," so you may determine that the speaker had a positive response to whatever the question was.** *(RL.6.5)*

40. **(C)** The word *envelop* is used as an action because the speaker is taking hold of someone's hand. Verbs are words that often indicate an action. *(L.6.4)*

41. Whispers are being personified because they are given the ability to shout, as if they have mouths and can speak. The speaker is trying to convey the idea that although the room is silent, silence can sometimes be very loud. *(RL.6.5)*

42. To evaluate a source's credibility, you can look at the domain name. Avoid using sites that are blogs or appear to be biased or derogatory about religions. When paraphrasing, use your own words to deliver the basic meaning of the text without copying word for word. Quote when appropriate, and be sure to copy the text exactly as it appears and give credit to the site or author. *(W.6.8)*

43. **whom, he** Because Craig is asking the question, the person to whom he is asking the question is receiving the action, making whom (the objective pronoun) correct. Later in the sentence, you realize that Craig is completing the action—seeing—making "he" the subjective pronoun. *(L.6.1.A and C)*

44. **me, it** The pronoun is receiving the action, so the objective pronoun should be used. In the second sentence, *it* replaces "water bottle," which is a singular item. *(L.6.1.A and C)*

45. **it, its** A hurricane is a thing, so *it* is the appropriate pronoun to replace this antecedent. In the second pronoun, you must use the possessive form of the pronoun to show that it belongs to storm. *(L.6.1)*

46. **he, he, his, them** Robert is a singular name being used to identify a man. In the first two replacements, the pronoun is completing the action, so the subjective pronoun, *he*, is used. In the third replacement, the pronoun needs to show ownership between the wife and Robert, so the possessive pronoun *his* is used. The books represent a plural antecedent, so you must use the objective pronoun, *them*. *(L.6.1.A and C)*

47. **himself** Father Bill is a priest in the church and plans to prepare the service. By placing the pronoun **himself** after his name, it emphasizes that even though he's very busy, he makes time to volunteer. *(L.6.1.B)*

48. **herself** The coach is a woman because the sentence says "she" had to forfeit the games. It will add impact to the sentence to explain that although the coach begged the players herself, they would not join the team. *(L.6.1.B)*

49. You may say a premonition is **a warning, a bad feeling,** or **an instinct**. Look at the example of the mirror crashing, which is a well-known superstition about bringing bad luck. Liz sees this as a sign or a warning that something may happen. In the second sentence she is worried about the future. *(L.6.4.B)*

50. **Singing to someone or entertaining** Use the context clue of the guitar to determine that the man will be doing something musical but more than just playing the guitar. It is a romantic gesture that will "sweep her off her feet," so it must be something heartfelt. These context clues help you determine an approximate definition. *(L.6.4.B)*

MATH

The Common Core mathematics standards are created to be building blocks between grade levels. The concepts learned in grades 4 and 5 are foundational skills necessary for students to master grade 6 concepts. This allows teachers to make sure that achievement gaps are closed and that students have prior knowledge to continue their learning with more challenging concepts.

The Common Core Standards in grade 5 allow students to develop fluency with addition and subtraction of fractions and develop understanding of the multiplication of fractions. In addition to extending division to 2-digit divisors, students begin to develop an understanding of volume. In grade 6, students connect ratio and rates to whole-number multiplication and division as well as learn to divide fractions. New to students in sixth grade is the introduction of negative numbers, writing and solving expressions and equations, and statistical thinking.

RATIOS AND RATES

6.RP.A.1 Understand the concept of a ratio and use ratio language to describe a ratio relationship between two quantities.

6.RP.A.2 Understand the concept of a unit rate a/b associated with a ratio a:b with b ≠ 0, and use rate language in the context of a ratio relationship.

1. For every 10 students there needs to be 1 chaperone during the trip to the museum. Which of the following ratios does not represent the student-to-chaperone ratio?

   (A) 1:10

   (B) 10 to 1

   (C) 10:1

   (D) $\frac{10}{1}$

REMEMBER

A unit rate is the amount per 1 unit. This means the amount per 1 hour, 1 day, 1 person, 1 trip, 1 anything!

2. Which of the following phrases correctly describes the ratio of $\frac{21}{3}$?

   (A) For every 3 cats Sarah has there are 21 fish in her tank.

   (B) When there are 21 children at the playground there needs to be 3 supervisors.

   (C) Three meals at a fast food restaurant totals $21.

   (D) Three walking laps on the track is to twenty-one laps around the track on a bike.

3. Students voted on their favorite subject at school. Math beat history class with two times as many votes. Which of the following ratios correctly represents the voting?

   (A) 2 history votes: 1 math vote

   (B) 1 math vote: 2 history votes

   (C) 2 math votes per 1 history vote

   (D) 1 vote for math per 2 votes for history

4. While running for a local mayoral election, it was concluded that the current mayor received only a quarter of the votes. Which of the following represents the ratio of the number of votes the current mayor received to the votes received by his opponent?

   (A) 1 to 3

   (B) 1 to 4

   (C) 4 to 1

   (D) 3 to 1

5. While shooting foul shots, the basketball player counted how many shots
   he made. The player determined that he made two-fifths of the foul shots.
   Write a ratio and draw a model that represents the number of shots the player
   made to the number he missed.

6. A civil engineer was monitoring the amount of water in a creek that flowed under a bridge
   to determine the safety for local residents. She determined that approximately 1,750
   gallons of water passed in 5 minutes. Which of the following is the unit rate that expresses
   the relationship in gal/min?
   Ⓐ 1,750 gallons in 5 minutes
   Ⓑ 5 minutes for 1,750 gallons
   Ⓒ 1 minute per 350 gallons
   Ⓓ 350 gallons per 1 minute

7. A snowmobile travels 625 feet in 13 seconds. Which of the following is the rate, to the
   nearest foot, at which the snowmobile travels in 1 second?
   Ⓐ 48 ft/sec
   Ⓑ 0.0208 ft/sec
   Ⓒ 625 ft/13 sec
   Ⓓ 10 ft/sec

8. A vendor at a farmer's market sells peaches for $2.38 per 2 pounds. Determine the unit
   rate for the peaches.

9. Which is the better deal to buy vegetables at the supermarket?
   $2.45/2.5 lb of potatoes or $0.98/lb of potatoes

(Answers are on page 187.)

REAL WORLD RATIO AND RATE PROBLEMS

> **6.RP.A.3** Use ratio and rate reasoning to solve real-world and mathematical problems, e.g., by reasoning about tables of equivalent ratios, tape diagrams, double number line diagrams, or equations.
>
> **6.RP.A.3.A** Make tables of equivalent ratios relating quantities with whole-number measurements, find missing values in the tables, and plot the pairs of values on the coordinate plane. Use tables to compare ratios.

1. The number of words per minute that Andrew can type is $\frac{30}{1}$. Which of the following ratios is equivalent to Andrew's rate?

   (A) 0.5 words/minute

   (B) 30 words/hour

   (C) 60 words/minute

   (D) 1,800 words/hour

2. Complete the chart by creating equivalent ratios to the first ratio given.

3	6		33	
7		70		140

3. Samantha said that she could complete 5 math problems in 4 minutes. She estimated that she could finish the entire worksheet of 25 problems in 20 minutes, assuming that all the problems were the same type and length. Explain how Samantha determined that she would be done with her math homework in 20 minutes.

4. Which of the following tables correctly displays equivalent ratios?

   (A)

1	5	10
3	15	20

   (B)

3	1	9
9	3	3

   (C)

2	6	10
3	9	15

   (D)

5	10	50
3	15	30

5. The table below shows how many cupcakes are sold compared to the number of cookies sold at the local bakery.

Part A. Complete the table by creating equivalent ratios. In the last double blank on the chart, you can determine your own ratio that is equivalent to 12:10.

cupcakes	12	36		
cookies	10		50	

Part B. Explain what constant of proportionality or scale factor you used to complete the last double blank.

6. Complete the equivalent ratio table and plot the ratios on the grid below.

x	y
1	2
2	4
3	6
4	8
5	

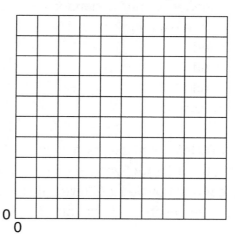

0
0

7. Complete the chart to determine how many minutes it will take Dakota to run 6 miles if he maintains his current rate.

Be careful! The left side of the chart is not in consecutive order.

Miles	Minutes
1	13
2	
4	
6	

(Answers are on page 187.)

UNIT RATE

6.RP.A.3 Use ratio and rate reasoning to solve real-world and mathematical problems, e.g., by reasoning about tables of equivalent ratios, tape diagrams, double number line diagrams, or equations.

6.RP.A.3.B Solve unit rate problems including those involving unit pricing and constant speed.

1. It takes a race car 40 seconds to make 1 lap around a 2.5 mile track. At this rate, how many minutes and seconds will it take to drive 9 miles?

2. Three and three-quarter pounds of bananas are sold for $2.25. Which of the following is the unit price for the bananas?
   - Ⓐ $1.67 per pound
   - Ⓑ $0.60 per pound
   - Ⓒ $1.44 per pound
   - Ⓓ $0.69 per pound

3. You and your family left the house for a vacation at 8 A.M. You promptly fell asleep in the car. Upon waking up at 10 A.M., you asked your mother how far you had traveled. She replied that the car had traveled 124 miles. If you continue at this average rate of speed, how far will you have driven in 3 hours and 15 minutes?

4. Which of the following companies offers the least expensive deal for its
    baby food per ounce (oz)?

Healthy Babies	$5.76 for 12 oz
Top Baby Food	$4.23 for 9 oz
Baby Puree	$0.92 for 1.5 oz
Yummy Baby	$2.08 for 4 oz

Ⓐ Healthy Babies   Ⓒ Baby Puree
Ⓑ Top Baby Food   Ⓓ Yummy Baby

5. You decide to mow your neighbor's lawn this summer. Before deciding on a fair price
    to charge your neighbor, you decide you should estimate how many hours it takes to
    mow a lawn. You time yourself mowing your own lawn, and it takes you 45 minutes.
    The approximate sizes of the lawns are shown in the diagrams below. Based on how
    long it took you to mow your own lawn, determine how long it will take you to mow your
    neighbor's lawn.

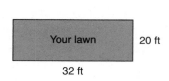
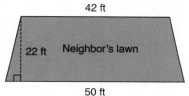

6. Which of the following is equivalent to 7.3 centimeters of snow in $2\frac{1}{4}$ hours?

    Ⓐ 2.25 cm in 7.3 hours
    Ⓑ 3.25 cm in 1 hour
    Ⓒ 14.6 cm in 4.5 hours
    Ⓓ 28.3cm in 9 hours

7. It takes Jim one hour to paint two walls in his house. If the rest of the walls are
    approximately the same size as the two walls he has already painted, how many walls
    can he finish painting in three and a half hours? Which of the following proportions
    can be used to solve the problem?

    Ⓐ $\dfrac{2}{1} = \dfrac{x}{3.5}$ Ⓒ $\dfrac{2}{1} = \dfrac{3.5}{x}$

    Ⓑ $\dfrac{1}{2} = \dfrac{x}{3.5}$ Ⓓ $\dfrac{1}{3.5} = \dfrac{x}{2}$

(Answers are on page 188.)

FINDING A PERCENT
OF A QUANTITY

6.RP.A.3.C Find a percent of a quantity as a rate per 100 (e.g., 30% of a quantity means 30/100 times the quantity); solve problems involving finding the whole, given a part and the percent.

1. If 45% of 350 students participate in after-school activities, which of the following approximately represents the number of students who participate in after-school activities?
   Ⓐ 7
   Ⓑ 45
   Ⓒ 350
   Ⓓ 158

2. Ninety percent of the students will pass their science test in Mr. Reynolds' class. If he has 120 students, how many will NOT pass their test?
   Ⓐ 10
   Ⓑ 12
   Ⓒ 30
   Ⓓ 90

3. An 8% sales tax is added to the price of your new video game. Which of the following represents the total price of the purchase with tax if the game was $54.99?
   Ⓐ $4.30
   Ⓑ $43.99
   Ⓒ $50.59
   Ⓓ $59.39

4. In an hour, Bella recorded that 11 minutes of television was devoted to commercials. Approximately what percent of the hour is devoted to commercials?
   Ⓐ 18%
   Ⓑ 11%
   Ⓒ 60%
   Ⓓ 5%

5. On your last math test you received an 80% for a score. You noticed that the teacher gave you 12 points on the entire test. Determine the total number of points that you could have earned on this particular test.

6. You decide to buy your grandmother a bracelet for her birthday. Upon entering the store, you notice a sign that says there is a 30% discount today. You find a bracelet with a ticket price of $45.99. Determine the sale price of the bracelet before tax.
   (A) $13.80
   (B) $32.19
   (C) $34.45
   (D) $59.79

7. In a bee hive, 10% of the bees are drones. What is the total number of bees in the hive if 1,200 are drones?

8. Starting next month, the physical therapist will receive a 2.5% increase in the number of patients she helps, which is 5 people. What is the number of patients she helps currently?

(Answers are on page 189.)

RATIOS AND CONVERTING MEASUREMENT UNITS

6.RP.A.3 Use ratio and rate reasoning to solve real-world and mathematical problems, e.g., by reasoning about tables of equivalent ratios, tape diagrams, double number line diagrams, or equations.

6.RP.A.3.D Use ratio reasoning to convert measurement units; manipulate and transform units appropriately when multiplying or dividing quantities.

1. 77 quarts is equivalent to how many gallons?
   - Ⓐ 19.25 gallons
   - Ⓑ 308 gallons
   - Ⓒ 38.5 gallons
   - Ⓓ 154 gallons

2. Complete the table below.

Pounds	2,000			6,000		13,500
Tons		2	2.5		5.5	

3. 12.7 Liters of water is equal to _____ milliliters.
   - Ⓐ 1.27
   - Ⓑ 127
   - Ⓒ 1,270
   - Ⓓ 12,700

4. Which is more, 7 feet 9 inches or 100 inches?

5. A 46-ounce fish was caught on your uncle's last fishing trip. How many pounds is 46 oz?

6. $1\frac{1}{3}$ gallons of heavy cream is needed to prepare dessert for a large party. You notice the store only sells heavy cream in quarts. How many quarts is $1\frac{1}{3}$ gallons equal to?

7. Three milliliters of water drip from a leaky faucet in one hour. How many liters are lost in one day?

8. The length and width of a rectangular garden was measured in inches. The building supply store sells fencing only in feet. Determine how many feet of fencing are needed to fence the perimeter of the garden, rounded to the nearest tenth.

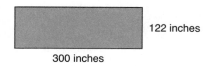

122 inches

300 inches

9. Complete the following conversions.

35 km   =   _____ cm

42 pts   =   _____ qts

16 cm   =   _____ mm

78 g   =   _____ kg

98 mi   =   _____ ft

16 fl oz   =   _____ c

(Answers are on page 190.)

READING, WRITING, AND EVALUATING EXPRESSIONS

6.EE.A.1 Write and evaluate numerical expressions involving whole-number exponents.

6.EE.A.2 Write, read, and evaluate expressions in which letters stand for numbers.

1. Evaluate the following expression: $2(17 - 1)$
   - (A) 32
   - (B) 33
   - (C) 34
   - (D) 216

2. Evaluate the following expression: $\frac{10}{5} + 2 \cdot 7 - 3^2$
   - (A) 19
   - (B) 10
   - (C) 7
   - (D) 4

3. Evaluate the following expression: $5^2 + 2^3 (9)$
   - (A) 64
   - (B) 79
   - (C) 97
   - (D) 82

4. Which of the following expressions results in a value of 5?
   - (A) $16 - 6 \div 2$
   - (B) $\frac{25}{5}(2^3 - 7)$
   - (C) $45 \cdot \frac{1}{9} + 1^2$
   - (D) $2^2 + 1 \div 5$

5. Emily was trying to figure out where she went wrong on a math problem. Find her error. Describe what she did incorrectly and explain how to finish the problem correctly.

$90 - 5 \times 7 + 10$

$90 - 35 + 10$

$90 - 45$

45

6. Which of the following expressions represents "a number decreased by 3 times another number"?

   Ⓐ $3x - y$
   Ⓑ $y - 3x$
   Ⓒ $3(x - y)$
   Ⓓ $3 - (y - x)$

7. Which of the following expressions represents "Christian is 5 years of age less than Keegan is in age"?

   Ⓐ $k + 5$
   Ⓑ $5 - k$
   Ⓒ $k - 5$
   Ⓓ $-(k - 5)$

8. Which of the following translations represents the verbal expression "twice a number y increased by 7"?

   Ⓐ $7 + 2y$
   Ⓑ $2(y + 7)$
   Ⓒ $2(7) + y$
   Ⓓ $2y + 14$

9. Translate the following expression: "a quarter of the students (s) and half of the teachers (t) went on the trip."

10. Write a verbal expression that describes:

$3x - 4$ _____

$\dfrac{x}{3}$ _____

(Answers are on page 191.)

PARTS OF EXPRESSIONS

> **6.EE.A.2.B** Identify parts of an expression using mathematical terms (sum, term, product, factor, quotient, coefficient); view one or more parts of an expression as a single entity.

1. In the expression $5(x + 2)$, which part represents a sum?

   Ⓐ 5

   Ⓑ $x + 2$

   Ⓒ x

   Ⓓ 2

2. In the expression $xy + 2y - \frac{x}{5}$, which part represents a quotient?

   Ⓐ xy

   Ⓑ $2y$

   Ⓒ $\frac{x}{5}$

   Ⓓ $xy + 2y - \frac{x}{5}$

3. What are the coefficients in the following expression?
$$-2y + 4z + 9 - yx$$

   Ⓐ 9 and 4

   Ⓑ -2, 4, and 9

   Ⓒ 2, 9, 4, and y

   Ⓓ -2 and 4

4. If $x = 2$, $y = 3$, and $z = 2$, which term in the expression below is the greatest?
$$3y - 4z + 2 + x^3$$

   Ⓐ $4z$

   Ⓑ 2

   Ⓒ $3y$

   Ⓓ x^3

5. When you use the distributive property to simplify $3(y - 7)$, the result is $3y - 21$.

Part A. In the nonsimplified expression, what are the factors? _____

What term represents a difference? _____

Part B. In the simplified expression, what are the factors? _____

What represents the difference? _____

6. Part A. Sort the following expression into its parts by completing the chart below.

$$2(y + 4) + \frac{3z + 12}{3} + 5y + yz + 6$$

Terms	Coefficients	Sums	Constants	Factors	Quotients	Products

Part B. Simplify the expression in Part A, and then complete the chart below using the simplified expression.

Terms	Coefficients	Sums	Constants	Factors	Quotients	Products

Part C. Discuss the similarities and differences between the charts from Part A and Part B.

(Answers are on page 192.)

EVALUATE EXPRESSIONS

1. Evaluate the following expression when $a = 2$ and $b = 5$.

   $5a - b + b^2$

   Ⓐ   57   Ⓒ   15

   Ⓑ   30   Ⓓ   72

   > Remember order of operation rules.

2. Evaluate the following expression when $a = 3$ and $b = 10$.

   $9a - b + 2b^2$

   Ⓐ   123   Ⓒ   417

   Ⓑ   217   Ⓓ   483

3. Evaluate the following expression when $x = 5$, $y = 6$, and $z = 2$.

   $$\frac{3y}{z} + y^2 + y(z - x)$$

   Ⓐ   87   Ⓒ   27

   Ⓑ   63   Ⓓ   12

4. Evaluate the following expression when $x = \frac{1}{2}$, $y = 4$, and $z = \frac{1}{4}$.

   $20z + y^3 + 40x(x - z)$

   Ⓐ   79   Ⓒ   22

   Ⓑ   69   Ⓓ   74

5. Evaluate the following expression when $c = 0.6$, $d = 2.1$, and $e = \frac{1}{3}$.

   $cd + d^3 + 9e(4c - d)$

   Ⓐ   11.421   Ⓒ   16.401

   Ⓑ   8.46   Ⓓ   13.321

6. Simplify the following expression when $a = 5$ and $b = 24$.

$$2a + a^2 - b$$

7. Carrie's deck is in the shape of a trapezoid. The area of her deck can be found using the formula $A = \frac{1}{2}h(b_1 + b_1)$. Find the area of Carrie's deck if its bases are 28.25 and $20\frac{1}{2}$ feet and its height is 8 feet.

8. Since all 6 sides are identical, to find the surface area of a cube you can multiply the area of one side by 6. The formula for this is $SA = 6s^2$.

Part A. What is the surface area for a cube that measures 5 inches?

Part B. What is the surface area for a cube that measures $5\frac{1}{4}$ inches?

Part C. Is the difference between the cubes' surface areas $\frac{1}{4}$ of an inch? Explain why or why not.

(Answers are on page 193.)

125

Expressions and Equations

EQUIVALENT EXPRESSIONS

> **6.EE.A.3** Apply the properties of operations to generate equivalent expressions.
>
> **6.EE.A.4** Identify when two expressions are equivalent (i.e., when the two expressions name the same number regardless of which value is substituted into them).

1. Which of the following expressions is equivalent to $7(y - 6)$?
   - Ⓐ $7y - 6$
   - Ⓑ $7y + 6$
   - Ⓒ $7y - 42$
   - Ⓓ $7y + 42$

   > Often students find success when they draw arrows from the first factor to each of the numbers inside the parentheses.
   >
   >
   > $2(x + 8)$

2. Which of the following expressions is equivalent to $5(4x + 9)$?
   - Ⓐ $20x + 45$
   - Ⓑ $20x + 9$
   - Ⓒ $5(13x)$
   - Ⓓ $65x$

3. Which of the following expressions is equivalent to $x(8 + 12)$?
   - Ⓐ $8x + 12$
   - Ⓑ $x + 12$
   - Ⓒ $20x$
   - Ⓓ $96x$

   > You can verify if the expressions are equivalent by picking a value for the variable(s) and substituting it into both the original and new expressions. The value to each should be the same!

4. Which of the following expressions is equivalent to $5r + 7 - r + 10 + 2r$?
   - Ⓐ $8r + 17$
   - Ⓑ $6r + 17$
   - Ⓒ $25r$
   - Ⓓ 25

   > If there is no number in front of the variable, then the coefficient is 1, $y = 1y$

5. Write 2 equivalent expressions for $3x + 8 - x$. The first expression should be the most simplified (standard form). The second expression can be anything as long as it is equivalent. Verify that each of your expressions is equal to the original expression if $x = 2$.

6. Sort the following expressions into the Yes or No chart based on if they are equivalent to $6r + 7r + 10 - 2r + 25 - 2$.

$15r + 23$ $20r - 9r + 66 - 33$ $10r + r + 3(11)$

$11r + 33$ $15r + 8$ $11r + 35$

$2(5.5r + 16.5)$ $44r$ $11(r + 3)$

$52r$ $15r + 33$ $\frac{1}{2}(22r + 66)$

$\frac{44r}{4} + \frac{99}{3}$

Yes	NO

(Answers are on page 194.)

SOLVING EQUATIONS

> **6.EE.B.5** Understand solving an equation or inequality as a process of answering a question: which values from a specified set, if any, make the equation or inequality true. Use substitution to determine whether a given number in a specified set makes an equation or inequality true.

1. Which of the following values makes the equation true?

    $x - 7 = 10$

    Ⓐ 3
    Ⓑ 17
    Ⓒ 27
    Ⓓ 70

2. Which of the following is a solution to the equation $90 = 80 + x$?

    Ⓐ 10
    Ⓑ −10
    Ⓒ −170
    Ⓓ 170

3. Which of the following values is a solution to the equation $\frac{y}{2} = 50$?

    Ⓐ 25
    Ⓑ 52
    Ⓒ 48
    Ⓓ 100

4. Which of the following values is a solution to the equation $5x - 10 = 50$?

    Ⓐ 8
    Ⓑ 12
    Ⓒ 200
    Ⓓ 300

5. Which of the following is a solution to the inequality $x + 8 > 20$?

    Ⓐ 10
    Ⓑ 11
    Ⓒ 12
    Ⓓ 13

6. Which of the following is NOT a solution to the inequality $9c \leq 72$?

   (A) 6

   (B) 7

   (C) 8

   (D) 9

7. Which of the following sets of numbers could be solutions to the inequality $90 < x$?

   (A) 90, 91 , 92

   (B) 90, 89, 87

   (C) 91, 92, 93

   (D) 89, 87, 86

8. Which of the following sets of numbers could be solutions to the inequality $100 > 2t$?

   (A) 50, 51 , 52

   (B) 50, 49, 47

   (C) 51, 52, 53

   (D) 49, 47, 46

(Answers are on page 194.)

VARIABLES AND EQUATIONS

1. Which of the following expressions could represent the perimeter of any square with side length s?
   Ⓐ s^2
   Ⓑ $s \cdot s$
   Ⓒ $4 + s$
   Ⓓ $4s$

2. Which of the following represents the height of a triangle if the area is 20 and the base is 4? The formula to find the area of a triangle is $A = \frac{1}{2}bh$.
   Ⓐ 2
   Ⓑ 10
   Ⓒ 20
   Ⓓ 40

3. Which of the following represents the width of a rectangle if the perimeter is 140 and the length is 10? The formula to find the perimeter of a rectangle is $P = 2l + 2w$.
   Ⓐ 60
   Ⓑ 10
   Ⓒ 240
   Ⓓ 300

4. Your little sister wants to sell brownies for $2.25 each and cupcakes for $3.50 each. She wrote an expression to represent how much she should charge for each depending on how many brownies, b, and cupcakes, c, she sells. Your uncle wants to buy 4 brownies and 2 cupcakes. Which of the following choices correctly represents the expression used and how much money your uncle owes?
   Ⓐ $b + c + 2.25 + 3.50$; $11.75
   Ⓑ $2.25b + b + 3.50c + c + c$; $29.25
   Ⓒ $2.25b + 3.50c$; $16.00
   Ⓓ $3.50b + 2.25c$; $18.50

5. An online company charges $75 per ticket for a concert plus a flat shipping and handling fee of $5. Which of the following equations represents the cost, C, when t tickets are bought from the online company?

Ⓐ 75t + 5

Ⓑ 5t + 75

Ⓒ C = 75t + 5

Ⓓ C = 5t + 75

6. Part A. Write an expression representing the amount Justin would owe if he bought a pair of sneakers for $50 and a pair of boots for $90.

Part B. Use the expression in Part A to determine the cost if Justin bought 2 pairs of sneakers and 3 pairs of boots.

7. Solve the following equation and check your answer.

$$4x + 2.50 = 20$$

8. Twice Brayton's age, a, increased by 5 results in 49.

Part A. Write an equation that represents the above situation.

Part B. Determine Brayton's age by solving the equation in part A.

(Answers are on page 195.)

WRITE INEQUALITIES

6.EE.B.8 Write an inequality of the form $x > c$ or $x < c$ to represent a constraint
or condition in a real-world or mathematical problem. Recognize that inequalities
of the form $x > c$ or $x < c$ have infinitely many solutions; represent solutions of
such inequalities on number line diagrams.

1. The mathematical expression $x > 7$ could represent which of the following situations?
   - (A) You must be less than 7 years old to see the creature feature.
   - (B) You must be older than 7 years old to see the creature feature.
   - (C) You must be 7 years old or older to see the creature feature.
   - (D) You must be 7 years old or younger to see the creature feature.

2. The mathematical expression $x \le 55$ could represent which of the following situations?
   - (A) You must drive less than 55 miles per hour on the street.
   - (B) You must score a minimum of 55 to retake the assessment.
   - (C) You must be 55 years old or older to retire from your job.
   - (D) You must be at most 55 inches tall to ride the amusement park ride.

3. The solution set of integers $\{x: 5, 4, 3, 2, 1, 0, \ldots\}$ can be represented by which of the following inequalities?
   - (A) $x > 5$
   - (B) $x \le 5$
   - (C) $x \ge 5$
   - (D) $x < 5$

4. The solution set of integers $\{r: 3, 4, 5, 6, \ldots\}$ can be represented by which of the following inequalities?
   - (A) $3 > r$
   - (B) $3 < r$
   - (C) $3 \le r$
   - (D) $3 \ge r$

5. Which of the following number lines represents $x \leq -1$?

Ⓐ
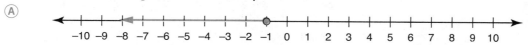

Ⓑ
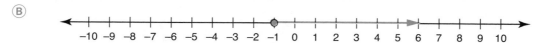

Ⓒ
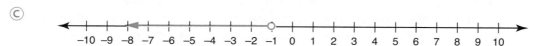

Ⓓ
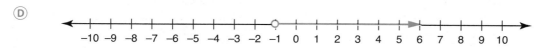

6. The Solar Sun Panel Company claims that its competitor's solar panels only work when the panels receive at minimum 50 percent of the incoming sun's rays. Write an inequality that represents this situation.

_____

7. Paul was giving a list of integers, n, to his son. He wrote down –2, –1, 0, 1, 2 . . . .

Write 2 inequalities representing integers based on Paul's list.

_____   _____

8. Vicki and Rich were playing a number guessing game. Vicki said that she was thinking of a number less than 9.

Part A. Write an inequality to represent the number that Vicki may be thinking of.

Part B. Draw the solution on a number line that represents the number that Vicki could be thinking of.

(Answers are on page 196.)

DEPENDENT AND INDEPENDENT VARIABLES

6.EE.C.9 Use variables to represent two quantities in a real-world problem that change in relationship to one another; write an equation to express one quantity, thought of as the dependent variable, in terms of the other quantity, thought of as the independent variable. Analyze the relationship between the dependent and independent variables using graphs and tables, and relate these to the equation.

1. Sam wants to ride a fast roller coaster. He gathers data with his science teacher and they determine that the taller the roller coaster, the faster speed it will have. Which of the following would be the dependent variable in this study?
   - (A) speed
   - (B) height
   - (C) weight
   - (D) angles

2. Dora was comparing the shoe size and foot length of her grandsons. She noticed that as their foot size increased, their shoe size also increased. If she were to create an equation to represent this relationship, which of the following would be the independent variable?
   - (A) age
   - (B) foot length
   - (C) weight
   - (D) shoe size

3. Given the table of values below, determine which of the following equations could represent the data.

r	s
5	15
10	30
12	36
50	150

   - (A) $r + 10 = s$
   - (B) $s = 3r$
   - (C) $s - 20 = r$
   - (D) $\dfrac{r}{3} = s$

4. Based on the graph below, answer the following questions about attending the local carnival.

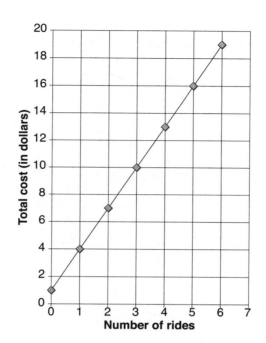

A. What is the dependent variable? _____

B. What is the independent variable?_____

C. If you ride 5 rides, what is the total cost to attend the carnival? _____

D. If you have $10 to spend, how many rides can you go on? _____

E. Describe what the point (5, 16) represents. _____

F. Describe what the point (0, 1) represents. _____

   Give an explanation as to how this could occur. _____

G. Could either $C = 4r$ or $C = 3r + 1$ represent the data given in the graph? Justify your answer.

(Answers are on page 197.)

DIVISION OF FRACTIONS

6.NS.A.1 Interpret and compute quotients of fractions, and solve word problems involving division of fractions by fractions, e.g., by using visual fraction models and equations to represent the problem.

Do not use a calculator for these problems.

1. Which of the following is the simplified quotient of $\frac{6}{17} \div \frac{3}{5}$?

   Ⓐ $\frac{2}{12}$

   Ⓑ $\frac{10}{17}$

   Ⓒ $\frac{18}{85}$

   Ⓓ $\frac{30}{51}$

2. Which of the following methods will NOT result in the correct answer to $\frac{4}{5} \div \frac{10}{40}$?

   Ⓐ $\frac{4}{5} \cdot \frac{20}{5}$

   Ⓑ $\frac{4 \times 40}{5 \times 10}$

   Ⓒ $\frac{4}{5} \times \frac{1}{4}$

   Ⓓ $\frac{0.8}{0.25}$

3. Which of the following is the simplified quotient of $2\frac{1}{4} \div \frac{2}{5}$?

   Ⓐ $5\frac{5}{8}$

   Ⓑ $2\frac{5}{8}$

   Ⓒ $\frac{18}{20}$

   Ⓓ $\frac{9}{10}$

4. Jordan needs to cut $3\frac{1}{2}$ pans of brownies into 24 pieces for his class. What portion of the brownies will each person get?

Ⓐ $\frac{7}{48}$

Ⓑ $6\frac{1}{2}$

Ⓒ $6\frac{6}{7}$

Ⓓ $\frac{48}{7}$

5. $10\frac{8}{10}$ divided by $4\frac{1}{2}$ results in _____ .

6. $5\frac{1}{3}$ gallons of punch need to be poured into $5\frac{1}{2}$ ounce glasses for the teenagers to drink at their Valentine's Day Dance. Determine the number of full glasses that will be poured for the party.

7. Hamburger meat needs to be divided into equal portions at the restaurant to make $\frac{1}{4}$ pound burgers. Determine how many full burgers can be made if the restaurant has $10\frac{1}{3}$ pounds of hamburger meat.

8. Describe two different processes for dividing fractions.

9. Using fraction models, find the quotient of the following problem.

$$\frac{3}{4} \div \frac{1}{2}$$

(Answers are on page 197.)

WHOLE NUMBER DIVISION

6.NS.B.2 Fluently divide multi-digit numbers using the standard algorithm.

1. Which of the following numbers is the quotient of 125,980 and 5?

   Do not use a calculator
   for these problems.

   Ⓐ 25,196
   Ⓑ 629,900
   Ⓒ 125,985
   Ⓓ 125,975

2. The answer to $\dfrac{20,475}{63}$ is _____ .

3. Which of the following values is the solution to the equation $24x = 5,040$?

   Ⓐ 120,960
   Ⓑ 5,064
   Ⓒ 4,830
   Ⓓ 210

4. The area of a rectangular soccer field is supposed to be 5,400 square meters. If the length is 120 meters, what must the width be to adhere to the correct area?

   Ⓐ 45 meters
   Ⓑ 5,280 meters
   Ⓒ 5,520 meters
   Ⓓ 648,000 meters

5. Two hundred seventy-six students will go on a field trip. If there are twelve teacher chaperones, how many students will each teacher have to supervise?

6. Geoff wanted to know about how many miles he drove each month for the last six months. He recorded his data in the table below.

Month	Miles
April	1,256
May	2,399
June	3,892
July	3,678
August	2,356
September	1,984

Which of the following values is a good estimate for his mean monthly mileage in the last six months?

Ⓐ 15,565

Ⓑ 2,594

Ⓒ 2,378

Ⓓ 2,636

7. Using the data from the chart in question 6, about how many more times is Geoff's highest mileage month compared to his lowest mileage month?

Ⓐ 1.5

Ⓑ 2

Ⓒ 2.5

Ⓓ 3

8. The area of a parallelogram is 450 ft^2. If the base of the parallelogram is 18 feet, determine the height of the parallelogram.

9. $15,192 \div 211 =$ _____

10. Describe a strategy that would help you quickly divide $\dfrac{28,000}{1,400}$.

(Answers are on page 199.)

OPERATIONS
WITH DECIMALS

6.NS.B.3 Fluently add, subtract, multiply, and divide multi-digit decimals using
the standard algorithm for each operation.

Emily went to the store and bought groceries.
Use her receipt below to answer questions 1–5.

Do not use a calculator
for these problems.

Milk	$4.25
Bread	$2.30
Eggs	$1.89
Can of soup	$0.99
2 lbs of deli meat	$5.88
3 containers of yogurt	$2.97

1. What was Emily's total bill for the groceries?

2. If Emily paid with a $50 bill, how much change did she receive?

3. How much more money did the bread cost than the eggs?

4. If she bought the same deli meat, what would $3\frac{1}{2}$ pounds of deli meat have cost Emily?

5. Determine the cost of one container of yogurt.

Perform the given operations.

6. 5 + 0.546 + 1.2 + 0.007

7. 125 − 0.0056

8. 7.2 × 1.067

9. 245 ÷ 0.05

10. $\dfrac{3.432}{2.2}$

(Answers are on page 200.)

GCF AND
DISTRIBUTIVE PROPERTY

6.NS.B.4 Find the greatest common factor of two whole numbers less than or equal to 100 and the least common multiple of two whole numbers less than or equal to 12. Use the distributive property to express a sum of two whole numbers 1–100 with a common factor as a multiple of a sum of two whole numbers with no common factor. For example, express 36 + 8 as 4 (9 + 2).

1. Which of the following numbers is the greatest common factor of 18 and 54?
   - (A) 3
   - (B) 6
   - (C) 9
   - (D) 18

2. What should you divide by to reduce $\frac{36}{48}$ so that you have to divide the numerator and denominator only once to get the fraction in simplest form?
   - (A) 6
   - (B) 2
   - (C) 12
   - (D) 8

3. Leah said that $\frac{21}{30} = \frac{7}{10}$. Is she correct? Justify your answer by explaining how the greatest common factor can help prove or disprove Leah's assertion.

4. Which of the following numbers is the least common multiple of 6 and 15?
   - (A) 3
   - (B) 30
   - (C) 60
   - (D) 90

5. Sam goes to his fishing hole in the woods every other day starting on the first day of the month. Jim goes to hunt in the same woods as Sam every third day starting on the first day of the month. Carrie wants to meet them and bring them lunch. When is the next day that both Jim and Sam will be in the woods at the same time?

6. The science club meets every 4 days and the math club meets every 6 days. When is the next time that the math and science club will meet on the same day?
    Ⓐ Day 6
    Ⓑ Day 8
    Ⓒ Day 12
    Ⓓ Day 24

7. If 10 + 35 is rewritten using the distributive property, it would be_____.
    Ⓐ 5(2 + 7)
    Ⓑ 45
    Ⓒ 10(1) + 5(7)
    Ⓓ 2(35 − 10)

8. Which of the following numbers makes this statement true: $x(4 + 3) = 12 + 9$?
    Ⓐ $x = 21$
    Ⓑ $x = 3$
    Ⓒ $x = 6$
    Ⓓ $x = 4$

9. Using the distributive property and GCF, determine another way to write:

    A. 55 + 77 = _____   B. $2x + 4$ = _____

(Answers are on page 201.)

RATIONAL NUMBERS— INTEGERS

6.NS.C.5 Understand that positive and negative numbers are used together to describe quantities having opposite directions or values (e.g., temperature above/below zero, elevation above/below sea level, credits/debits, positive/ negative electric charge); use positive and negative numbers to represent quantities in real-world contexts, explaining the meaning of 0 in each situation.

1. Sort the following values into the chart below.

Deposit of $45	8 degrees below zero	Elevation of 5,456 feet
Charge of an electron	Withdraw $5	95°F
203 feet below sea level	Loss of 7 pounds	Debt of $450

Negative Values	Positive Values

2. Translate the following verbal expressions into numeric values.
   A. 10 degrees below zero
   B. Owe your mother $75
   C. Withdraw $20 from your bank account
   D. Gained 10 pounds

3. While hiking in the Grand Canyon you realize that your elevation is 2,400 feet. Is this elevation below sea level? Explain.

4. The Dead Sea is 422 meters below sea level. Circle the integers that represent this depth.

   Positive 422   +422   −422   Negative 422

(Answers are on page 202.)

RATIONAL NUMBERS ON NUMBER LINES

6.NS.C.6 Understand a rational number as a point on the number line. Extend number line diagrams and coordinate axes familiar from previous grades to represent points on the line and in the plane with negative number coordinates.

1. On the number line below, place the following integers in their correct location. Use a dot, and label each dot with the integer it represents.

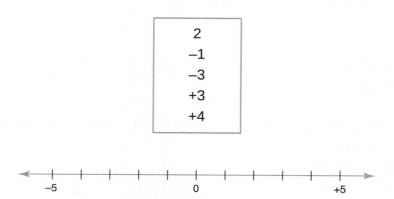

2
−1
−3
+3
+4

2. On the number line below, place the following integers in their correct location. Use a dot, and label each dot with the integer it represents.

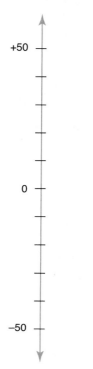

Owe $15
−(−25)
35 degrees below zero
40 feet above sea level

(Answers are on page 202.)

OPPOSITES ON
A NUMBER LINE

6.NS.C.6.A Recognize opposite signs of numbers as indicating locations on opposite sides of 0 on the number line; recognize that the opposite of the opposite of a number is the number itself, e.g., $-(-3) = 3$, and that 0 is its own opposite.

1. Lynn was looking at her outside thermometer on a cold winter day and wondered what the opposite of 3°F below zero would be. Which of the following temperatures represents the *opposite of* 3°F below zero?

   Ⓐ 3°C

   Ⓑ −3°F

   Ⓒ 3°C above zero

   Ⓓ 3°F above zero

2. Which of the following integers are all equivalent to "*the opposite of negative 8*"?

   Ⓐ +8, −(−8), positive 8

   Ⓑ −8, −(+8), negative 8

   Ⓒ −(−8), positive 8, −8

   Ⓓ negative 8, +8, −(+8)

3. Place the following numbers correctly on the number line.

   +3, −3, +4, −4, 0, −2.5, +2.5, +1.1, −1.1

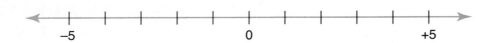

4. Describe what you notice about where the numbers are placed in relation to their opposites.

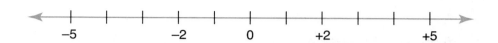

5. Which of the following is NOT the opposite of owing your friend $30?
   Ⓐ +$30
   Ⓑ −$30
   Ⓒ −(−$30)
   Ⓓ $30

6. Which of the following integers are equivalent to "*the opposite of 9*"?
   Ⓐ +9, −(−9), positive 9
   Ⓑ −9, −(+9), positive 9
   Ⓒ −(+9), negative 9, −9
   Ⓓ negative 9, +9, −(+9)

(Answers are on page 203.)

ORDERED PAIRS AND THE COORDINATE PLANE

6.NS.C.6.B Understand signs of numbers in ordered pairs as indicating locations in quadrants of the coordinate plane; recognize that when two ordered pairs differ only by signs, the locations of the points are related by reflections across one or both axes.

1. Which of the following coordinates could be used to create a square when graphed on a coordinate plane?

   Ⓐ (0, 0),(1, 1), (2, 2), (3, 3)

   Ⓑ (3, 2), (3, −2), (−1, 2), (−1, −2)

   Ⓒ (4, 5), (5, 4),(−5, −4), (−4, −5)

   Ⓓ (6, −4), (4, −6), (5, 4), (−4, −5)

> **TIP**
> Draw a grid to help you answer each question.

2. Explain how the point (3, –4) is related to (3, 4) and how (–7, 2) is related to (–7, –2) in regard to each pair's position when graphed.

3. Describe how the point (2, –4) is related to (–2, –4) and how (–1, 3) is related to (1, 3) in regard to each pair's position when graphed.

(Answers are on page 203.)

RATIONAL NUMBERS AND INTEGERS ON NUMBER LINES AND COORDINATE PLANES

> **6.NS.C.6.C** Find and position integers and other rational numbers on a horizontal or vertical number line diagram; find and position pairs of integers and other rational numbers on a coordinate plane.

1. On the number line below, place the following rational numbers in their correct location. Use a dot, and label each dot with the rational number it represents.

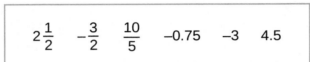

2. Determine which quadrant each of the following points falls within on the coordinate plane.

_____ (3, –7)   _____ (–4, 8)   _____ (–2, –10)

_____ (4, 7)   _____ (–32, –80)   _____ (positive integer, negative integer)

3. Describe the sign of the x-coordinate and the sign of the y-coordinate in each of the Quadrants.

Quadrant I _____   Quadrant II _____

Quadrant III _____Quadrant IV _____

4. Graph each of the following ordered pairs correctly on the coordinate plane
below. Be sure to label each point with its corresponding letter on the
coordinate plane. Next to each point determine the quadrant that it falls
in or the axis it falls on.

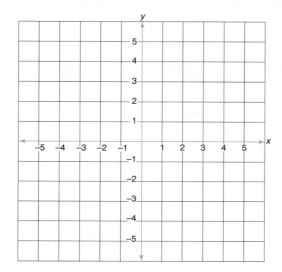

A (5, 3)   _____

B (−1, 4)   _____

C (0, 0)   _____

D (−3, 0)   _____

E (−5, −2)   _____

F (0, −2)   _____

G (6, −6)   _____

H (−3, −1)   _____

5. Part A. On the set of axes below, draw your own Rectangle *ABCD,* and label each point
with its coordinate.

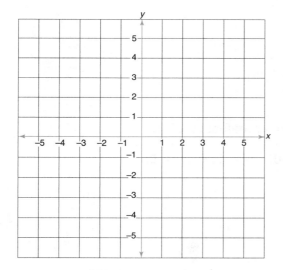

A _____

B _____

C _____

D _____

Part B. Determine the area of your rectangle.

Part C. On the same set of axes, draw a different rectangle, leaving two of the coordinates
exactly the same as the rectangle that you drew in Part A.

Part D. Explain how the absolute value plays an important role in calculating the area of
the rectangle.

(Answers are on page 203.)

ABSOLUTE VALUE

6.NS.C.7 Understand ordering and absolute value of rational numbers.

1. What is the absolute value of negative 7? _____

2. What is the absolute value of positive 32? _____

3. What is the absolute value of $-\frac{1}{2}$? _____

4. $|-87|$ is equivalent to all of the following EXCEPT?
    - Ⓐ -87
    - Ⓑ 87
    - Ⓒ $-|-87|$
    - Ⓓ $|+87|$

5. $-|-5|$ is equivalent to
    - Ⓐ 5
    - Ⓑ -5
    - Ⓒ $|5|$
    - Ⓓ $|-5|$

6. Arrange the following integers in order from greatest to least.

    $$-23,\ 9,\ -6,\ +2,\ -89,\ +67,\ 0,\ 91,\ -3,\ 11$$

7. Which of the following lists of integers is in order from least to greatest?
    - Ⓐ $-2, 5, 0, -9, 6$
    - Ⓑ $-9, -2, 0, 5, 6$
    - Ⓒ $-2, -9, 5, 0, 6$
    - Ⓓ $6, 5, 0, -2, -9$

8. Which of the following lists of rational numbers is in order from least to greatest?

   Ⓐ $-3, -\dfrac{1}{3}, +4, -1, -0.3, -|-2|$

   Ⓑ $+4, -3, -1, -|-2|, -0.3, -\dfrac{1}{3}$

   Ⓒ $-3, -|-2|, -1, -0.3, -\dfrac{1}{3}, +4$

   Ⓓ $-3, -|-2|, -1, -\dfrac{1}{3}, -0.3, +4$

9. Order the following rational numbers from least to greatest:

$$+2, -\dfrac{2}{3}, +4, 1, -0.6, -|-4|, 0$$

(Answers are on page 205.)

INEQUALITIES

6.NS.C.7.A Interpret statements of inequality as statements about the relative position of two numbers on a number line diagram. For example, interpret $-3 > -7$ as a statement that -3 is located to the right of -7 on a number line oriented from left to right.

1. Which of the following statements is equivalent to the inequality $|-5| < 10$?
   - (A) Negative five is greater than ten.
   - (B) Negative five is less than negative ten.
   - (C) Five is more than negative ten.
   - (D) Five is less than ten.

2. Sort the following statements into the correct categories based on their validity.

   | $|-9| < 11$ | $7 > 4$ | $|-5| < 10$ | $-3 > |-12|$ |
   | $-2 < 0$ | $6 < -7$ | $|-25| = 25$ | $-32 = |-32|$ |

True	False

3. Which of the following numbers makes $x < -2$ true?
   - (A) 3
   - (C) −1
   - (B) −3
   - (D) 1

4. Which of the following numbers makes $x \geq |-356|$ true?
   - (A) 355
   - (C) 356
   - (B) −355
   - (D) −356

5. Which of the following numbers makes $-7 > x$ true?
   - (A) −8
   - (C) −6
   - (B) −7
   - (D) −5

   > $x > 3$ is the same as $3 < x$.

(Answers are on page 205.)

INTERPRETING ORDER OF RATIONAL NUMBERS

6.NS.C.7.B Write, interpret, and explain statements of order for rational numbers in real-world contexts. For example, write $-3°C > -7°C$ to express the fact that $-3°C$ is warmer than $-7°C$.

1. The coaches determined that to be eligible for MVP of a football game a player must not have lost any yards while running the ball. Which of the following inequalities could represent the yards of a player eligible for MVP?

   Ⓐ $x > |-1|$ yds   Ⓒ $x < -1$ yds

   Ⓑ $x < |1|$ yds   Ⓓ $x > -1$ yds

2. Describe in words a situation the following inequality could represent, and provide a value that makes it true and a value that makes it false. $x < -9$

3. Write an inequality that represents the following: *You must be at least 18 years old to vote.*

4. Complete the table below. In the last row, create your own entries for each category.

Inequality	Verbal Description	Integer Values that Satisfy the Inequality
$x < -50$		
	Must be less than 50 pounds to ride the swings	
		3, 4, 5, 6, 7 . . .
$x > |-2|$		

(Answers are on page 206.)

GRAPHING ON THE COORDINATE PLANE

6.NS.C.8 Solve real-world and mathematical problems by graphing points in all four quadrants of the coordinate plane. Include use of coordinates and absolute value to find distances between points with the same first coordinate or the same second coordinate.

Directions: Use of the following coordinate plane is optional for questions 1–3.

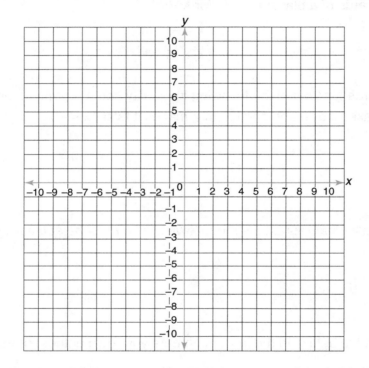

1. Which of the following represents the distance between the points (4, –6) and (4, 7) when graphed on a coordinate plane?

   (A) 1   (C) 6

   (B) 7   (D) 13

2. What is the distance between the points (–2, –6) and (3, –6) when graphed on a coordinate plane?

_____

3. What is the distance between the points (−1, −5) and (−6, −5) when graphed
on a coordinate plane?

_____

For questions 4 and 5, use the map of Jim's neighborhood, which is placed over the
coordinate plane below. The grid lines represent roads and are worth one mile
each. In each situation, Jim starts out from his house.

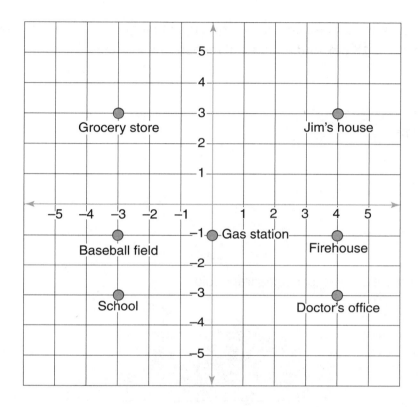

4. Determine the shortest distance Jim should take to travel from his house to school.
Make sure you show work or explain the process you used to determine your answer.

5. Determine the shortest distance for Jim to go to the firehouse if he must get groceries and
gas before arriving at the firehouse. Justify your answer using work and/or an explanation.

(Answers are on page 206.)

AREA OF POLYGONS

6.G.A.1 Find the area of right triangles, other triangles, special quadrilaterals, and polygons by composing into rectangles or decomposing into triangles and other shapes; apply these techniques in the context of solving real-world and mathematical problems.

1. What is the area, in square centimeters, of a right triangle with a height measuring 10 cm, a base measuring 13 cm, and a diagonal measuring 16.4 cm?

   Ⓐ 39.4 cm^2

   Ⓑ 65.0 cm^2

   Ⓒ 32.5 cm^2

   Ⓓ 130.0 cm^2

2. Determine the area of the isosceles trapezoid.

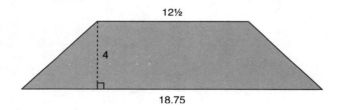

12½

4

18.75

3. An interior designer is tiling a bathroom using tile shaped like a parallelogram. The entire wall is 8 feet by 10 feet. The measurements of the tile are shown below.

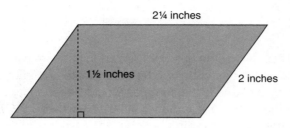

2¼ inches

1½ inches

2 inches

Part A. Determine the minimum number of tiles needed to cover the entire wall.

Part B. If each tile is $1.29 and there is 8% tax, determine the minimum amount the interior designer will pay to tile the wall.

(Answers are on page 207.)

VOLUME OF RIGHT RECTANGULAR PRISMS

6.G.A.2 Find the volume of a right rectangular prism with fractional edge lengths by packing it with unit cubes of the appropriate unit fraction edge lengths, and show that the volume is the same as would be found by multiplying the edge lengths of the prism. Apply the formulas $V = lwh$ and $V = Bh$ to find volumes of right rectangular prisms with fractional edge lengths in the context of solving real-world and mathematical problems.

1. Determine the volume of a rectangular prism that measures 12.6 cm by $3\frac{1}{3}$ cm by 9.75 cm.

> When the Bh is used for volume, the capital B does NOT stand for base. It stands for the area of the entire base.

2. Which of the following choices is the volume of a box that measures 8 inches tall by 4 inches wide by 5 inches deep?
   Ⓐ   20 square inches
   Ⓑ   160 square inches
   Ⓒ   20 cubic inches
   Ⓓ   160 cubic inches

3. Which of the following formulas cannot be used to find the volume of a rectangular prism?
   Ⓐ $V = Bh$
   Ⓑ $V = lwh$
   Ⓒ $V = bh$
   Ⓓ $\frac{V}{l} = wh$

4. The base of a rectangular prism has an area of 45 square units. The prism is 10 units in height. Which of the following choices is the volume of the prism?
   Ⓐ   450 units^2
   Ⓑ   55 units^2
   Ⓒ   450 units^3
   Ⓓ   55 units^3

5. Which of the following choices is the volume of the rectangular prism shown?

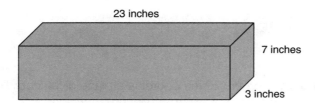

23 inches

7 inches

3 inches

Ⓐ   502 cubic inches
Ⓑ   483 cubic inches
Ⓒ   44 cubic inches
Ⓓ   33 cubic inches

6. Which of the following choices is the volume of the rectangular prism shown below?
Ⓐ   111.19921 cubic units
Ⓑ   193.5034 cubic units
Ⓒ   22.52 cubic units
Ⓓ   57.869 cubic units

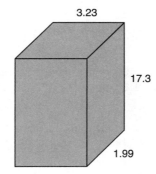

3.23

17.3

1.99

7. The volume of a rectangular prism is 459 cubic feet. If the length is 3 feet and the width is 30 feet, what is the height of the prism?
Ⓐ   41,310 feet
Ⓑ   426 feet
Ⓒ   13.9 feet
Ⓓ   5.1 feet

8. Which of the following expressions can be used to find the volume of the puzzle cube shown below?
Ⓐ s^3
Ⓑ bh
Ⓒ $s + s + s$
Ⓓ $2lw + 2lh + 2hw$

(Answers are on page 208.)

DRAWING POLYGONS ON COORDINATE PLANES

6.G.A.3 Draw polygons in the coordinate plane given coordinates for the vertices; use coordinates to find the length of a side joining points with the same first coordinate or the same second coordinate. Apply these techniques in the context of solving real-world and mathematical problems.

1. Part A. Graph the following coordinates on the grid below.
   (4, 3), (4, –5), (–2, 3), and (–2, –5)

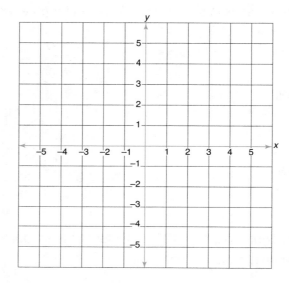

Part B. Determine the perimeter of the polygon.

Part C. Determine the area of the polygon.

2. Part A. Graph the following coordinates on the grid below.
   (–3, –2), (3, –2), (–1, 2), and (5, 2)

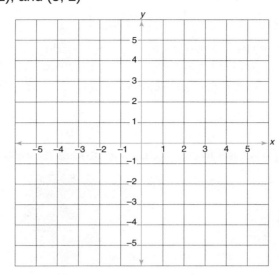

Part B. Determine the area of the polygon.

Part C. On the grid, draw a rectangle that has the same area as the polygon you drew from Part A. State the coordinates of the rectangle you drew.

3. Part A. Graph the following coordinates on the grid below.
   (0, 4), (0, –2), and (3, –2)

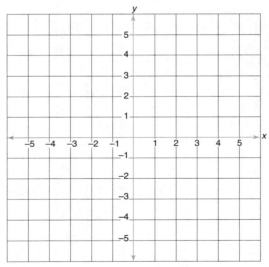

Part B. Determine the area of the polygon.

Part C. On the grid, draw another right triangle that has the same area but different dimensions.

(Answers are on page 209.)

SURFACE AREA AND NETS

1. Which of the following nets will fold to make a triangular prism?

    Ⓐ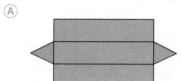

    Ⓑ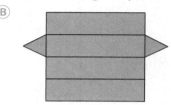

    Ⓒ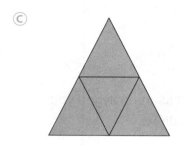

    Ⓓ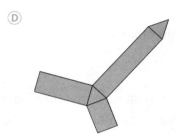

2. Which of the following nets will fold to make a square pyramid?

    Ⓐ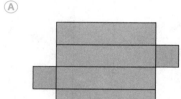

    Ⓑ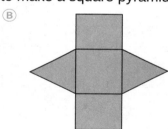

    Ⓒ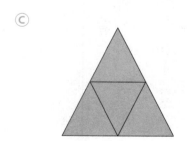

    Ⓓ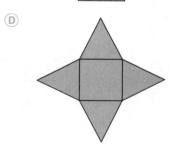

3. This net will fold into which of the following three-dimensional shapes?

    Ⓐ Square pyramid   Ⓒ Rectangular prism

    Ⓑ Triangular prism   Ⓓ Triangular pyramid

4. A net of a rectangular prism will consist of
   - Ⓐ 5 rectangles and 0 triangles
   - Ⓒ 6 rectangles and 0 triangles
   - Ⓑ 4 rectangles and 2 triangles
   - Ⓓ 3 rectangles and 2 triangles

5. Which of the following is not a triangular pyramid net?

   Ⓐ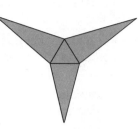

   Ⓑ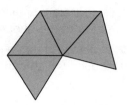

   Ⓒ

   Ⓓ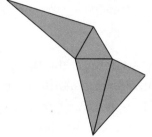

6. What is the surface area of an equilateral triangular pyramid if one triangle's base is 6 centimeters and its height is about 5.2 centimeters?
   - Ⓐ 15.6 cm^2
   - Ⓒ 31.2 cm^2
   - Ⓑ 62.4 cm^2
   - Ⓓ 124.8 cm^2

7. Which process would NOT result in finding the surface area of a triangular prism?
   - Ⓐ area of 2 triangles + area of 3 rectangles
   - Ⓑ $lw + lw + \left(\frac{1}{2}\right)bh + lw + \left(\frac{1}{2}\right)bh$
   - Ⓒ $lwh + 2\left(\frac{1}{2}\right)bh$
   - Ⓓ $bh + lw + lw + lw$

8. A pasta manufacturing company wants to know how much cardboard is needed to make a box for its pasta. A sketch of the pasta box is below. Determine how much cardboard, to the nearest eighth of an inch, is needed to make one box.

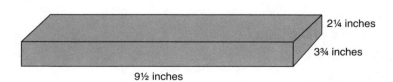

2¼ inches

3¾ inches

9½ inches

(Answers are on page 210.)

STATISTICS, MEASURES OF CENTER, AND VARIATION

> **6.SP.A.1** Recognize a statistical question as one that anticipates variability in the data related to the question and accounts for it in the answers.
>
> **6.SP.A.2** Understand that a set of data collected to answer a statistical question has a distribution which can be described by its center, spread, and overall shape.
>
> **6.SP.A.3** Recognize that a measure of center for a numerical data set summarizes all of its values with a single number, while a measure of variation describes how its values vary with a single number.

1. A biologist collected data on the number of bacteria cells on different kitchen tables. Which of the following questions is appropriate to ask to statistically analyze this data?
   - Ⓐ What kind of bacteria was there?
   - Ⓑ How many bacteria cells were there on each table?
   - Ⓒ What color was the bacteria?
   - Ⓓ Where were the houses located?

2. An engineer was curious as to the amount of stress a new metal could withstand when pressure is applied to it. Which of the following data sets is appropriate to gather to statistically analyze this data?
   - Ⓐ types of machines applying the pressure
   - Ⓑ color of the metal
   - Ⓒ pounds of pressure applied to the metal when it broke
   - Ⓓ weight in pounds of the metal

3. Using which of the following questions can you anticipate getting variability in your data?
   - Ⓐ How old is my homeroom teacher?
   - Ⓑ What are the heights of students in my class?
   - Ⓒ How many vehicles does my family own now?
   - Ⓓ What is my eye color?

4. When statistically analyzing data, a researcher would not look to study which of the following statistics?
   - Ⓐ central tendencies of the data
   - Ⓑ variability in the data
   - Ⓒ spread of the data
   - Ⓓ time it took to collect the data

5. When analyzing the data in the graph below, which of the following questions would be most beneficial to study?

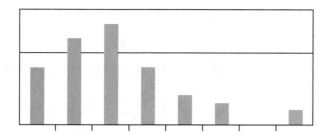

Ⓐ What is the range?
Ⓑ Why is the data skewed?
Ⓒ Where was the data collected?
Ⓓ What is the interquartile range?

6. The graph to the right represents data collected on diners at a restaurant in one day. On average, what conclusion can be made by looking at the graph?

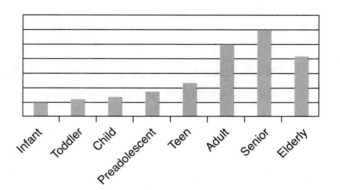

Ⓐ Most people were younger than teens.
Ⓑ Most people were teens.
Ⓒ Most people were older then teens.
Ⓓ Most people ranged from child to teen.

7. According to the line plot below, which of the following statements is true?

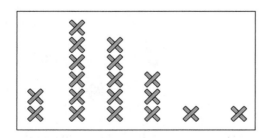

Ⓐ The data is symmetric.   Ⓒ The data is skewed right.
Ⓑ The data is biased.   Ⓓ The data is skewed left.

(Answers are on page 211.)

DOT PLOTS, HISTOGRAMS, AND BOX PLOTS

6.SP.B.4 Display numerical data in plots on a number line, including dot plots, histograms, and box plots.

1. Joe collected data on the number of gallons of gas he used in his truck each week over the last few months.

    20, 35, 7, 23, 16, 8 ,17, 9, 11

    Part A. Create a box and whisker plot of the data.

    Part B. Based on the data, Joe can plan that 50 percent of the time he will use what range of gallons of gas per week?

    _____

    Part C. Determine the Interquartile Range

    _____

    Part D. Explain what the different lengths of the lines (whiskers) represents.

    > The variation in the lengths on a box and whisker plot shows how spread or clustered the data is.

2. The ages of students at opening day of little league who bought food at the concession stand are listed below.

5, 7, 6, 8, 9, 5, 6, 4, 10, 12, 11, 6, 7, 8, 9, 5, 6,
6, 7, 8, 9, 12, 5, 6, 8, 9, 11, 10, 5, 7, 4, 6, 13

Part A. Create a histogram of the data.

Age Interval	Tally	Frequency
4–5		
6–7		
8–9		
10–11		
12–13		

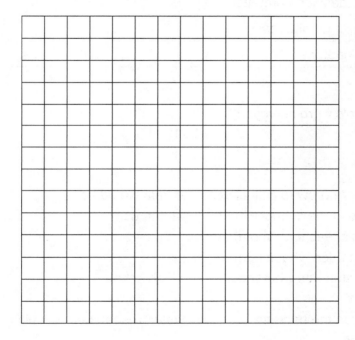

Part B. The median age can be found in what age interval? _____

Part C. What does the shape of the data tell the concession stand manager? How could this information be beneficial to the manager?

(Answers are on page 212.)

REPORTING OBSERVATIONS AND ATTRIBUTES

6.SP.B.5 Summarize numerical data sets in relation to their context, such as by:

6.SP.B.5.A Reporting the number of observations.

6.SP.B.5.B Describing the nature of the attribute under investigation, including how it was measured and its units of measurement.

Andrew collected data on the popular types of technology used in schools, and he recorded his data below.

tablets	126
desktop computers	450
smartphones	98
laptops	324

1. How many schools were surveyed?

    Ⓐ 4
    Ⓑ 990
    Ⓒ 250
    Ⓓ 998

2. The best way for Andrew to collect accurate data would be to

    Ⓐ ask students at the school what they want to use.
    Ⓑ ask the music teachers what they use.
    Ⓒ ask administration what it currently uses.
    Ⓓ ask college students what they used in high school.

3. To analyze data on the bacteria in the city water, researchers should take samples from

    Ⓐ 1,000 houses.
    Ⓑ 1,000 businesses.
    Ⓒ 100 houses and 100 businesses.
    Ⓓ 1,000 houses and 1,000 businesses.

4. When researchers analyze data on the health of students, which of the following measureable attributes would NOT be appropriate to gather data on?

    Ⓐ time spent exercising
    Ⓑ shoe size
    Ⓒ weight
    Ⓓ caloric intake

5. To find the average height of students in 6th grade, which of the following is the best unit to measure and record as data?

ⓐ inches ⓒ pounds

ⓑ yards ⓓ liters

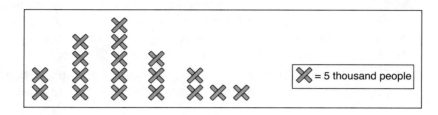

6. How many people were surveyed to create the graph above?

ⓐ 5 ⓒ 5,000

ⓑ 18 ⓓ 90,000

7. Company A claimed that it sold more products than Company B. List some questions that Company B could use to question the validity of Company A's claim.

8. If you were Company B, fill in the table to make a reliable, unbiased plan that tests the validity of Company A's claims.

Who would you ask?	
How would you ask?	
What would you ask?	
What units would you measure in?	
Where would you ask?	
What other characteristics should you take into consideration about this data collection?	

(Answers are on page 213.)

SHAPE AND PATTERNS IN DATA

6.SP.B.5.C Giving quantitative measures of center (median and/or mean) and variability (interquartile range and/or mean absolute deviation), as well as describing any overall pattern and any striking deviations from the overall pattern with reference to the context in which the data were gathered.

6.SP.B.5.D Relating the choice of measures of center and variability to the shape of the data distribution and the context in which the data were gathered.

Emily counted how many books she had to read last year in college. The information is recorded in the chart below.

American Literature	5
Biology	2
History of Western Civilization	3
World War II	4
Micro-Economics	1
Poetry	2
Statistics	0

1. According to the data, which of the following values represents the mean number of books per class?
   - Ⓐ 2.4
   - Ⓑ 17
   - Ⓒ 7
   - Ⓓ 0.4

2. Determine the mean absolute deviation of the data to the nearest tenth.

3. Explain what the mean absolute deviation means in reference to the number of books Emily had to read.

4. When is the median a better measure of center to use to represent data than the mean?
   - (A) It is never better.
   - (B) It is always better.
   - (C) It is better when there is an outlier.
   - (D) It is better when there is a mean absolute deviation.

5. When the data is evenly distributed, which measure of center or variability is more appropriate to use to represent the data?
   - (A) Mean
   - (B) Median
   - (C) Mode
   - (D) Range

(Answers are on page 214.)

MATH PRACTICE TEST

My Name: _____

Today's Date: _____

1. For every 15 children there needs to be 2 adults at the day care. Which of the following ratios represents the adult to children ratio?

   Ⓐ 15:2

   Ⓑ 2:15

   Ⓒ 15 to 2

   Ⓓ $\dfrac{15}{2}$

2. A motorcycle travels $3\dfrac{1}{8}$ miles in 2.5 minutes. Which of the following represents the rate, to the nearest mile, at which the motorcycle travels in 1 hour?

   Ⓐ 1.25 mi/hr

   Ⓑ 0.896 mi/hr

   Ⓒ 75 mi/hr

   Ⓓ 4,500 mi/hr

3. Which is the better deal to buy peaches at the farmers' market?

   $2.19 for $1\dfrac{1}{4}$ lb of peaches or $0.88 for $\dfrac{1}{2}$ lb of peaches

4. Keegan said that he could wash 3 cars in 36 minutes at the school car wash fundraiser. He estimated that he could wash the 7 teachers' cars in less than an hour and a half, assuming that all the cars were similar. Determine if Keegan is correct and explain how to determine that estimate.

5. Complete the equivalent ratio table and plot the ratios on the grid below.

x	y
1	0.5
2	1
3	1.5
4	2
5	
6	

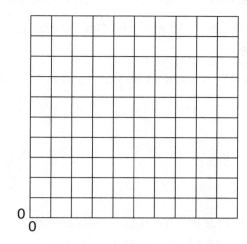

6. Which of the following delis offers the least expensive cost per pound for deli meat?

Healthy Deli	$9.92 per 2 pounds
David's Deli	$9.38 per 1.5 pounds
Meat & More	$4.75 for $\frac{1}{2}$ pound
Top Deli	$1.25 for 4 ounce

(A) Healthy Deli   (C) Meat & More

(B) David's Deli   (D) Top Deli

7. You decide to paint your neighbor's garage. Before settling on a fair price to charge your neighbor, you decide you should estimate how many hours it will take to paint one side. You remember from painting your bedroom that it takes about 40 minutes to paint one wall. The approximate sizes of the walls in your bedroom and sides, of the garage are shown in the diagrams below. Based on how long it took you to paint one wall in your room, determine to the nearest hour how long it will take you to paint all four sides of your neighbor's garage if all four sides are congruent.

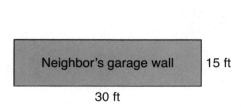

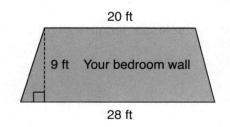

175

8. It takes Scot $\frac{3}{4}$ of an hour to rake $\frac{2}{3}$ of his yard. The weather report on the radio said a storm would arrive in about 50 minutes. Scot wants to know if he can finish raking before the storm will arrive.

Which of the following proportions can be used to solve the problem?

(A) $\dfrac{45}{50} = \dfrac{x}{\frac{2}{3}}$

(C) $\dfrac{45}{x} = \dfrac{50}{\frac{2}{3}}$

(B) $\dfrac{50}{\frac{2}{3}} = \dfrac{45}{x}$

(D) $\dfrac{45}{\frac{2}{3}} = \dfrac{50}{x}$

9. You have a fish tank that you need to fill and notice that the hose you attached to it has a slow flow rate. You want to go outside to play ball but don't want to keep checking on the tank. You decide to estimate the time it will take to fill the tank if the flow rate stays constant. Determine how much longer it will take you to fill the tank if in 15 minutes you only filled the tank 15 percent of the way.

10. Which of the following represents the amount of sales tax on a $35.00 shirt if the tax rate is 7%?
    (A) $2.45
    (B) $1.07
    (C) $37.45
    (D) $32.55

11. Approximately 85% of students play sports in the middle school. If there are 250 students that play sports, about how many students are in the middle school?
    (A) 3
    (B) 34
    (C) 213
    (D) 294

12. 33 pints is equivalent to how many cups?
    (A) 66 cups
    (B) 16.5 cups
    (C) 8.25 cups
    (D) 132 cups

13. Which is the lesser length? 9 feet 2 inches or 115 inches?

14. The length and width of a child's outdoor play area was measured in feet. The building supply store only sells the fencing in rolls of 96 inches. Determine how many full rolls of fencing are needed to fence in the play area.

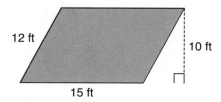

15. Which of the following verbal expressions represents a negative integer?
    Ⓐ 4 degrees below zero
    Ⓑ Increase in your allowance
    Ⓒ Climbed to an elevation of 100 feet above sea level
    Ⓓ Gained 5 pounds

16. On the number line below, place the following integers in their correct location. Use a dot and label each dot with the integer it represents.

| 1   −2   −3   0   +2   −1 |

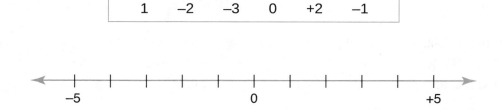

17. Which of the following integers are all equivalent to "the opposite of negative 5"?
    Ⓐ negative 5, +5, −(+5)   Ⓒ −5, −(+5), negative 5
    Ⓑ +5, −(−5), positive 5   Ⓓ −(−5), positive 5, −5

18. Which of the following coordinates could be used to create a square when graphed on a coordinate plane?
    Ⓐ (0, 0), (1, 1), (2, 2), (3, 3)   Ⓒ (4, 5), (5, 4), (−5, −4), (−4, −5)
    Ⓑ (4, 2), (4, −2), (0, 2), (0, −2)   Ⓓ (6, −4), (4, −6), (5, 4), (−4, −5)

For questions 19 and 20 refer to the graph below.

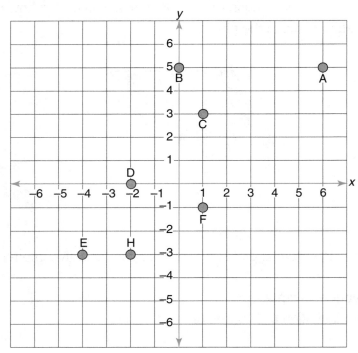

19. Which of the following coordinates represents point *D*?
    Ⓐ (0, –2)
    Ⓑ (–2, 0)
    Ⓒ (2, 0)
    Ⓓ (0, 2)

20. Which of the following sets of points is 4 units away from each other?
    Ⓐ Points *B* and *A*
    Ⓑ Points *C* and *F*
    Ⓒ Points *H* and *E*
    Ⓓ Points *D* and *H*

21. |–19| is equivalent to all of the following EXCEPT:
    Ⓐ –19
    Ⓑ 19
    Ⓒ – –19
    Ⓓ |+19|

22. Which of the following lists of rational numbers is in order from least to greatest?

    Ⓐ $+1, -2, -|-5|, -\frac{2}{3}, -0.6, -9$

    Ⓑ $-|-5|, +1, -9, -\frac{2}{3}, -2, -0.6$

    Ⓒ $-9, -|-5|, -2, -\frac{2}{3}, -0.6, +1$

    Ⓓ $-9, -|-5|, -2, -0.6, -\frac{2}{3}, +1$

23. Which of the following numbers makes $-10 > x$ true?

Ⓐ -11 Ⓒ -8

Ⓑ -9 Ⓓ -7

24. In order to be eligible for an award at school, the teachers determined that a student must have completed more than 15 assignments correctly in one month. Which of the following inequalities could represent this situation?

Ⓐ $x > |-15|$ Ⓒ $x \le 15$

Ⓑ $x < |15|$ Ⓓ $x \ge 15$

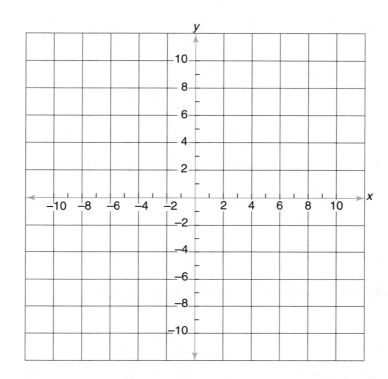

25. Which of the following numbers represents the distance between the points $(-3, -4)$ and $(-7, -4)$ when graphed on a coordinate plane?

Ⓐ 0   Ⓒ 3

Ⓑ 4   Ⓓ 7

26. Evaluate $\dfrac{15}{5} + 40 \cdot 7 - 3^4$.

Ⓐ 271   Ⓒ 220

Ⓑ 202   Ⓓ 289

27. Which of the following expressions represents "a third of the difference of 3 and m"?

    Ⓐ $3(3 - m)$ Ⓒ $\frac{1}{3}(3 - m)$

    Ⓑ $\frac{1}{3}3 - m$ Ⓓ $3 - 3m$

28. In the expression $3(5x + 2)$, which part represents a sum?

    Ⓐ 3   Ⓒ $x + 2$

    Ⓑ $5x + 2$ Ⓓ $5x$

29. In the expression $ab + c - \dfrac{d}{f}$, which part represents a product?

    Ⓐ ab Ⓒ $\dfrac{d}{f}$

    Ⓑ c Ⓓ $ab + c - \dfrac{d}{f}$

30. Evaluate the following expression when $x = \dfrac{1}{2}$, $y = 4$, and $z = \dfrac{1}{3}$.

    $9z + y^3 + 60x(x - z)$

    Ⓐ 98   Ⓒ 97

    Ⓑ 20   Ⓓ 72

31. Which of the following expressions is equivalent to $x(2 + 10)$?

    Ⓐ $2x + 10$ Ⓒ $12x$

    Ⓑ $x + 12$ Ⓓ $20x$

32. Sue and Lynn were discussing if $3x + 9$ is equivalent to $3(x + 3)$. Using $x = 2$, determine if they are equivalent and show work that Lynn could use to verify.

33. Which of the following values is the solution to the equation below?

$$4x - 10 = 30$$

- Ⓐ 5
- Ⓑ 10
- Ⓒ 80
- Ⓓ 160

34. What is the height of a triangle if the area is 55 and the base is 10?
- Ⓐ 1,100
- Ⓑ 550
- Ⓒ 275
- Ⓓ 11

35. Part A. Write an equation representing the amount a babysitter charges, *C,* if she charges $10 for the snacks she brings and $5 per hour, *h,* she babysits.

Part B. Determine how many hours your aunt can hire a babysitter if she has $50 to spend.

36. Which of the following number lines represents $x \geq -1$?

Ⓐ
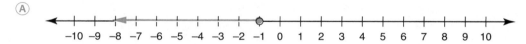

Ⓑ
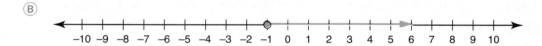

Ⓒ
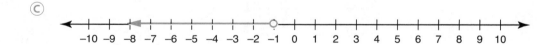

Ⓓ

37. A restaurant serves many different hamburgers. Noah wants to buy 4 of the same hamburger and use a $2 coupon at the restaurant. There is no tax, and he has no more than $9 to spend.

Part A. Write an inequality that could be solved to determine the amount that each hamburger could cost so that Noah does not spend more than $9.

Part B. Solve the inequality that you wrote in Part A to determine the amount he could spend on each hamburger.

Part C. Draw the solution on a number line that represents the cost of the hamburgers.

38. Part A. Given the table of values below, determine which of the following equations could represent the data.

a	b
5	16
6	19
20	61
50	151

Ⓐ $a + 11 = b$

Ⓑ $b = 13 + a$

Ⓒ $3a + 1 = b$

Ⓓ $\dfrac{b}{10} = a$

Part B. The letter b in the chart above represents the _____.

Ⓐ Independent variable

Ⓑ Dependent variable

Ⓒ Input

Ⓓ Domain

39. Cookie dough needs to be divided into equal portions at the bakery to make $\frac{1}{8}$ pound cookies. Determine how many full cookies can be made if the bakery has $5\frac{1}{2}$ pounds of cookie dough.

40. Mimi was noticing that a stray cat walked by her kitchen window every 2 minutes, a bird flew by every 6 minutes, and her dog came to look out the window every 9 minutes. When is the first time that the cat, dog, and bird will all be at the window at the same time?
    - (A) 2 minutes
    - (B) 12 minutes
    - (C) 18 minutes
    - (D) 36 minutes

41. If $20x + 44$ is rewritten using the distributive property, it would be _____.
    - (A) $20(x + 44)$
    - (B) $64x$
    - (C) $(20 + 44)x$
    - (D) $4(5x + 11)$

42. Determine the volume of a rectangular prism that measures 2.5 cm by $4\frac{1}{3}$ cm by $9\frac{1}{5}$ cm.

43. Which of the following expressions can be used to find the volume of a rectangular prism?
    - (A) Bh
    - (B) S^3
    - (C) bh
    - (D) $l = wh$

44. Part A. Graph the following coordinates on the grid below.

(3, 2), (3, –2), (–4, –2), (–4, 2)

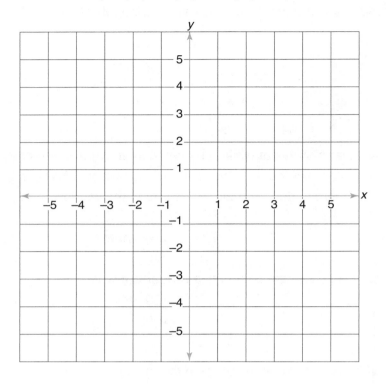

Part B. Determine the perimeter of the polygon.

Part C. Determine the area of the polygon.

45. Which of the following nets will fold to make a triangular pyramid?

Ⓐ Ⓐ

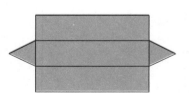

Ⓒ

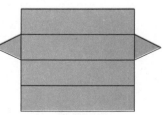

Ⓑ

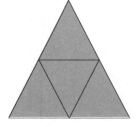

Ⓓ

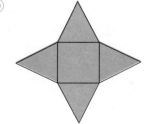

46. A cereal box company wants to know how much cardboard is needed to make a box for its cereal. A sketch of the cereal box is below. Determine the amount of cardboard to the nearest eighth of an inch they will need to make one box.

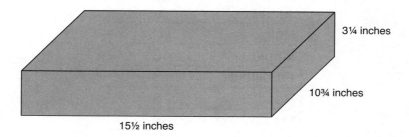

3¼ inches

10¾ inches

15½ inches

47. Using which of the following questions can you anticipate getting variability in your data?

Ⓐ How old is my aunt today?

Ⓑ What are the weights of students in my class?

Ⓒ How many people are in the room now?

Ⓓ What is my hair color?

48. The ages of the patients that visited a pediatrician's office in one day are shown below.

2, 4, 1, 6, 1, 2, 3, 7, 13, 14, 11, 8, 9, 1, 2, 1, 15

Which of the following box plots is correctly drawn based on the data the pediatrician collected?

Ⓐ
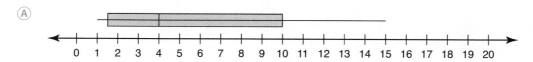

Ⓑ
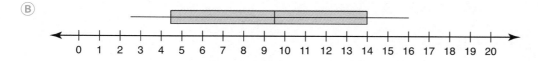

Ⓒ
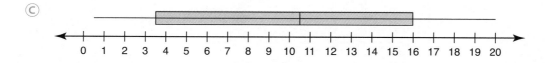

Ⓓ
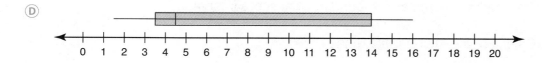

49. Meyers' Landscaping logged the types of shrubs and trees they sold last year in the chart below. Determine the mean absolute deviation of the data to the nearest tenth.

Spruce	10
Juniper	23
Holly	13
Maple	8
Forsythia	3
Rose	5
Oak	6

50. The scores of 6th grade math students in Mrs. Yerdon's class are recorded below.

94, 65, 78, 90, 99, 76, 89, 87, 60, 73, 84, 88, 90, 95, 97, 81, 96

Part A. Create a histogram of the data.

Test Scores	Tally	Frequency
60–69		
70–79		
80–89		
90–99		

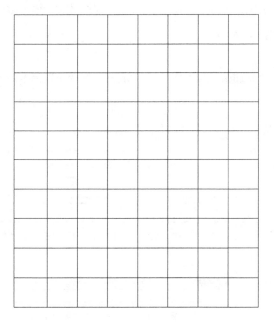

Part B. The median score can be found in what score interval?

Part C. Calculate the interquartile range (IQR).

Part D. Describe the spread of the data.

(Answers are on page 214.)

MATH ANSWERS EXPLAINED

Ratios and Rates, page 110

1. **(A)** Ratios are written in the order stated. Because the word *student* appears first and the word *chaperone*, appears second, the ratio could be written as 10:1, 10 to 1, or $\frac{10}{1}$. However, the question asks for the ratio that does *not* represent the student-to-chaperone ratio, which is choice **A**.

2. **(B)** All choices use the numbers 21 and 3; however, notice that in the fraction the number 21 is listed on the top. Therefore, 21 must be mentioned first when describing the ratio.

3. **(C)** Math gets 2 votes for every 1 vote history class receives. The only choice that matches this is choice C. The other choices all have 2 votes for history and 1 vote for math.

4. **(A)** A quarter can be thought of as $\frac{1}{4}$. If there were a total of 4 votes and the mayor received 1 for every 4, this leaves 3 votes out of 4 for his opponent. Make sure that the current mayor's votes are listed first.

5. **2 to 3, 2:3, or $\frac{2}{3}$** This question asks you to compare the number made to the number missed. If $\frac{2}{5}$ is the number of shots he makes, that means he makes 2 shots for every 5 total shots. If he makes 2 shots for every 5 shots, he must miss 3 for every 5 since 5 − 2 = 3. Be sure to list the number he made first.

6. **(D)** Writing the ratio as a fraction may help you start to solve this problem. Then divide both the top and bottom numbers by 5 to find out how many gallons of water pass in 1 minute.
$$\frac{1{,}750 \text{ gallons} \div 5}{5 \text{ minutes} \div 5} = \frac{350}{1}.$$
Choice C looks like a plausible answer; however, the question asks for the answer in gallons/minute, which means gallons must be written first.

7. **(A)** Unit rates express the rate as an amount per 1. In this case, that means per 1 second.
$$\frac{625 \text{ feet} \div 13}{13 \text{ seconds} \div 13} \approx \frac{48}{1}$$

8. **$1.19 per pound** This unit rate calls for the amount of money per 1 pound.
$$\frac{\$2.38 \div 2}{2 \text{ pounds} \div 2} = \frac{1.19}{1}$$

9. **neither is better** They both are equivalent to $0.98 per pound once the unit rate of $2.45/2.5 lbs is calculated. Divide 2.45 by 2.5 to equal 0.98.
$$\frac{\$2.45 \div 2.5}{2.5 \text{ lb} \div 2.5} = \frac{\$0.98}{1 \text{ lb}}$$

Real World Ratio and Rate Problems, page 112

1. **(D)** The ratio is given as 30 words per minute. Choices A and C refer to words per minute but use the wrong number of words. Choice B has the correct number of words but the wrong time. Choice **D** is correct because to get 30 words per minute to equal an amount per hour, you would multiply by 60 since there are 60 minutes in 1 hour: 30 × 60 = 1,800.

2.

3	6	30	33	60
7	14	70	77	140
	Multiplied by 2	Multiplied by 10	Multiplied by 11	Multiplied by 20

3. Explanations will vary but should be similar to the following: Samantha realized that if she could do 5 problems in 4 minutes, she should multiply 5 problems by 5 to equal 25 problems. She then multiplied the 4 by 5 also, keeping the constant of proportionality or scale factor the same for both, resulting in 20. This is similar to finding equivalent fractions. This problem could also be solved by setting up a proportion and cross multiplying to find the unknown number.
$$\frac{\text{problems}}{\text{minute}} = \frac{5}{4} = \frac{25}{x}$$
$$\frac{100}{5} = \frac{5x}{5}$$
$$20 = x$$

4. (C) In choice **C** each ratio after 2:3 is multiplied using a constant number to get the next ratio. For example, to get 6:9, you multiply both 2 and 3 by 3. To get 10:15 you multiply 2 and 3 by 5. Another way to look at this problem is that both 6:9 and 10:15 can be reduced to 2:3, thus proving they are all equivalent.

5. Part A.

cupcakes	12	36	**60**	**6**	**24**
cookies	10	**30**	50	**5**	**20**

Part B. Answers can vary for the last blank. Given are two possible answers. Note that you can multiply or divide 12:10 by any number as long as you stay consistent for each part of the ratio. I **divided** 12 and 10 each by **2** to get 6 and 5. I **multiplied** 12 and 10 each by **2** to get 24 and 20.

6. Typically you graph by first going over on the *x*-axis the *x*-value stated in the table and then up or down the correct *y*-value on the vertical axis.

x	*y*
1	2
2	4
3	6
4	8
5	**10**

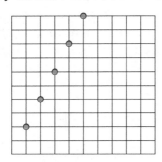

7. Each mile is multiplied by 13.

	Miles	Minutes
	1	13
2 × 13 = 26	2	**26**
4 × 13 = 52	4	**52**
6 × 13 = 78	6	**78**

Be careful! Do not just add 13 each time down the chart. The left side of the chart is not in consecutive order.

Unit Rate, page 114

1. **2 minutes 24 seconds** Find the unit rate, or number of seconds to drive 1 mile: divide 40 seconds by 2.5 miles. Once you find the unit rate, you can use that number to quickly multiply. So, if 1 mile is completed in 16 seconds, then 9 miles are completed in 144 seconds.

   40 seconds ÷ 2.5 miles = 16 seconds per 1 mile

   9 miles × 16 seconds = 144 seconds

   To change 144 seconds to minutes and seconds, subtract 60 seconds for every minute. The amount left over that cannot be subtracted by 60 would be the seconds.

   144 − 60 seconds = 2 minutes 24 seconds

2. (B) To find the unit rate, calculate the cost for 1 unit, or 1 pound of bananas. To find the unit rate, divide the $2.25 price by 3.75 pounds. This results in $0.60 per 1 pound. Choice A is a distractor because it is the answer if you divide 3.75 by 2.25.

3. **201.5 miles** Find the unit rate, or number of miles that was driven in 1 hour. Divide 124 miles by the 2 hours that you traveled (from 8 A.M. to 10 A.M.): 124 ÷ 2 = 62. Use the unit rate to quickly multiply. So, if 62 miles is completed in 1 hour, then in 3 hours and 15 minutes (3.25 hours), 201.5 miles are driven: 62 × 3.25 = 201.5.

4. (B) Since all the prices are given in different amounts, it is difficult to compare them. Divide each of the prices by the number of ounces given to get the unit rate, or the amount it costs for only 1 ounce. Then they will be easy to compare.

Healthy Babies	$5.76 for 12 oz $5.76 ÷ 12 oz	$0.48/oz
Top Baby Food	$4.23 for 9 oz $4.23 ÷ 9 oz	$0.47/oz
Baby Puree	$0.92 for 1.5 oz $0.92 ÷ 1.5 oz	$0.61/oz
Yummy Baby	$2.08 for 4 oz $2.08 ÷ 4 oz	$0.52/oz

5. **Approximately 1 hour and 11 min** Find a unit rate based on how many square feet you can mow in 1 hour.

   Step 1: Determine the area of your rectangular lawn using the formula $A = bh$. The area of your lawn is 32 × 20, or 640 square feet or 640 ft^2.

Step 2: Using the area from Step 1 and the 45 minutes given in the problem, determine the unit rate, or amount of square feet you can mow in 1 hour. Convert 45 minutes to a decimal:

$$\frac{45}{60} = \frac{3}{4} = 0.75.$$

640 square feet ÷ 0.75 hours ≈ 853 ft² per hour

Step 3: Determine the area of the neighbor's lawn. Substitute, or plug in, the numbers from the diagram under the corresponding variables in the formula and then use order of operations.

$$A = \frac{1}{2}h(b_1 + b_2)$$

$$A = \frac{1}{2}22(50 + 42)$$

$$A = 11(92)$$

$$A = 1,012$$

Step 4: Using the unit rate from Step 2, determine how long it will take to mow 1,012 ft². Make sure you convert the decimal portion of your answer to minutes by multiplying by 60.

1,012 square feet ÷ 853 ft² per hour

≈ 1.1864 hours

0.1864 × 60 ≈ 11 minutes

1 hour and 11 minutes

6. **(C)** There are multiple ways to solve this problem. One way is to set up proportions and see if their cross products are equal. The other way is to see if a constant of proportionality is used consistently for each answer choice provided.

$\frac{cm}{hours} \frac{7.3}{2.25} = \frac{2.25}{7.3}$	$\frac{cm}{hours} \frac{7.3}{2.25} = \frac{14.6}{4.5}$
5.0625 ≠ 53.29	32.85 = 32.85
$\frac{cm}{hours} \frac{7.3}{2.25} = \frac{3.25}{1}$	$\frac{cm}{hours} \frac{7.3}{2.25} = \frac{28.3}{9}$
7.3125 ≠ 7.3	63.675 ≠ 65.7

7. **(A)** When setting up proportions, you need to make sure you place the numbers in a constant pattern. Look for the constant pattern by writing the words they represent. For example, in choice A, 2 is written over 1, which is 2 walls over 1 hour. Look at the second ratio and see if it is walls over hours, which it is because 3.5 is hours and on the bottom of the ratio.

1. **(D)** To solve a percent problem you can translate the words to an equation to solve or you can set up a proportion to solve. If you set up a proportion, this format may help you:

$$\frac{is}{of} = \frac{\%}{100}$$ The number after the word *is* goes on top (numerator) of the first fraction: the number after the word *of* goes on the bottom (denominator). The number that is with the percent sign (%) is placed in the top of the second fraction, and 100 is always the bottom because percents are out of the total number 100. One of the four places will be represented by an unknown letter, typically x or n.

$$\frac{x}{350} = \frac{45}{100}$$

$$\frac{100x}{100} = \frac{15,750}{100}$$

$x = 157.5$ or about 158

2. **(B)** Notice that the problem gives information on how many students pass, but the question actually asks for how many will *not* pass. You are looking for 10% of 120 students, not 90% of 120 students.

$$\frac{x}{120} = \frac{10}{100}$$

$$\frac{100x}{100} = \frac{1,200}{100}$$

$x = 12$

3. **(D)** To determine tax, you must first calculate 8% of 54.99, and then add that answer onto 54.99. You can use the proportion method or translate it to an equation and solve. Remember to add the tax you calculated to the price of the game.

$$\frac{x}{54.99} = \frac{8}{100}$$

$$\frac{100x}{100} = \frac{439.92}{100}$$

$x = 4.3992$ or $4.40 when rounded

$4.40 + 54.99 = 59.39

4. **(A)** Using a proportion, find the percent.

$$\frac{is}{of} = \frac{\%}{100}$$

$$\frac{11}{60} = \frac{x}{100}$$

$$\frac{60x}{60} = \frac{1,100}{60}$$

$x = 18.\overline{3}$ or 18% when rounded

5. **15** As you determine where to place the numbers in the proportion, remember that the word *is* represents the *part,* and the word *of* represents *out of the total or whole.*

$$\frac{\text{is (part)}}{\text{of (whole)}} = \frac{\%}{100}$$

$$\frac{12}{x} = \frac{80}{100}$$

$$\frac{80x}{80} = \frac{1,200}{80}$$

$$x = 15$$

6. **(B)** To calculate the sale price, the 30% discount must be found first. Then the difference between the original price and the discount must be found.

Step 1. Think of the problem as "30% off of 45.99 is what amount?"

$$\frac{\text{is (part)}}{\text{of (whole)}} = \frac{\%}{100}$$

$$\frac{x}{45.99} = \frac{30}{100}$$

$$\frac{100x}{100} = \frac{1379.7}{100}$$

$$x = 13.797 \text{ or } 13.80 \text{ rounded}$$

Step 2. The discount is $13.80, yet the problem asks for the sale price. Subtract the discount from the original price. $45.99 − $13.80 = $32.19

7. **12,000 bees** Think of the problem as "10% of what amount is 1,200?"

$$\frac{\text{is (part)}}{\text{of (whole)}} = \frac{\%}{100}$$

$$\frac{1,200}{x} = \frac{10}{100}$$

$$\frac{10x}{10} = \frac{120,000}{10}$$

$$x = 12,000$$

8. **200** Think of the problem as "2.5% of what amount is 5?"

$$\frac{\text{is (part)}}{\text{of (whole)}} = \frac{\%}{100}$$

$$\frac{5}{x} = \frac{2.5}{100}$$

$$\frac{2.5x}{2.5} = \frac{500}{2.5}$$

$$x = 200$$

Ratios and Converting Measurement Units, page 118

1. **(A)** To convert, you need to know that there are 4 quarts in 1 gallon. From there, set up a proportion to convert.

$$\frac{\text{quarts}}{\text{gallons}}\frac{4}{1} = \frac{77}{x}$$

$$\frac{4x}{4} = \frac{77}{4}$$

$$x = 19.25$$

2. Use proportional reasoning to complete the chart. See chart at bottom of this page.

3. **(D)** To convert you need to know there are 1,000 ml in 1 L. Set up a proportion to convert.

$$\frac{\text{ml}}{\text{L}}\frac{1,000}{1} = \frac{x}{12.7}$$

$$\frac{1x}{1} = \frac{12,700}{1}$$

$$x = 12,700$$

4. **100 inches** To convert, you need to know there are 12 inches in 1 foot. Set up a proportion to convert. Convert one of the given measurements to the other's units. Convert 7 feet 9 inches to all inches to compare it to 100 inches.

Pounds	2,000	**4,000**	**5,000**	6,000	**11,000**	13,500
Tons	**1**	2	2.5	**3**	5.5	**6.75**
Explanation	**Conversion rule**	Multiply 2,000 by 2	Multiply 2,000 by 2.5	Divide 6,000 by 2,000	Multiply 2,000 by 5.5	Divide 13,500 by 2,000

$$\frac{\text{inches}}{\text{feet}} \quad \frac{12}{1} = \frac{x}{7}$$

$$\frac{1x}{1} = \frac{84}{1}$$

x = 84 inches plus the extra 9 inches = 93 inches

5. **2.875 pounds** Set up a proportion and convert. There are 16 ounces in 1 pound.

$$\frac{\text{ounces}}{\text{pounds}} \quad \frac{16}{1} = \frac{46}{x}$$

$$\frac{16x}{16} = \frac{46}{16}$$

x = 2.875 pounds

6. $5\frac{1}{3}$ **quarts** For every 1 gallon there are 4 quarts. For every 2 gallons there are 8 quarts. The answer must be between 1 and 8 quarts because $1\frac{1}{3}$ is between 1 and 2. The constant of proportionality is to multiply every gallon by 4.

$$1\frac{1}{3} = \frac{4}{3}$$

$$\frac{4}{3} \times 4 = \frac{16}{3}$$

$$\frac{16}{3} = 5\frac{1}{3}$$

7. **0.072 L/day** This is a two-step problem in which milliliters need to be converted to liters and hours need to be converted to days.

Step 1: Convert ml to L. There are 1,000 ml in 1 L.

$$\frac{\text{liters}}{\text{ml}} \quad \frac{1}{1,000} = \frac{x}{3}$$

$$\frac{1,000x}{1,000} = \frac{3}{1,000}$$

$$x = 0.003 \text{ L/hr}$$

Step 2: Convert the L/hr to liters per day. There are 24 hours in a day. $0.003 \times 24 = .072$ L/day

8. **70.3 feet** The problem should be completed using 2 steps. Step 1 is to find the perimeter. A rectangular perimeter can be found by adding all sides or by using the formula $P = 2L + 2W$.

$$P = 2L + 2W$$
$$P = 2(300) + 2(122)$$
$$P = 600 + 244$$
$$P = 844 \text{ inches}$$

Step 2 is to convert to feet. There are 12 inches in 1 foot.

$$\frac{\text{feet}}{\text{inches}} \quad \frac{1}{12} = \frac{x}{844}$$

$$\frac{12x}{12} = \frac{844}{12}$$

$$x = 70.33 \text{ feet}$$

9.

35 km =	**3,500,000 cm**	Multiply by 100,000 (1 km = 100,000 cm)
42 pts =	**21 qts**	Divide by 2 (2 pts = 1 qt)
16 cm =	**160 mm**	Multiply by 10 (1 cm = 10 mm)
78 g =	**0.078 kg**	Divide by 1,000 (1 g = .001 kg)
98 mi =	**517,440 ft**	Multiply by 5,280 (5,280 ft = 1 mile)
16 fl oz =	**2 c**	Divide by 8 (8 fl oz = 1 c)

Reading, Writing, and Evaluating Expressions, page 120

1. **(A)** You must perform the order of operations to solve this problem.

$$2(17-1)$$
$$2(16)$$
$$32$$

2. **(C)** You must perform the order of operations to solve this problem.

$$\frac{10}{5} + 2 \cdot 7 - 3^2$$
$$\frac{10}{5} + 2 \cdot 7 - 9$$
$$2 + 2 \cdot 7 - 9$$
$$2 + 14 - 9$$
$$16 - 9$$
$$7$$

3. **(C)** Use order of operations to evaluate. You must perform the exponent operations first, then multiplication, and finally addition. Remember, $2^3 = 2 \cdot 2 \cdot 2$ and $5^2 = 5 \cdot 5$.

$$5^2 + 2^3(9)$$
$$25 + 8(9)$$
$$25 + 72$$
$$97$$

4. **(B)**

$$\frac{25}{5}(2^3 - 7)$$

$$\frac{25}{5}(8-7)$$

$$\frac{25}{5}(1)$$

$$5(1)$$

$$5$$

5. Emily added before she should have. She should have subtracted 35 from 90, as shown in the work below. The misconception that Emily had was that she should add before subtracting. Subtraction can be done before addition if it comes first in the problem when reading it left to right.

$$90 - 5 \times 7 + 10$$
$$90 - 35 + 10$$
$$55 + 10$$
$$65$$

6. (B) *Decreased* means to subtract. Choice A is a distractor because reversing the order of subtraction is the most common error for students to make. Since the problem references two different unknown numbers, you need to use two different variables.

7. (C) Five years less means to subtract 5 from k. Choice B is a distractor because reversing the order of subtraction is the most common error for students to make.

8. (A) *Twice* means to multiply by 2, and *increased* means to add. Choice A is written using the commutative property, which allows us to switch the order and keep the same result.

9. Answers will vary. However, the most common ones are: $\frac{1}{4}s + \frac{1}{2}t$, $.25s + .5t$, $\frac{s}{4} + \frac{t}{2}$. You can verify that the expression you wrote is

equivalent to the given expression by picking a number to represent each variable and substituting the numbers into both expressions. The two expressions will result in the same answer if they are equivalent.

10. Answers will vary. The most common answers are: The product of x and 3 decreased by 4; four less than the product of 3 and x; 3 times x less 4; 3 times x decreased by 4; my aunt is 4 years younger than 3 times my age. Something (x) is divided by 3; the pizza was shared by 3 people.

Parts of Expressions, page 122

1. (B) A *sum* is the answer to addition. Of the choices, $x + 2$ is the only sum.

2. (C) A *quotient* is the answer to division, which is $\frac{x}{5}$.

3. (D) *Coefficients* are the numbers that are in front of variables. The only numbers that are in front of variables are -2 and 4.

4. (C) A *term* is a part of an expression separated by addition or subtraction signs. To determine the greatest term, you need to substitute in x-, y-, and z-values given in the problem. So, $3y = 9$ when you multiply 3(3), $4z = 8$ when you multiply 4(2), and $x^3 = 8$ when you multiply $2 \times 2 \times 2$.

5. Part A. The *factors* are **3 and (y − 7)** because they are the 2 parts that you multiply together. The term **(y − 7)** represents the *difference*, which is the answer to a subtraction problem.

   Part B. The *factors* are **3 and y**. The entire expression, **3y − 21**, represents the difference.

6. Part A. See chart below.

Terms	Coefficients	Sums	Constants	Factors	Quotients	Products
$2(y + 4)$	2	$(y + 4)$		2 and $(y + 4)$		$2(y + 4)$
$\frac{3z+12}{3}$	3	$3z + 12$		3 and z	$\frac{3z+12}{3}$	$3z$
$5y$	5			5 and y		$5y$
yz				y and z		yz
6		$2(y + 4) + \frac{3z+12}{3}$ $+ 5y + yz + 6$	6			

Part B. **7y + z + yz + 18**

$2(y + 4) + \dfrac{3z+12}{3} + 5y + yz + 6$	Perform the distributive property on $2(y + 4)$ to get $2y + 8$
$2y + 8 + z + 4 + 5y + yz + 6$	Reduce the quotient by dividing both coefficients 3 and 12 by 3 to get $z + 4$
$7y + z + yz + 18$	Combine like terms, which are $2y + 5y$ and then $8 + 4 + 6$

Terms	Coefficients	Sums	Constants	Factors	Quotients	Products
$7y$	7			7 and y	none	$7y$
z						
yz				y and z		yz
18		$7y + z + yz + 18$	18			

Part C. Answers will vary; this is a suggested response. There are many differences in the charts because the simplification process creates fewer parts. Each category, except the quotient, still exists but with different numbers. The only similarity is yz remained as a term, as factors and as a product because it did not have a like term to be combined with.

Evaluate Expressions, page 124

1. (B)
$$5a - b + b^2$$
$$5(2) - 5 + 5^2$$
$$5(2) - 5 + 25$$
$$10 - 5 + 25$$
$$5 + 25$$
$$30$$

2. (B)
$$9a - b + 2b^2$$
$$9(3) - 10 + 2(10)^2$$
$$27 - 10 + 2(100)$$
$$27 - 10 + 200$$
$$17 + 200$$
$$217$$

3. (C)
$$\frac{3y}{z} + y^{(2)} + y(z - x)$$
$$\frac{3(6)}{2} + 6^2 + 6(2 - 5)$$
$$\frac{3(6)}{2} + 36 + 6(2 - 5)$$
$$\frac{18}{2} + 36 + 6(2 - 5)$$
$$9 + 36 + 6(2 - 5)$$
$$9 + 36 + 12 - 30$$
$$45 + 12 - 30$$
$$57 - 30$$
$$27$$

4. (D)
$$20z + y^3 + 40x(x - z)$$
$$20(\tfrac{1}{4}) + 4^3 + 40(\tfrac{1}{2})(\tfrac{1}{2} - \tfrac{1}{4})$$
$$20(\tfrac{1}{4}) + 4^3 + 40(\tfrac{1}{2})(\tfrac{1}{4})$$
$$20(\tfrac{1}{4}) + 64 + 40(\tfrac{1}{2})(\tfrac{1}{4})$$
$$5 + 64 + 40(\tfrac{1}{2})(\tfrac{1}{4})$$
$$5 + 64 + 20(\tfrac{1}{4})$$
$$5 + 64 + 5$$
$$64 + 10$$
$$74$$

5. (A)
$$cd + d^3 + 9e(4c - d)$$
$$0.6(2.1) + 2.1^3 + 9(\tfrac{1}{3})(4(0.6) - 2.1)$$
$$0.6(2.1) + 2.1^3 + 9(\tfrac{1}{3})(2.4 - 2.1)$$
$$0.6(2.1) + 2.1^3 + 9(\tfrac{1}{3})(0.3)$$
$$0.6(2.1) + 9.261 + 9(\tfrac{1}{3})(0.3)$$
$$1.26 + 9.261 + 9(\tfrac{1}{3})(0.3)$$
$$1.26 + 9.261 + 3(0.3)$$
$$1.26 + 9.261 + 0.9$$
$$2.16 + 9.261$$
$$11.421$$

6. 11
$$2a + a^2 - b$$
$$2(5) + 5^2 - 24$$
$$2(5) + 25 - 24$$
$$10 + 25 - 24$$
$$35 - 24$$
$$11$$

7. **195 square feet**

$A = \frac{1}{2}h(b_1 + b_1)$

$A = \frac{1}{2}(8)(28.25 + 20\frac{1}{2})$

$A = \frac{1}{2}(8)(48.75)$

$A = 4(48.75)$

$A = 195$ square feet

8. Part A. **150 square inches**

$A = 6s^2$

$A = 6(5)^2$

$A = 6(25)$

$A = 150$ square inches

Part B. **165.375 square inches**

$A = 6s^2$

$A = 6(5.25)^2$

$A = 6(27.5625)$

$A = 165.375$ square inches

Part C. **No. The difference between a side of 5 and a side of $5\frac{1}{4}$ results in a difference in area of 15.375 square inches.** There is a difference per side of 2.5625 square inches, and there are 6 sides, resulting in a greater difference in terms of area.

Equivalent Expressions, page 126

1. **(C)** Use the distributive property to simplify the expression to form an equivalent expression. Multiply 7 and y and then 6 and 7. Be sure to keep the terms separate. Because they are *not* like terms, you cannot combine them. Don't forget that there is a subtraction sign inside the parentheses that must remain in the final answer.

2. **(A)** Use the distributive property to simplify the expression to form an equivalent expression. In this case, you are multiplying 5 and $4x$ and then 5 and 9. Be sure to keep the terms separate. Because they are *not* like terms, you cannot combine them. Choice C mistakenly combines $4x$ and 9 to be $13x$ and choice D combines $20x$ and 45 to be $65x$, even though they should *not* have been combined because they are not like terms. Choice B is another common error because the factor was distributed to only the first number inside the parentheses.

3. **(C)** Use the distributive property and then combine like terms to simplify the expression to form an equivalent expression. When you use the distributive property, you are multiplying x and 8 to get $8x$ and then x and 12 to get $12x$. This results in $8x + 12x$. Since both terms have the variable x, they are like terms and should be combined: $8x + 12x = 20x$.

4. **(B)** Combine like terms to simplify the expression to form an equivalent expression. Like terms end in the same variable. In this particular expression, the terms ending in r are the like terms: $5r - 1r + 2r = 6r$. Make sure you know that $-r$ means $-1r$. The constants 7 and 10 are also like terms and should be added together: $7 + 10 = 17$.

5. **$2x + 8$. Answers will vary for the second expression.** Some examples are $x + x + 8$, $2x + 4 + 4$, $10x - 8x + 10 - 2$, or $\frac{10x}{5} + 8$. Use substitution and order of operations to verify the expressions. Each expression should result in the same final value if they are truly equivalent.

$3x + 8 - x$	$2x + 8$	$x + x + 8$
$3(2) + 8 - 2$	$2(2) + 8$	$2 + 2 + 8$
$6 + 8 - 2$	$4 + 8$	$4 + 8$
$14 - 2$	**12**	**12**
12		

6.

Yes	No
$11r + 33$	$15r + 23$
$10r + r + 3(11)$	$15r + 8$
$11(r + 3)$	$11r + 35$
$2(5.5r + 16.5)$	$15r + 33$
$20r - 9r + 66 - 33$	$52r$
$\frac{1}{2}(22r + 66)$	$44r$
$\frac{44r}{4} + \frac{99}{3}$	

Solving Equations, page 128

1. **(B)** You can check to see if a value is the solution to an equation by substituting it into the equation and performing the order of operations. When $x = 17$, the equation is true.

$$x - 7 = 10$$
$$17 - 7 = 10$$
$$10 = 10$$

When $x = 70$, the equation is not true.

$$x - 7 = 10$$
$$70 - 7 = 10$$
$$63 \neq 10$$

2. **(A)** Substitute the value into the equation and perform the order of operations. When $x = 10$, the equation is true.

$$90 = 80 + x$$
$$90 = 80 + 10$$
$$90 = 90$$

3. **(D)** Substitute the value into the equation and perform the order of operations. When $y = 100$, the equation is true.

$$\frac{y}{2} = 50$$
$$\frac{100}{2} = 50$$
$$50 = 50$$

4. **(B)** Substitute the value into the equation and perform the order of operations. When $x = 12$, the equation is true.

$$5x - 10 = 50$$
$$5(12) - 10 = 50$$
$$60 - 10 = 50$$
$$50 = 50$$

5. **(D)** Substitute the value into the inequality and perform the order of operations. Be sure to read the inequality symbol correctly. Inequalities can have more than one answer. When x is 13, the inequality is true.

$$x + 8 > 20$$
$$13 + 8 > 20$$
$$21 > 20$$

When x is 12, the inequality is not true.

$$x + 8 > 20$$
$$12 + 8 > 20$$
$$20 = 20$$

20 is not greater than 20.

When x is 11, the inequality is not true.

$$x + 8 > 20$$
$$11 + 8 > 20$$
$$19 < 20$$

19 is not greater than 20.

6. **(D)** Substitute the value into the inequality and perform the order of operations. This question is asking for the one solution that does *not* check. Remember that the symbol $\leq$ is read "less than or equal to." In this particular inequality, that means

that 8 can be a solution because it produces a statement that is equal to the inequality. When c is 9, the inequality is not true.

$$9c \leq 72$$
$$9(9) \leq 72$$
$$81 > 72$$

81 is not less than or equal to 72; it is greater than 72.

7. **(C)** Substitute the values into the inequality. Be sure to read the inequality symbol correctly. In this particular problem, the variable is written last. Read it as "90 is less than a number." It may be easier for you to read it from right to left, starting with the variable, "a number is greater than 90." Inequalities can have more than one answer. This question is asking for the solutions that do check. There are more possible solutions but the question gives you only a partial set to check. Choice C is the only one with all numbers greater than 90 or where 90 is less than all the numbers.

8. **(D)** Substitute the values into the inequality. Be sure to read the inequality symbol correctly. In this particular problem, the variable is written last, so read it as "100 is greater than twice a number." It may be easier for you to read it from right to left, starting with the variable: "Twice a number is less than 100." This question is asking for the solutions that do check. Choice D is the only one with all numbers that check in the inequality: $100 > 2(49)$; $100 > 2(47)$; $100 > 2(46)$.

Variables and Equations, page 130

1. **(D)** The perimeter of a square is found by adding all four sides ($s + s + s + s$) or by multiplying one side by four ($s \times 4$, or $4s$) since the four sides are all the same length. Choices A and B refer to the area of a square and not to the perimeter.

2. **(B)** Substitute the numbers into the correct variables. The area is given and you need to solve for h, which means you must isolate the variable and use inverse operations.

$$A = \frac{1}{2}bh$$
$$20 = \frac{1}{2}4h$$
$$20 = 2h$$
$$\frac{20}{2} = \frac{2h}{2}$$
$$10 = h$$

3. (A) Substitute the numbers into the correct variables. The area is given. You need to solve for *w*, which means you must isolate the variable and use inverse operations.

$$P = 2l + 2w$$
$$140 = 2(10) + 2w$$
$$140 = 20 + 2w$$
$$\underline{-20 \quad -20}$$
$$\frac{120}{2} = \frac{2w}{2}$$
$$60 = w$$

4. (C) Write an expression to represent the situation and then substitute the numbers into the correct variables. Then perform the order of operations. In this problem, brownies are $2.25 each, so $2.25b$ represents brownies. Cupcakes are $3.50 each, so $3.50c$ represents cupcakes. To find the total, add the cost of the brownies to the cost of the cupcakes: $2.25b + 3.50c$

$$2.25b + 3.50c$$
$$2.25(4) + 3.50(2)$$
$$9 + 7$$
$$16$$

5. (C) The cost is represented by adding the number of tickets and the shipping cost. Each ticket is $75. Because the number of tickets that can be bought changes, you represent this by multiplying the number of tickets, *t*, by 75, and then adding the extra $5. Choice A looks like a good choice, but it is an expression, *not* an equation.

6. Part A. **50s + 90b** The problem does not specify which variables to use. State what variables you are using: Let *s* = sneakers and *b* = boots.

   Part B. **$370** Substitute the numbers 2 and 3 into the correct variables and then perform the order of operations.

$$50s + 90b$$
$$50(2) + 90(3)$$
$$100 + 270$$
$$370$$

7. **4.375**

$$4x + 2.50 = 20$$
$$4x + 2.50 = 20$$
$$\underline{-2.50 \quad -2.50}$$
$$\frac{4x}{4} = \frac{17.50}{4}$$
$$x = 4.375$$

To check your answer, substitute the value you got for *x* into the equation to see if the statement is true. If the statement is not true, then an error occurred and you should go back to find and fix the error.

$$4x + 2.50 = 20$$
$$4(4.375) + 2.50 = 20$$
$$17.5 + 2.50 = 20$$
$$20 = 20$$
$$\text{true}$$

8. Part A. **2a + 5 = 49**, Part B. **a = 22**

$$2a + 5 = 49$$
$$2a + 5 = 49$$
$$\underline{-5 \quad -5}$$
$$\frac{2a}{2} = \frac{44}{2}$$
$$a = 2$$

Write Inequalities, page 132

1. (B) The > symbol means *greater than*. Therefore, in this particular problem you must be greater, or older, than 7.

2. (D) The ≤ symbol means *less than or equal to*. Therefore, in this particular problem you are looking for the situation to be less than 55 or equal to 55. Choice D says "at most," which means you can't go above 55. This means you must be 55 inches or shorter. The symbol ≤ includes 55 and less, so choices B and C are incorrect because they refer to 55 and more. Choice A is a good distractor since it mentions less than 55, but it does not include 55.

3. (B) The ≤ symbol means *less than or equal to*. Therefore, in this particular problem you are looking for the situation to be less than 5 or equal to 5 because 5 is included in the set. The 3 dots mean that the pattern continues into the negatives.

4. (C) In this particular problem you are looking for the situation to be greater than 3 or equal to 3 because 3 is included in the set. The 3 dots mean that the pattern continues higher. This problem can be tricky because the number is written before the variable. Choice C is read as "3 is less than or equal to *r*."

5. **(A)** The symbol ≤ means less than (to the left of the number) or equal to, which is shown as a filled in circle.

6. **$r \geq 50$** The key words in this situation are "at minimum." This means that you can include the value of 50 and higher.

7. **$r \geq -2$ and $r > -3$** The integers start at –2 and continue larger; therefore, you need to use a greater than symbol. The question refers to integers, which means positive or negative whole numbers. Since –2 is in the list, you can refer to –2 as the first integer and use that with ≥. The other option is to refer to integers greater than –3 but not equal to –3.

8. Part A. **$x < 9$**

   Part B. The circle should not be filled in since it is less than, *not* equal to.

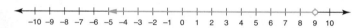

Dependent and Independent Variables, page 134

1. **(A)** Dependent variables change depending on the independent variable. In this particular scenario, the speed is dependent on the height. Choices B, C, and D could all be independent variables and will have an effect on the dependent variable.

2. **(B)** Independent variables effect the outcome of the dependent variable. In this particular scenario, the shoe size is dependent on the foot length, so the foot length is independent. Although age and weight may have something to do with shoe size and foot length, they are not part of this particular study.

3. **(B)** You will notice that the r values are all multiplied by 5 to result in the given s values. The s value equals the r value divided by 3. Choice A works only when r is 5 and s is 15. Choice C works only when r is 10 and s is 30. The equation must work for all the input and output values. Choice D does not work for any of the values; it would work if the s and r values were switched in position.

4. A. **Cost** is dependent upon how many rides you go on.

B. **Number of rides** is the independent variable, since that is the number you would input into the equation to determine the cost.

C. **$16.** Go along the horizontal axis to 5 and up until you hit the graphed line. Then go left to read what the vertical axis number is.

D. **3 rides** Go up to $10 on the vertical axis and then go to the right until you hit the graphed line. From there, go down to read how many rides you can go on.

E. **The point represents 5 rides, which cost $16.**

F. **The point represents 0 rides, which cost $1.** Explanations can vary. A possible one is given. This seems not to make sense because if you are not going on a ride, you would not pay. However, there may be an admission fee to get into the carnival or a parking fee that could cost $1.

G. **$C = 3r + 1$ is the only equation that can be used to represent all the data.** Justifications will vary, but a suggested justification is provided. You can see from the work below that $C = 4r$ does not check when r is 3 and c is 10. Those values, and *all* the other values, do check in $C = 3r + 1$. All the values given in the graph need to check in the equation for the equation to represent the data.

$C = 4r$	$C = 3r + 1$
$10 = 4(3)$	$10 = 3(3) + 1$
$10 \neq 12$	$10 = 9 + 1$
	$10 = 10$

Division of Fractions, page 136

NOTE: You should *not* use a calculator for these problems.

1. **(B)** Be careful—the question asks for the simplified answer, so you must reduce the answer completely, and choice D does not reduce it completely. You can divide fractions by multiplying the first fraction (dividend) by the reciprocal of the second fraction (divisor). This is shown below. You can also divide fractions by multiplying the numerator of the first fraction by the denominator of the other fraction. This product becomes the new numerator. Then multiply the denominator of the first fraction by the numerator of the

other fraction. This product becomes the new denominator.

$$\frac{6}{17} \div \frac{3}{5}$$

$$\frac{6}{17} \cdot \frac{5}{3}$$

$$\frac{30}{51} = \frac{10}{17}$$

2. **(C)** Choices A, B, and D result in the same answer of 3.2 or $3\frac{1}{5}$. Remember, the question asks for the method that does *not* result in the correct answer. There are different methods for dividing fractions. Choice C did not flip (take the reciprocal of) the second fraction. Therefore it is incorrect.

3. **(A)** Dividing fractions can be done by multiplying the first fraction (dividend) by the reciprocal of the second fraction (divisor). This is shown below. You need to change the mixed number into an improper fraction.

$$2\frac{1}{4} \div \frac{2}{5}$$

$$\frac{9}{4} \div \frac{2}{5}$$

$$\frac{9}{4} \cdot \frac{5}{2}$$

$$\frac{45}{8} = 5\frac{5}{8}$$

4. **(A)**

$$3\frac{1}{2} \div 24$$

$$\frac{7}{2} \div \frac{24}{1}$$

$$\frac{7}{2} \cdot \frac{1}{24}$$

$$\frac{7}{48}$$

5. $2\frac{2}{5}$

$$10\frac{8}{10} \div 4\frac{1}{2}$$

$$\frac{108}{10} \div \frac{9}{2}$$

$$\frac{108}{10} \cdot \frac{2}{9}$$

$$\frac{216}{90} = \frac{12}{5} = 2\frac{2}{5}$$

6. **124 full glasses.** Remember, the question asks for *full* glasses. You must first set up a proportion to convert the gallons to fluid ounces. There are 128 fluid ounces in 1 gallon.

$$\frac{1 \text{ gallon}}{128 \text{ fl oz}} = \frac{5\frac{1}{3}}{x}$$

$$5\frac{1}{3} \times 128$$

$$\frac{16}{3} \times \frac{128}{1}$$

$$\frac{2048}{3} = 682\frac{2}{3} \text{ fluid ounces}$$

Then you must divide the total fluid ounces by $5\frac{1}{2}$ for each glass.

$$682\frac{2}{3} \div 5\frac{1}{2}$$

$$\frac{2048}{3} \div \frac{11}{2}$$

$$\frac{2048}{3} \cdot \frac{2}{11}$$

$$\frac{4096}{33} = 124\frac{4}{33}$$

7. **41 full burgers** Remember, the question asks for how many *full* burgers. You should divide $10\frac{1}{3}$ by $\frac{1}{4}$.

$$10\frac{1}{3} \div \frac{1}{4}$$

$$\frac{31}{3} \div \frac{1}{4}$$

$$\frac{31}{3} \cdot \frac{4}{1}$$

$$\frac{124}{3} = 41\frac{1}{3}$$

8. Answers can vary. Suggested responses are provided. You may want to show some specific math problems to enhance your description. One method of dividing fractions can be found by multiplying the first fraction (dividend) by the reciprocal of the second fraction (divisor). Another method is to multiply the numerator of the first fraction by the denominator of the other fraction. This product becomes the new numerator. Then multiply the denominator of the first fraction by the numerator of the other fraction. This product becomes the new denominator. A third method is to draw fraction models to divide fractions.

9. $1\frac{1}{2}$

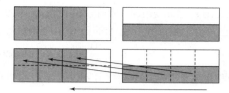

Step 1: Draw models for $\frac{3}{4}$ and $\frac{1}{2}$.

Step 2: Find common denominators by cutting the fourths model in half and the half model in fourths. Now you have made the pieces into eighths.

Step 3: See how many of the 4 units fit into the $\frac{6}{8}$. The four pieces fit into the other 1 time and will have 2 left over, or $1\frac{2}{4}$, which is $1\frac{1}{2}$.

Whole Number Division, page 138

NOTE: You should *not* use a calculator for these problems.

1. (A) A *quotient* is the answer to a division problem. You should set up the long division with 125,980 inside the division bracket (dividend) and 5 on the outside (divisor).

$$
\begin{array}{r}
25{,}196 \\
5\overline{)125{,}980} \\
-10 \\
\hline
25 \\
-25 \\
\hline
09 \\
-5 \\
\hline
48 \\
-45 \\
\hline
30 \\
-30 \\
\hline
0
\end{array}
$$

2. 325 You should set up the long division with 20,475 inside the division bracket (dividend) and 63 on the outside (divisor).

$$
\begin{array}{r}
325 \\
63\overline{)20{,}475} \\
-189 \\
\hline
157 \\
-126 \\
\hline
315 \\
-315 \\
\hline
0
\end{array}
$$

3. (D) To solve the equation for *x*, you must isolate the variable by performing inverse operations. Since 24*x* is multiplication, the inverse is division. You need to divide both sides by 24. Set up the long division with 5,040 inside the division bracket (dividend) and 24 on the outside (divisor).

$$
\begin{array}{r}
210 \\
24\overline{)5{,}040} \\
-48 \\
\hline
24 \\
-24 \\
\hline
0
\end{array}
$$

4. (A) Area is found by multiplying the length by the width. Since the area is given and you are trying to find a missing width, you would divide the area by the length. Set up the long division with 5,400 inside the division bracket (dividend) and 120 on the outside (divisor).

$$
\begin{array}{r}
45 \\
120\overline{)5{,}400} \\
-480 \\
\hline
600 \\
-600 \\
\hline
0
\end{array}
$$

5. 23 students In this particular problem you need to write the words in their standard numeric form. To solve this problem, divide the number of students by the number of teachers. Set up the long division with 276 as the dividend (inside the division bracket) and 12 as the divisor (on the outside).

$$
\begin{array}{r}
23 \\
12\overline{)276} \\
-24 \\
\hline
36 \\
-36 \\
\hline
0
\end{array}
$$

6. (B) *Mean* is another word for average. To find the mean, add up all the values and divide the sum by the number of values added. In this case, the sum is 15,565. Notice that this is choice A. It was put there as an option to distract you! After you add the numbers and get 15,565, you need to divide it by 6, since there were 6 values. Set up long division with 15,565 in the division bracket (dividend) and 6 on the outside (divisor). Notice that the question asks you for "about" and the answers do not have decimals. As you divide, you

can stop once you reach the tenths place and then round. Choice C is the median and choice D is the range. These were also given as options to distract you.

$$\begin{array}{r} 2{,}594 \\ 6\overline{)15{,}565} \\ -12 \\ \hline 35 \\ -30 \\ \hline 56 \\ -54 \\ \hline 25 \\ -24 \\ \hline 1 \end{array}$$

7. **(D)** To solve this problem, you first need to locate the highest mileage month, June, and the lowest mileage month, April. From there you need to divide 3,892 by 1,256. This gives you about 3.09, so the answer is 3.

$$\begin{array}{r} 3.09 \\ 1{,}256\overline{)3{,}892.00} \\ -3{,}768 \\ \hline 124.0 \\ -0 \\ \hline 124.00 \\ -113.04 \\ \hline 10.96 \end{array}$$

Since the question says *about* and the answer choices are rounded to whole or tenth, you should divide out to hundredth, then round.

8. **25 ft** The formula for the area of a parallelogram is $A = bh$. Substitute 450 for A and 18 for b. Then, solve by inverse operations. You must divide 450 by 18, as shown below.

$$\begin{array}{r} 25 \\ 18\overline{)450} \\ -36 \\ \hline 90 \\ -90 \\ \hline 0 \end{array}$$

9. **72** Set up the long division with 15,192 as the divisor (inside the division bracket) and 211 as the divisor (on the outside).

$$\begin{array}{r} 72 \\ 211\overline{)15{,}192} \\ -14\,77 \\ \hline 422 \\ -422 \\ \hline 0 \end{array}$$

10. Answers will vary. A suggested response is provided. One strategy is to notice that both numbers end in zeros. You can reduce the number of zeros by canceling from the top to the bottom, resulting in $\frac{280}{14}$. This is an easier problem to divide: 14 can go into 280, 20 times!

Operations with Decimals, page 140

NOTE: You should not use a calculator for these problems.

1. **$18.28** Line up the decimal points and add the price of each item.

$$\begin{array}{r} 4.25 \\ 2.30 \\ 1.89 \\ 0.99 \\ 5.88 \\ +\,2.97 \\ \hline 18.28 \end{array}$$

2. **$31.72** Subtract the total spent, $18.28, from $50. Be sure to line up the decimal points.

$$\begin{array}{r} {\scriptstyle 49\ 91} \\ 50.00 \\ -\,18.28 \\ \hline 31.72 \end{array}$$

3. **$0.41** Line up the decimal points and subtract.

$$\begin{array}{r} {\scriptstyle 1\ \ 12\ 1} \\ 2.30 \\ -\,1.89 \\ \hline 0.41 \end{array}$$

4. **$10.29** Set up a proportion and cross multiply. Convert $3\frac{1}{2}$ to 3.5.

$$\frac{\text{pounds}}{\$} \quad \frac{2}{5.88} = \frac{3.5}{x}$$

$$\frac{20.58}{2} = \frac{2x}{2}$$

$$10.29 = x$$

$$\begin{array}{r} 5.88 \\ \times\ 3.5 \\ \hline 2940 \\ +\,17640 \\ \hline 20.580 \end{array} \qquad \begin{array}{r} 10.29 \\ 2\overline{)20.58} \\ -2 \\ \hline 005 \\ -4 \\ \hline 18 \\ -18 \\ \hline 0 \end{array}$$

5. **$0.99** To solve this problem you must see that the given price of $2.97 was the total for 3 containers. You need to divide 2.97 by 3 to find the cost of 1. This is also how you find the unit rate.

$$\begin{array}{r} 0.99 \\ 3\overline{)2.97} \\ -27 \\ \hline 27 \\ -27 \\ \hline 0 \end{array}$$

6. **6.753** Make sure you line up the decimal points. Remember that the decimal point on 5 is at the end, as in 5.0

$$\begin{array}{r} 5.000 \\ 0.546 \\ 1.200 \\ + 0.007 \\ \hline 6.753 \end{array}$$

7. **124.9944** Make sure that you line up the decimal points. The decimal point is at the end of 125, as in 125.0000. You will need to borrow across the zeros. Make sure 125 is on top of 0.0056 as you line up to subtract.

$$\begin{array}{r} {}^{4\ 9\ 9\ 9\ 1} \\ 12\cancel{5}.\cancel{0}\cancel{0}\cancel{0}\cancel{0} \\ - 0.0056 \\ \hline 124.9944 \end{array}$$

8. **7.6824** Multiplication is commutative, so you can place the numbers in any order. Typically, you place the longer number on top. To decide where the decimal point goes in the final answer (product), you must first count how many decimal places there are in both numbers you are multiplying. In this particular case, there is 1 decimal place in 7.2 and 3 decimal places in 1.067. So 1 + 3 = 4 decimal places in the final answer.

$$\begin{array}{r} 1.067 \\ \times\ \ 7.2 \\ \hline 2134 \\ 74690 \\ \hline 7.6824 \end{array}$$

9. **4,900** To divide the values, you need to put 245 in the division bracket (dividend) and 0.05 outside the division bracket (divisor). You must divide by a whole number, so you need to move the decimal place over two times to the right to make 0.05 the

number 5. You must keep the problem balanced, so you also need to move the decimal point to the right two times on the number inside the bracket. Remember that 245 has a decimal point at the end.

$$\begin{array}{r} 4900. \\ .05\overline{)245.00} \\ -20 \\ \hline 45 \\ -45 \\ \hline 00 \\ -0 \\ \hline 00 \\ -0 \\ \hline 0 \end{array}$$

10. **1.56**

$$\begin{array}{r} 1.56 \\ 2.2\overline{)3.432} \\ -22 \\ \hline 123 \\ -110 \\ \hline 132 \\ -132 \\ \hline 0 \end{array}$$

GCF and Distributive Property, page 142

1. **(D)** The greatest common factor, or GCF, is the largest number that can go into both numbers without a remainder. Choices A, B, and C are all factors that can go into 18 and 54. However, the question asked for the greatest, which is 18. You can list all the factors to help you:
   54: 1, 2, 3, 6, 9, <u>18</u>, 27, 54
   18: 1, 2, 3, 6, 9, <u>18</u>

2. **(C)** Find the greatest common factor (GCF) of 36 and 48. You can list all the factors of each and look for the largest one in both lists.
   36: 1, 2, 3, 4, 6, 9, <u>12</u>, 36
   48: 1, 2, 3, 4, 6, 8, <u>12</u>, 16, 24, 48.

3. **Leah is correct.** Justifications will vary; a suggested explanation is given. Leah is correct that the two fractions are equal since $\frac{7}{10}$ is the simplified version of $\frac{21}{30}$. The greatest common factor of 21 and 30 is 3. When you reduce 21 by 3 and 30 by 3 you get $\frac{7}{10}$. The GCF helps you reduce the fraction by dividing only one time.

4. **(B)** The least common multiple is the smallest number that both numbers have as their multiples. If you list the multiples of each number, you eventually will come to a common number. If you list the multiples in order from least to greatest, you want the first common number in the list because it is smallest: 6: 6, 12, 18, 24, <u>30</u>, 36, 42, 48, 54, 60,... and 15: 15, <u>30</u>, 45, 60, ...

5. **Day 7** You can set up a calendar and mark every other day and then mark every third day. Both people will be there on the first day. Look to see when they will be there on the same day again. You can also solve this problem by extending the patterns. Every other day starting on day 1 is really just listing the odd numbers, 1, 3, 5, 7, 9, 11, 13, 15, ... Every third day starting on day 1 is like adding 3 to the previous number (1, 4, 7, 10, 13, ...).

6. **(C)** You can make a calendar and mark every fourth day and every sixth day to see what day falls under both. The other method is to make a list of the multiples of 4 and 6. 4: 4, 8, <u>12</u>, 16, 20, 24, ... and 6: 6, <u>12</u>, 18, 24, ...)

7. **(A)** To rewrite the expression as an expression with the distributive property, you need to find the GCF. Put the GCF outside the parentheses. Divide both numbers (10 and 35) by the GCF you chose and place them inside the parentheses. In this problem, the GCF of 10 and 35 is 5. Then, 10 divided by 5 is 2 and 35 divided by 5 is 7, so (2 + 7) are inside the parentheses.

8. **(B)** In this particular problem we are looking to see what value x equals. x represents the GCF of 12 and 9, which is 3. If you substitute 3 where x is and perform the distributive property, you will get 12 + 9 as your check.

9. Part A. **11(5 + 7)** The GCF of 55 and 77 is 11, which is the largest number that goes into 55 and 77 or that 55 and 77 are divisible by. Divide 55 by 11 to get 5 and 77 by 11 to get 7.

   Part B. **2(x + 2)** The GCF of 2x and 4 is 2. Divide 2x by 2 to get x and 4 by 2 to get 2.

Rational Numbers—Integers, page 144

1.

Negative Values	Positive Values
8 degrees below zero	Deposit of $45
Withdraw $5	95°F
203 feet below sea level	Elevation of 5,456
Charge of an electron	feet
Loss of 7 pounds	
Debt of $450	

2. Remember that drops, losses, owing money, debts, below sea level, and below zero are all negatives. A. –10 degrees; B. –$75; C. –$20; D. +10 pounds

3. Since 2,400 feet is a positive number, it is *not* below sea level. A number less than 0 or with a negative sign is below sea level.

4. **Negative 422 and –422** Remember that below sea level is a negative number.

Rational Numbers on Number Lines, page 145

1.

Compare each number to the other numbers. Each tick mark represents a unit of 1. You can see where zero and positive and negative 5 are placed. Remember that negatives are to the left of zero and positives are to the right.

2.

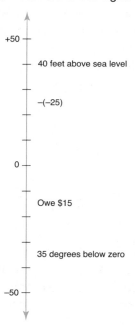

A vertical number line is similar to a thermometer or to altitude, where below sea level and below zero are negative numbers, and above sea level is a positive number. Also remember that the opposite of an opposite or the negation of a negative is equivalent to a positive: $-(-25) = +25$. Recall that owing money is represented with a negative sign. The tick marks represent units of 10; therefore, some of the values fall between the tick marks.

Opposites on a Number Line, page 146

1. **(D)** This answer is written in mathematical language instead of mathematical notation. Be sure to notice that the question asks for the *opposite* of 3 below zero. Numbers below zero are negative numbers. The opposite of negative numbers are positive numbers. Because the original question was given in Fahrenheit, Celsius has nothing to do with this question and is there only to distract you.

2. **(A)** Remember that the opposite of negative 8 is positive 8 or +8. The opposite of the opposite of a number is the number itself, therefore, $-(-8)$ also equals +8. In choice B, all are equivalent to negative 8. Choices C and D include only one or two correct choices.

3.

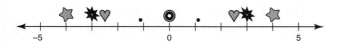

4. Answers will vary. You should discuss that opposites like +2 and −2 are located on the opposite sides of zero. Negatives are on the left of zero and positives are to the right of zero. They are located the same distance away from zero but on opposite sides. You could also describe the opposite numbers as symmetric if the number line was folded at zero.

5. **(B)** Be sure to notice that the question asks for *not* the opposite of owing $30. Owing money is considered a negative number. The opposite of negative numbers are positive numbers. This question asks for *not* the opposite, so you are actually looking for the choice that represents owing $30.

6. **(C)** Remember that the opposite of positive 9 is negative 9 or −9. The opposite can also be represented by a negative in front of the positive sign like in − (+9). In choice C, all options are equivalent to negative 9.

Ordered Pairs and the Coordinate Plane, page 148

1. **(B)** You can sketch or use graph paper to prove that a square is formed, all sides are congruent, four right angles are present, and opposite sides are parallel. For choice B, you need to realize that the length of the right side is 4 units and, therefore, all the other coordinates allow the other sides to also be 4 units long.

2. You could use a grid to graph each set of points *or* you could notice that the points are reflections over the *x*-axis and that the *y*-coordinate's signs change but the numbers remain the same. You should explain how the numbers are in opposite quadrants and how the numbers remain the same but the signs change.

3. You could use a grid to graph each set of points. You could also notice that the points are reflections over the *y*-axis and that the *x*-coordinate's sign changes but the numbers remain the same. You should explain how the numbers are in opposite quadrants and how the numbers remain the same but the signs change.

Rational Numbers and Integers on Number Lines and Coordinate Planes, page 150

1.

Compare each number to the other numbers. One way to do this is to convert all the numbers to decimals and compare them in their decimal form. For example, $-\frac{3}{2} = -1.5$ and $\frac{10}{5}$ is equivalent to 2. Each tick mark represents a unit of 1 because you can see where zero and positive and negative 5 are placed. Remember that negatives are to the left of zero and positives are to the right. Also, make sure that you place −0.75 closer to −1 than −0.5 would be. Think of it as going deeper in debt (negative), which moves you more to the left.

2. __IV__ (3, –7) __II__ (–4, 8) __III__ (–2, –10)
   __I__ (4, 7) __III__ (–32, –80) __IV__ (positive integer, negative integer)

A	(5, 3)	__I__
B	(–1, 4)	__II__
C	(0, 0)	**origin – located at the intersection of the x- and y-axes**
D	(–3, 0)	__x-axis__
E	(–5, –2)	__III__
F	(0, –2)	__y-axis__
G	(6, –6)	__IV__
H	(–3, –1)	__III__

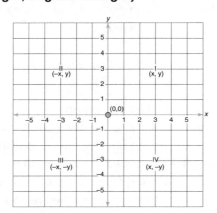

Ordered pairs are written with parentheses as (x, y). The first number in the ordered pair represents the number for the x-axis (the horizontal axis). You should move left or right along the x-axis first. The second number represents the y-coordinate for the y-axis (vertical axis). You should move up or down along the y-axis second. Quadrants are labeled with Roman numerals and are numbered in a counterclockwise rotation.

3. Quadrant I: The x- and y-coordinates are both positive

   Quadrant II: The x-coordinate is negative and the y-coordinate is positive.

   Quadrant III: The x- and y-coordinates are both negative.

   Quadrant IV: The x-coordinate is positive and the y-coordinate is negative.

   Remember that the origin is (0, 0) and that some points can fall on each axis. Points (–3, 0) and (5, 0) fall on the x-axis and the points (0, 7) and (0, –8) fall on the y-axis.

4.

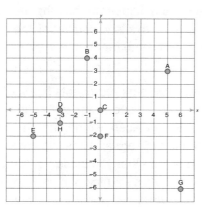

5. Part A. Answers will vary. You can draw any rectangle as long as it is a rectangle and not a square or parallelogram. Opposite sides should be parallel and congruent, and there should be 4 right angles. Points A, B, C, and D should be labeled appropriately with parentheses (x, y). Make sure that the coordinates match the rectangle formed and correspond to the correct letters.

Part B. Answers will vary depending on what was drawn in Part A. You can use the formula $A = bh$ or $A = lw$ and substitute the values for the length and width, then perform the order of operations. Because there is no defined unit label for each small grid square, you should count using the grid lines. The final label will be square units or units^2.

You could also choose, instead of using the formula, to simply count the total number of boxes within the lines of the rectangle. The final label will be square units or units^2.

Part C. Answers will vary. You need to leave two points the same that are on the same side of your original rectangle to maintain a rectangular shape.

Part D. Answers will vary. Your explanation should include that to find distance, the absolute value is used because distance cannot be a negative number. When the rectangle's length or width is drawn in Quadrants II, III, or IV (which use negative numbers), the signs need to be ignored for the purpose of finding distance.

Absolute Value, page 152

1. **7 or |–7|.** The absolute value is the distance from zero, regardless of the direction, negative or positive.

2. **32 or |+32|**

3. $\frac{1}{2}$ or $\left|-\frac{1}{2}\right|$

4. **(A)** |–87| = 87. Choice A is the only answer that does not equal 87.

5. **(B)** –|–5| = –5. To find the value, first take the absolute value of –5, which is 5. Since there is another negative sign in front of the absolute value bars, you must place that on your answer. Only take the absolute value of what is inside of the absolute value bars.

6. **91, +67, 11, 9, +2, 0, –3, –6, –23, –89** First, notice that it says greatest to least, which means you need to start by listing the largest positive integers first. Negative integers are smaller than positive integers.

7. **(B)** First, notice that the question asks for least to greatest, which means you need to start by listing the negatives first. Notice that choice D is in order from greatest to least. Don't get distracted by it!

8. **(D)** First, notice that the question asks for least to greatest, which means you need to start by listing the negatives first. A strategy to help determine in which order to place them is to simplify the fractions and turn them into decimals: –|–2| = –2 and $-\frac{1}{3}$ = –.3333. One of the trickiest rational numbers to determine placement of is $-\frac{1}{3}$ and –0.3. Because $-\frac{1}{3}$ = –.3333, it is more "in debt" than –0.3. Because the numbers are negative, $-\frac{1}{3}$ is less than –0.3. If these numbers were positive, the ordering would be reversed. You can visualize a number line to help you order the integers. Numbers to the right of another number are always greater.

9. $-|-4|, -\frac{2}{3}, -0.6, 0, 1, +2, +4$

   First, notice that the question asks for least to greatest, which means you need to start by listing the negatives first. A strategy to help determine in which order to place the numbers is to simplify them and turn the fractions into decimals: –|–4| =

–4 and $-\frac{2}{3}$ = $-.\overline{6666}$. One of the trickiest rational numbers to determine placement of is $-\frac{2}{3}$ and –0.6. Because $-\frac{2}{3}$ = $-.\overline{6666}$, it is more "in debt" than –0.6. Because the numbers are negative, $-\frac{2}{3}$ is less than –0.6.

Inequalities, page 154

1. **(D)** |–5| is equal to 5, not –5. Make sure you read the question carefully. It is asking which one is equivalent to or the same as. You are really looking at 5 < 10, which is read as "5 is less than 10."

2. The way you would read the given statement is shown below in quotes.

   True

   |–9| < 11 "Nine is less than 11."

   7 > 4 "7 is greater than 4."
   |–5| < 10 "5 is less than 10."
   –2 < 0 "Negative 2 is less than 0."
   |–25| = 25 "25 is equal to 25."

   False

   6 < –7 "6 is less than negative 7" is not true.
   –3 > |–12| "Negative 3 is greater than 12" is not true.
   –32 = |–32| "Negative 32 equals 32" is not true.

3. **(B)** If you place the numbers on a number line, you need to find the number that is less than or to the left of –2. The only one to the left is –3.

4. **(C)** The absolute value of –356 is 356; |–356| = 356. The inequality says "x is greater than or equal to." The only choice that is greater than or equal to 356 is choice C, 356.

5. **(A)** This inequality is written backwards to the typical inequalities we see. Typically, the variable is written first. Be careful on these! This is read "–7 is greater than x," which means if –7 is greater than x, then x is less than –7. Choice A would read that –7 > –8, which is the only true selection. Remember that x > 3 is the same as 3 < x.

Interpreting Order of Rational Numbers, page 155

1. **(A)** Look for an inequality that shows only positive values. Choice A is equivalent to $x > 1$ once you simplify the absolute value signs. The other choices all have values that have negatives in them.

2. Answers can vary. Some acceptable answers may include:

   - When the outside temperature is less than –9, the school closes. True value is –10 degrees and a false value is –8 degrees.
   - When digging a ditch 9 feet below sea level, there is concern for ground water to fill the ditch. True value is –10 feet and a false value is –8 feet.

3. $x \geq 18$ At least 18 means you can be 18 *or* older. You need to use the $\geq$ (greater than or equal to sign) so 18 can be included in the values.

4. See chart at the bottom of this page.

Graphing on the Coordinate Plane, page 156

1. **(D)** If you graph the two points on the grid, you can count the number of spaces from –6 to 7. From –6 to the x-axis, which is zero, is a distance of 6 units. You would disregard the negative sign because distances are not negative and instead use the absolute value of –6. From the x-axis to 7 is a total of 7 units. So, the total distance is 13, or 6 + 7 = 13.

2. **5** If you graph the two points on the grid, you can count the number of spaces from –2 to 3. From

Inequality	Verbal Description	Integer Values that Satisfy the Inequality (Make sure you use positive and negative whole numbers)
$x < -50$	**Answers can vary:** *Less than 50 feet below sea level there are interesting species of fish.*	**–51, –52, –53, –54 . . .**
$x < 50$	Must be less than 50 pounds to ride the swings.	**49, 48, 47, 46 . . .**
$x > 2$ or $x \geq 3$ *Either of these are acceptable since the values are stated as integers.*	**Children over the age of 2 must be in a booster seat.** *or* **Families with 3 or more animals can receive a coupon at the pet store.**	3, 4, 5, 6, 7 . . .
$x > \|-2\|$	**"An account balance greater than the absolute value of –2 will not require the bank to close the account."** *or* **If the absolute value bars are simplified it would read:** **"An account balance greater than 2 will not require the bank to close the account."**	**3, 4, 5, 6, 7 . . .**
Answers will vary.	*Answers will vary.*	*Answers will vary.*

−2 to the *y*-axis, which is zero, it is a distance of 2 units. You would disregard the negative sign because distances are not negative and instead use the absolute value of −2. From the *y*-axis to 3 is a total of 3 units. So, the total distance is 5, or 2 + 3 = 5.

3. **5** If you graph the two points on the grid, you can count the number of spaces from −1 to −6. From −1 to −6 there is a distance of 5 units. You would disregard the negative signs because distances are not negative and instead use the absolute value of both numbers. So, the total distance is 5.

4. **13 miles** Road paths can vary. One example is to leave Jim's house and travel down to the doctor's office and left to school. Another option is to travel left to the grocery store and down to the school. Another option is to travel to the firehouse, then left to the gas station, and then down to the point (0,−3), and then left to the school. Discussion of work could include lines drawn on the grid to show the path. You must remember that although there are negative numbers on some of the coordinates, distances are not negative, and you should use the absolute value for the distance. 6 + 7 = 13

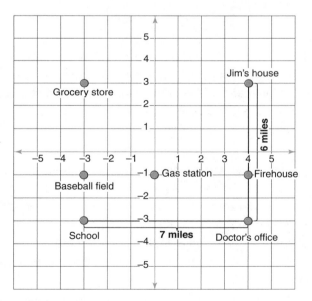

5. **18 miles** The lines on the following grid show the paths that go through the specified locations with the minimal distances. 7 + 4 + 7 = 18 miles

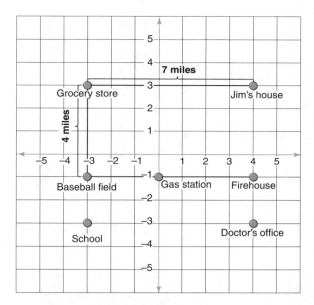

You must remember that although there are negative numbers on some of the coordinates, distances are not negative, and you should use the absolute value for the distance.

Area of Polygons, page 158

1. **(B)** The formula for the area of a triangle is $A = \frac{1}{2}bh$. This problem gives you the dimensions of all three sides but the formula only uses the height and base. You should only use 10 and 13 in the formula.

$$A = \frac{1}{2}bh$$

$$A = \frac{1}{2}13 \cdot 10$$

$$A = \frac{1}{2}130 \quad \text{or} \quad A = 13 \cdot 5$$

$$A = 65 \text{ cm}^2$$

2. **62.5 units squared** You can use the trapezoid formula, or you can break the shape into 2 triangles and 1 rectangle. With either method, you must know that isosceles means to have two congruent (equal in measure) sides. In this case, those are the diagonals. This information is helpful because if the sides are congruent, then the bases of the two small triangles are also congruent.

$A = \frac{1}{2}h(b_1+b_2)$ $A = \frac{1}{2}4(18.75+12.5)$ $A = \frac{1}{2}(4)(31.25)$ $A = 2(31.25)$ $A = 62.5$ units squared	$A = bh$ $A = 12.5(4)$ $A = 50$ $A = \frac{1}{2}bh$ $A = \frac{1}{2}(4)3.125$ $A = (2)\,3.125$ $A = 6.25$ There are 2 triangles, so $6.25 + 6.25 = 12.5$ 2 triangles plus rectangle $= 12.5 + 50 = 62.5$ units^2

3. Part A. **3,414 tiles** First you need to find the area of 1 tile. The formula for the area of a parallelogram is $A = bh$. Be sure to use the height (1.5 inches) and the base (2.25 inches).

$$A = bh$$
$$A = 1.5(2.25)$$
$$A = 3.375 \text{ in}^2$$

Then you need to figure out the area of the wall. First, convert the feet measurements to inches. There are 12 inches in 1 foot. $8 \times 12 = 96$ and $10 \times 12 = 120$.

$$A = bh$$
$$A = 120(96)$$
$$A = 11,520 \text{ in}^2$$

Finally, divide the area of the wall by the area of 1 tile: $\frac{11,520}{3.375} = 3,413.\overline{3}$

The interior designer would need at least 3,414 tiles. He may need more since he may have to cut them to fit, but 3,414 is the minimum number he would need.

Part B. **$4,756.38** You need to multiply by $1.29 per tile. So $1.29 \times 3,414 = \$4,404.06$. Next, add tax onto the price. There are multiple ways to do this. One way is to set up a proportion and cross multiply and then add the tax onto the cost of the tile.

$$\frac{8}{100} = \frac{x}{4,404.06}$$

$$\frac{35,232.48}{100} = \frac{100x}{100}$$

$$x = 352.3248$$

$$x \approx 352.32$$

$$352.32 + 4,404.06 = \$4,756.38$$

1. **$409\frac{1}{2}$ cm^3** Since $\frac{1}{3}$ is a repeating decimal, you should keep it as a fraction and use your fraction skills in the volume formula. Convert 12.6 to $12\frac{6}{10} = 12\frac{3}{5}$ and 9.75 to $9\frac{75}{100} = 9\frac{3}{4}$. Also convert the mixed numbers to improper fractions. If you can cross reduce ahead of time, it will help make the numbers smaller and more manageable.

$$V = lwh$$

$$V = 12\frac{3}{5} \times 3\frac{1}{3} \times 9\frac{3}{4}$$

$$V = \frac{63}{5} \times \frac{10}{3} \times \frac{39}{4}$$

$$V = \frac{63}{\underset{1}{5}} \times \frac{\overset{2}{10}}{\underset{1}{3}} \times \frac{\overset{13}{39}}{4}$$

$$V = \frac{63}{1} \times \frac{2}{1} \times \frac{13}{4}$$

$$V = \frac{1638}{4}$$

$$V = 409\frac{2}{4} = 409\frac{1}{2}$$

2. **(D)** To find the volume of a box, use the formula $V = lwh$. $V = 8(4)(5)$, which is 160. Volume uses cubic measures, so make sure you chose choice D and not choice B. Choice B refers to square units, which are for area.

3. **(C)** This formula is used to find the area of rectangles and parallelograms. The question asked for the formula that *cannot* be used. All the other formulas are versions of $V = lwh$, which is choice B. Choice A is $V = Bh$ and is used for volume. The capital B stands for the area of the base of the prism. Choice D is an equivalent form of $V = lwh$.

4. **(C)** The volume can be found with the formula $V = Bh$, where B represents the area of the base of the prism. The area of the base of the prism, B, is given as 45 square units in the problem. 45 times 10 results in 450. You must choose 450 cubic units or 450 units^3, not square units.

5. **(B)** To find the volume of a rectangular prism, you need to use the formula $V = lwh$. This means to multiply all three dimensions together. $V = 23(3)(7)$, which is 483. Volume uses cubic measures, so make sure your answer is labeled with cubic inches.

6. **(A)** To find the volume of a rectangular prism, you need to use the formula $V = lwh$. This means to multiply all three dimensions together. $V = 1.99(3.23)(17.3)$, which is 111.19921. Volume uses cubic measures, so make sure your answer is labeled with cubic units.

7. **(D)** In this problem you are trying to find the missing height. Because the volume is given, you will divide by the product of 3 and 30 to find the third number that would result in 459 when multiplied by all three dimensions. You should substitute the values into the equation and use inverse operations to solve for h.

$$V = lwh$$
$$459 = 3(30)h$$
$$\frac{459}{90} = \frac{90h}{90}$$
$$5.1 = h$$

8. **(A)** The volume of a rectangular prism can be found with the formula $V = lwh$. Because all sides of a cube are the same length, you could also write it as $V = sss$ or $V = s^3$. Choice B is the formula for the area of a rectangle or square and choice D is the surface area formula for a rectangular prism.

Drawing Polygons on Coordinate Planes, page 162

1. Part A. The coordinates are plotted for you in the grid at the top of the next column.

   Part B. **28 units.** The distance from point to point can be found by counting the squares in between. The perimeter is found by adding up the lengths of all the sides: $6 + 6 + 8 + 8 = 28$

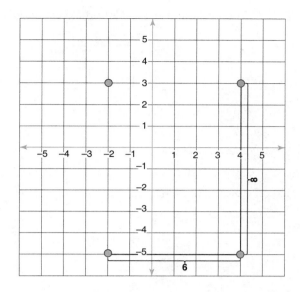

Part C. **48 square units**

$$A = bh$$
$$A = 6(8)$$
$$A = 48$$

2. Part A. The coordinates are plotted for you below.

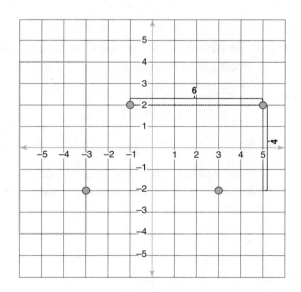

Part B. **24 units²**

$$A = bh$$
$$A = 6(4)$$
$$A = 24$$

Part C. Any rectangle can be drawn as long as the area remains 24 units². Some dimensions could be 2×12, 3×8, 6×4.

3. Part A. The coordinates are plotted for you below.

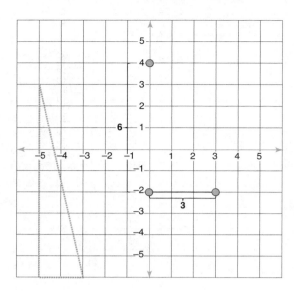

Part B. **9 units²**

$$A = \frac{1}{2}bh$$

$$A = \frac{1}{2}6(3)$$

$$A = 3(3)$$

$$A = 9$$

Part C. Any Triangle can be drawn as long as the area remains 9 units², and it has a right angle. Some dimensions could be 2×9, 4×4.5, 12×1.5.

Surface Area and Nets, page 164

1. **(A)** A triangular prism has two bases made from triangles and the sides are rectangles. It will fold into this shape:

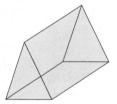

2. **(D)** A square pyramid has a square base and triangles for the sides. It would fold into this polyhedra:

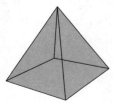

3. **(D)** The net will fold into a triangular pyramid.

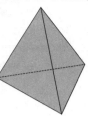

4. **(C)** The net of a rectangular prism can be different depending on the dimensions; however, it always will have 6 rectangles and 0 triangles. Two examples of rectangular prism nets are shown below.

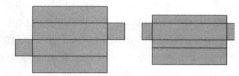

5. **(B)** Choice B is the only one that will *not* fold into a triangular pyramid. Although it has the correct number of triangles, the placement of the one on the bottom right will fold over one of the other sides, leaving a gap or no side on the left once it is folded.

6. **(B)** You need to find the area of 1 triangle and multiply by 4.

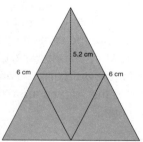

The area of 1 triangle:

$$A = \frac{1}{2}bh$$

$$A = \frac{1}{2}6(5.2)$$

$$A = 3(5.2)$$

$$A = 15.6 \text{ cm}^2$$

There are 4 triangles, so the total surface area is 4(15.6), or 62.4 cm².

7. **(C)** All of the other processes will result in the surface area of a triangular prism because there are 2 triangles and 3 rectangles. The question asked for the one that would *not* result in the surface area. Choice C uses the volume of a rectangular prism with the area of a triangle.

8. $130\frac{7}{8}$ inches^2

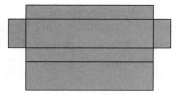

You can sketch a net of the box, label the dimensions, and then find the area of each rectangle. Then you need to find the total surface area by adding all the rectangles' areas together (see the chart below). You will notice that there are two of every type of rectangle; therefore, you can find the area of each type and double your answer.

Statistics, Measures of Center, and Variation, page 166

1. **(B)** When we want to statistically analyze data, we need to ask a question that enables us to gather numeric or quantitative data. This allows us to use the central tendencies or measures of variability to make conjectures about what we are studying. Although it may be important to know the kind

Side	Area work for one rectangle	Double the area of the one rectangle
Front of the box (same as the back)	$A = bh$ $A = 9\frac{1}{2} \cdot 2\frac{1}{4}$ $A = \frac{19}{2} \cdot \frac{9}{4}$ $A = \frac{171}{8}$	$\frac{171}{8} \cdot 2$ $\frac{342}{8}$
Right side (same as the left)	$A = bh$ $A = 3\frac{3}{4} \cdot 2\frac{1}{4}$ $A = \frac{15}{4} \cdot \frac{9}{4}$ $A = \frac{135}{16}$	$\frac{135}{16} \cdot 2$ $\frac{270}{16}$
Top side (same as the bottom)	$A = bh$ $A = 3\frac{3}{4} \cdot 9\frac{1}{2}$ $A = \frac{15}{4} \cdot \frac{19}{2}$ $A = \frac{285}{8}$	$\frac{285}{8} \cdot 2$ $\frac{570}{8}$
Find the total of all areas calculated:	$\frac{171}{8} + \frac{171}{8} + \frac{135}{16} + \frac{135}{16} + \frac{285}{8} + \frac{285}{8}$ This is adding each rectangle separately. Get common denominators.	You can add the doubled areas to be quicker. Get common denominators. $\frac{342}{8} + \frac{270}{16} + \frac{570}{8}$ $\frac{684}{16} + \frac{270}{16} + \frac{1140}{16}$ $\frac{2094}{16}$ $130\frac{14}{16}$ $130\frac{7}{8}$

of bacteria, the color, and where the houses are located, these questions don't ask for statistical data.

2. (C) When we want to statistically analyze data, we need to gather numeric or quantitative data. This allows us to use the central tendencies or measures of variability to make conjectures about what we are studying. Although it may be important to know the types of machines, color, and weight of the metal that is being tested, we cannot perform mathematical or statistical analysis on that type of information.

3. (B) Variability means that you will receive many different numeric numbers or data. Choices A, C, and D only refer to one person's answer and so there is no variability in the answers.

4. (D) When analyzing data, researchers and mathematicians look at the central tendencies (mean and median) and variability (interquartile range and/or mean absolute deviation) and spread and shape (bell shaped curve and/or skewedness) of the data when graphed. The amount of time it takes to collect the data is generally not of any value in the statistical analysis.

5. (B) The data is shifted to the right and is not symmetric. This is interesting data to analyze since it is skewed to the right (the long tail is to the right) or positively skewed. The skewedness is different from the bellshaped curve, which is a common shape to normal data. This will affect the mean and median (measures of center). More research and questioning should be done, and part of the analysis could be why it is skewed.

6. (C) By looking at the shape of the data and how it is shifted to the left (skewed left with the long tail to the left), we can conclude that most people were older than teenage. This shift and shape are important to notice.

7. (C) Since most of the x's are to the left, the tail is to the right, so this data is considered skewed to the right.

1. Part A. To create a box and whisker plot, you need to calculate the 5 statistical summary, as shown below. Then, plot those 5 pieces of data on a number line to create the box and whisker plot.

Minimum = 7
Q1 (lower quartile) = 8.5
Median = 16
Q3 (upper quartile) = 21.5
Maximum = 35

STEP 1: Place the numbers in order from least to greatest to find the minimum and maximum numbers. The median number is the one in the middle. If there are 2 middle numbers, you need to find their average (add them and divide by 2). STEP 2. To find the lower quartiles (Q1), you need to find the middle of the lower numbers, the numbers to the left of the median. To find the upper quartile (Q3), you need to find the middle of the upper numbers, the numbers to the right of the median. There are two middle numbers for the quartiles:

$$Q1 \ \frac{8+9}{2} = 8.5 \qquad Q3 \ \frac{20+23}{2} = 21.5$$

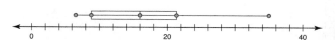

To create the graph, place dots on a number line for all 5 pieces of data. The number line should start with at least the minimum and go to at least the maximum number. Connect a line from the min to the max. The box is from Q1 to Q3 and a line goes in the box at the median.

Part B. There are 3 possible answers. Each section of the line, regardless of the length, shows 25%. One answer is that Joe can plan to use from 8.5 to 21.5 gallons of gas in a week since 50% of the data is represented by the box. Another group of 50% could be the first two sections of the graph 7 to 16. Finally, the last group of 50% could be from 16 to 35.

Part C. **13** The IQR is the upper quartile minus the lower quartile. In this case it is 21.5 − 8.5 = 13.

Part D. Explanations will vary. A suggested response is provided. Remember that the variation in the length on a box and whisker plot shows how spread or clustered the data is. The whiskers, or lines, have different lengths to show the spread of the data within that group of 25%. The shorter the whisker, the more compact the numbers are, and the longer the whisker, the more spread apart they are, even though there are the same number of values in each whisker. This concept also applies to the size of the box.

2. Part A.

Age Interval	Tally	Frequency
4–5	₩ II	7
6–7	₩ ₩ I	11
8–9	₩ III	8
10–11	IIII	4
12–13	III	3

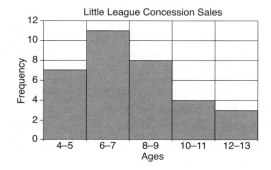

Part B. Age 6–7 is where the median number would lay. You can determine this by first counting the number of ages in the list, which is 33. Half of 33 is 16.5, so the median would fall between the 16th and 17th number. If you start from the youngest age interval, there are only 7 values and if you go into the next interval, there are 11 more, totaling 18 values from ages 4–7. Since there are 18 values in the first two bars and we want the value between the 16th and 17th values we know the value must lay in the 6–7 bar interval.

Part C. The shape of the data is skewed right since the long tail is to the right. Explanations can vary. A suggested response is provided. Since the shape of the data shows that the ages are skewed to the right, it seems that there are more younger children than older children buying food at the concession stand. This can help the manager understand who buys more food and can help him make future decisions on what to buy based on younger children's interests.

1. (D) To find the number of schools in the survey, you need to add the number of responses for each kind of technology because the question said Andrew collected data on the most popular type meaning that only one was recorded per school.

2. (C) There are many ways to collect accurate information. The best in this situation is to ask the administration for current information since it should know what is being used in its school. Former students and a music teacher may not know what everyone or most of the school uses, and asking students what they want is a different question than what is being used.

3. (D) The number of observations or samples is important when analyzing data for a purpose. Typically more samples are better, especially from a variety of places, to account for any variables or issues that may arise.

4. (B) Even though you can measure shoe size, it is not appropriate to measure in this investigation since researchers are looking to learn about the health of students. Time exercising, weight, and the number of calories in food are important to know.

5. (A) To measure height, a linear unit for length is needed, which in this case would be inches because yards are too large, leading to fractional answers. Pounds is a measure of weight, and liters is a measure of volume/capacity and is typically for liquids.

6. (D) The key shows that each **X** represents 5,000 people. There are 18 **X**s on the graph, so $18 \times 5,000 = 90,000$.

7. Answers will vary. Some suggested questions and the reasons are listed. How many adults were surveyed? The sample size question is important because good data analysis uses a large sample size. Company A could have asked only 10 adults, and 10 adults does not represent a national average. Who did you ask? How were they asked? Asking for more information on the characteristics of the data collected, and how, when, and where can show that some people

may have been excluded, making the data not representative of a national claim. Noticing that the survey was done only in December, for example, could also show bias because many people increase spending for the holidays. Also, there could have been a new game system or game released that particular month, leading to biased data.

8. The answers will vary. Some suggested responses are provided.

Who would you ask?	All purchasers of the company's merchandise
How would you ask?	Provide a survey online on a video game website; provide a phone number on the purchase receipts for a telephone survey
What would you ask?	How many products have you bought? How much money did you spend? How often do you buy merchandise?
What units would you measure in?	Number of products or dollars
Where would you ask?	Pick locations across the country so no one area is left out
What other characteristics should you take into consideration about this data collection?	Are there certain months that were more popular? If a new product is released and if there is a lot of hype for it

Shape and Patterns in Data, page 172

1. **(A)** To find the mean, add the number of books and divide by the number of classes Emily took.

$$\frac{5+2+3+4+1+2+0}{7} = \frac{17}{7} \approx 2.4$$

2. **1.3** Use the answer in question 1 for the mean. Subtract 2.4 from all the values. Use absolute value. For any value that is negative, drop the negative sign.

Value	Distance from the Mean (2.4)
5	2.6
2	0.4
3	0.6
4	1.6
1	1.4
2	0.4
0	2.4

Now calculate the mean of the deviations (distances from the mean).

$$\frac{2.6+0.4+0.6+1.6+1.4+0.4+2.4}{7} = \frac{9.4}{7} \approx 1.3$$

3. Answers will vary. A suggested response: The mean absolute deviation represents a value that shows how far away the data is from the mean. In the case of Emily reading books for college, 1.3 represents how far away the data is from the mean number of books. It helps show the spread or clustering of the data.

4. **(C)** The median is a better measure of center when there is an outlier. Outliers pull the mean up (if it's an outlier higher than the rest of the data) or pull the mean down (if it's a smaller number than the rest of the data). Since outliers are located at the ends of the data list, they have less impact on the median because it is in the middle of the set of data. When you calculate the mean, you add the number into the sum so it has a greater effect.

5. **(A)** When the data is evenly distributed, the shape is symmetric and typically has no outliers. Since there are no outliers, the mean is generally the best to use.

Math Practice Test, page 174

1. **(B)** Ratios can be written with a colon 2:15, with the word *to* as in 2 to 15, or as a fraction. Since the word *adult* appears before the word *children*, you should pick the answer that has the number of adults first, which is 2:15, 2 to 15, or $\frac{2}{15}$. (6.RP.A.1)

2. **(C)** Unit rates express the rate as an amount per 1. In this case, that means per 1 hour. You can convert $3\frac{1}{8}$ to decimal form, which is 3.125. Do this by dividing 1 by 8. Set up a proportion with miles over minutes. Then cross multiply and divide each side by 2.5:

$$\frac{3.125 \text{ miles}}{2.5 \text{ minutes}} = \frac{x}{60}$$

$$2.5x = 187.5$$

$$\frac{2.5x}{2.5} = \frac{187.5}{2.5}$$

$$x = 75 \qquad \text{(6.RP.A.2)}$$

3. **\$2.19 for $1\frac{1}{4}$ lb** The unit rate is calculated at \$1.75 per pound, and the \$0.88 per half of a pound has a unit rate of \$1.76 per pound. Divide 2.19 by 1.25:

$$\frac{\$2.19 \div 1.25}{1.25 \text{ lb} \div 1.25} = \frac{\$1.75}{1 \text{ lb}}$$

Divide 0.88 by $\frac{1}{2}$ or 0.5:

$$\frac{\$0.88 \div 0.5}{0.5 \text{ lb} \div 0.5} = \frac{\$1.76}{1 \text{ lb}}$$

(6.RP.A.3.B)

4. **Yes, Keegan will be done before $1\frac{1}{2}$ hours** It is estimated to take him 84 minutes. Keegan realized that if he could wash 3 cars in 36 minutes, he should multiply 7 cars by 12, which is the unit rate or constant of proportionality to determine how long it will take to wash 7 cars. This is similar to finding equivalent fractions. This problem could also be solved by setting up a proportion and cross multiplying to find the unknown number.

$$\frac{\text{cars}}{\text{min}} \frac{3}{36} = \frac{7}{x}$$

$$\frac{252}{3} = \frac{3x}{3}$$

$$84 = x$$

(6.RP.A.3)

5.

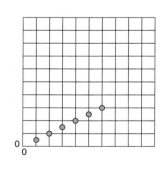

x	y
1	0.5
2	1
3	1.5
4	2
5	2.5
6	3

You need to find the constant of proportionality and multiply it by the x-values to get the y-values. To find the constant of proportionality, you can divide the y-value by the x-value. The constant of proportionality cannot change from the x-value; it must always be used for every value in the chart.

$1 \div 2 = 0.5$ or $\frac{1}{2}$. So the constant of proportionality is to multiply by 0.5 or $\frac{1}{2}$. Remember when you graph, the x-axis is the horizontal axis and the y-axis is the vertical axis. (6.RP.A.3.A)

6. **(A)** Since all the prices are given in different numbers of pounds or ounces, you must find the unit rate to compare. Divide each of the prices by the number of pounds given to get the unit rate, or the amount it costs for only 1 pound. For the deli whose price is written in ounces, convert that to 1 ounce and then multiply by 16 because 16 ounces are in 1 pound. (6.RP.A.3.B)

Healthy Deli	\$9.92 per 2 pounds	\$9.92 ÷ 2	\$4.96/lb
David's Deli	\$9.38 per 1.5 pounds	\$9.38 ÷ 1.5	\$6.25/lb
Meat & More	\$4.75 for $\frac{1}{2}$ pound	\$4.75 ÷ 0.5 oz	\$9.50/lb
Top Deli	\$1.25 for 4 ounces	\$1.25 ÷ 4 oz = 0.3125 0.3125 × 16 = 5.00	\$5.00/lb

7. **Approximately 6 hours** Finding a unit rate based on how many square feet you can paint in one hour will help you solve this problem.

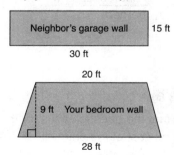

Step 1: Determine the area of your bedroom wall.

$$A = \frac{1}{2}h(b_1 + b_2)$$

$$A = \frac{1}{2}9(28 + 20)$$

$$A = \frac{1}{2}9(48)$$

$$A = 216$$

Step 2: Using the area from Step 1 and the 40 minutes given in the problem, determine the unit rate or number of square feet you can paint in 1 hour. Note: You need to change the 40 minutes to a decimal. $\frac{40}{60} = \frac{2}{3} \approx 0.67$. 216 square feet ÷ 0.67 hours ≈ 322 ft² per hour.

Step 3: Determine the area of one side of your neighbor's garage using the formula $A = bh$. The area is 30 times 15 or 450 square feet or 450 ft². Multiply 450 ft² by 4 because there are 4 sides to paint. Your result is 1,800 ft².

Step 4: Now, using the unit rate from Step 2, determine how long it will take to paint 1,800 ft². 1,800 square feet ÷ 322 ft² per hour ≈ 5.59 hours, which when rounded to the nearest hour is 6 hours. (6.RP.A.3.B and 6.G.A.1)

8. **(D)** When setting up proportions, make sure you place the numbers in a constant pattern. For example, in choice D, is written 45 over $\frac{2}{3}$, which is 45 minutes over $\frac{2}{3}$ of lawn. Look at the second ratio and see if it is minutes over lawn, which it is because 50 minutes is on the top of the ratio. (6.RP.A.2)

9. **85 minutes** Setting up a proportion and cross multiplying will help you solve the problem. There are two ways to do this: using the percent or using the fraction. The percent method is shown. Using 0.15 as the equivalent to 15% and 1 as the equivalent to 100%:

$$\frac{minutes}{percent}\ \frac{15}{.15} = \frac{x}{1}$$
$$\frac{15}{.15} = \frac{.15x}{.15}$$
$$100 = x$$

(6.RP.A.3.B)

10. **(A)** Note that the question asks for the sales tax, *not* the total cost of the shirt with tax. There are two ways to solve this problem: using an equation or using a proportion (shown).

$$\frac{x}{35} = \frac{7}{100}$$
$$\frac{245}{100} = \frac{100x}{100}$$
$$x = \$2.45$$

(6.RP.A.3.C)

11. **(D)** There are two ways to solve this problem: using an equation or using a proportion.

$$\frac{250}{x} = \frac{85}{100}$$
$$\frac{25,000}{85} = \frac{85x}{85}$$
$$x \approx 294$$

(6.RP.A.3.C)

12. **(A)** To convert you need to know that there are 2 cups in 1 pint. From there set up a proportion to convert.

$$\frac{cups}{pints}\ \frac{2}{1} = \frac{x}{33}$$
$$x = 66 \text{ cups}$$

(6.RP.A.3.D)

13. **9 feet 2 inches** To convert you need to know there are 12 inches in 1 foot. From there, set up a proportion to convert. Convert one of the given measurements to the other's units. Convert 9 feet 2 inches to all inches to compare it to 115 inches.

$$\frac{inches}{feet}\ \frac{12}{1} = \frac{x}{9}$$
$$\frac{1x}{1} = \frac{108}{1}$$

$x = 108$ inches plus the extra 2 inches, for a total of 110 inches

(6.RP.A.3.D)

14. **7 rolls** The problem should be completed using 3 steps.

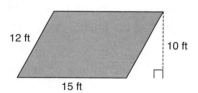

Step 1: Find the perimeter. A parallelogram's perimeter can be found by adding all sides or using the formula $P = 2L + 2W$. Make sure you use 12 feet and 15 feet since the 10 feet listed is used for the width when calculating area.

$$P = 2L + 2W$$
$$P = 2(15) + 2(12)$$
$$P = 30 + 24$$
$$P = 54 \text{ feet}$$

Step 2: Convert to inches. There are 12 inches in 1 foot.

$$\frac{\text{feet}}{\text{inches}}\frac{1}{12} = \frac{54}{x}$$

$$\frac{1x}{1} = \frac{648}{1}$$

$$x = 648 \text{ inches}$$

Step 3: Calculate how many rolls are needed. There are 96 inches in 1 roll.

$$\frac{648}{96} = 6.75 \text{ rolls}$$

7 rolls need to be bought because you can't buy part of a roll and because the question asks for full rolls. (6.RP.A.3.D and 6.G.A.1)

15. **(A)** Negative integers are whole numbers below zero. The other choices are all examples of positive integers. (6.NS.C.5)

16.

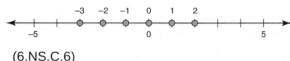

(6.NS.C.6)

17. **(B)** Remember that the opposite of negative 5 is positive 5 or +5. The opposite of the opposite of a number is the number itself; therefore, $-(-5)$ equals +5. (6.NS.C.6.A)

18. **(B)** You can sketch or use graph paper to prove that a square is formed, all sides are congruent, four right angles are present, and opposite sides are parallel. You could also visualize that there are two pairs of x-values that are the same and two pairs of y-values that are the same. (6.NS.C.6.B)

19. **(B)** Ordered pairs are written with parentheses as (x, y). The first number in the ordered pair represents the number for the x-axis (the horizontal axis), and you should move left or right along the x-axis first. The second number represents the y-coordinate for the y-axis (vertical axis), and you should move up or down second. In this case, point D is located 2 places left on the x-axis, so the x-value is -2. It does not go up or down the y-axis, so the y-value is 0. (6.NS.C.6.C)

20. **(B)** Points C and F are on the same vertical line, so you can count how many lines are between -1 and 3 vertically. You could also compare their coordinates and notice that the x-values are the same and that the y-values change: (1, 3) and

(1, –1). Because distances are not negative, you could take the absolute value of –1, which is 1, and add it to the 3 to get 4. (6.NS.C.6.C and 6.NS.C.8)

21. **(A)** $|-19| = 19$. Choice A is the only answer that does not equal 19. The question asks which one is *not* equivalent. The absolute value is represented symbolically with the vertical lines and is the distance from zero, regardless of the direction, negative or positive. You want to know how far away –19 is from zero. –19 is nineteen units away from zero. When determining absolute value, remove the positive/negative signs. (6.NS.C.7 and 6.NS.C.7.C)

22. **(C)** First you should notice that the question says least to greatest, which means you need to start by listing the negatives first. Negative integers are smaller than positive integers. A strategy to help determine which order to place the integers in is to simplify them and turn the fractions into decimals. $-|-5| = -5$ and $-\frac{2}{3} = -.\overline{666666}$ One of the trickiest rational numbers to determine placement of is $-\frac{2}{3}$ and $-.6$. Because $-\frac{2}{3} = -.\overline{666666}$, it is more "in debt" than -0.6. Because the numbers are negative, that means $-\frac{2}{3}$ is less than -0.6. (6.NS.C.7)

23. **(A)** This inequality is written backwards to the typical inequalities we see. Typically, the variable is written first. Be careful on these! This is read "-10 is greater than x," *which means if -10 is greater than x, then x is less than -10.* You can also think of it as reading backward from the x. Choice A reads that $10 > -11$, which is the only true selection. (6.NS.C.7.A and 6.NS.C.7.B)

24. **(A)** You are looking for an inequality that shows only positive values more than 15. Choice A is equivalent to $x > 15$ after you simplify the absolute value signs. *(6.NS.C.7.A and 6.NS.C.7.B)*

25. **(B)** If you graph the two points on the grid, you can count the number of spaces from –3 to –7. From –3 to –7 there is a distance of 4 units. Disregard the negative signs because distances are not negative. Instead, use the absolute value of both numbers. (6.NS.C.8)

26. (B) You must perform the order of operations to solve this problem.

$$\frac{15}{5} + 40 \cdot 7 - 3^4$$

$$\frac{15}{5} + 40 \cdot 7 - 81$$

$$3 + 40 \cdot 7 - 81$$

$$3 + 280 - 81$$

$$283 - 81$$

$$202$$

(6.EE.A.1)

27. (C) Recall that difference means to subtract. Since it says a third of the difference, that means to take a third after you subtract, so subtraction must go inside the parentheses. A third is represented by the fraction $\frac{1}{3}$. (6.EE.A.2)

28. (B) In this particular problem 3 is multiplied by the entire quantity of $5x + 2$, so both 3 and $(5x + 2)$ are factors of the final product. However, the problem asks for a sum, which means the answer to addition. $5x + 2$ is the only sum. (6.EE.A.2.B)

29. (A) The product is the answer to the multiplication part, which is ab. When letters are directly next to each other that means multiply. (6.EE.A.2.B)

30. (D) (6.EE.A.2)

$$9z + y^3 + 60x(x - z)$$

Substitute the numbers under the correct variables.

$$9\left(\frac{1}{3}\right) + 4^3 + 60\left(\frac{1}{2}\right)\left(\frac{1}{2} - \frac{1}{3}\right)$$

Use PEMDAS. First, perform operations in the parentheses. Get common denominators.

$$9\left(\frac{1}{3}\right) + 4^3 + 60\left(\frac{1}{2}\right)\left(\frac{3}{6} - \frac{2}{6}\right)$$

Solve what's in the parentheses:

$$\frac{3}{6} - \frac{2}{6} = \frac{1}{6}$$

$$9\left(\frac{1}{3}\right) + 4^3 + 60\left(\frac{1}{2}\right)\left(\frac{1}{6}\right)$$

Next, solve the exponents: $4 \times 4 \times 4 = 64$.

$$9\left(\frac{1}{3}\right) + 64 + 60\left(\frac{1}{2}\right)\left(\frac{1}{6}\right)$$

Then perform multiplication. Use mental math: a third is dividing by three. Half of 60 is 30.

$$3 + 64 + 30\left(\frac{1}{6}\right)$$

A sixth of 30 is 5.

$$3 + 64 + 5$$

Then perform addition.

$$67 + 5$$

$$72$$

31. (C) This problem requires you to use the distributive property. Then, you must combine like terms to simplify the expression to form an equivalent expression. When you use the distributive property, you are multiplying the front factor over every part of the other factor. In this case, you are multiplying x and 2 to get $2x$ and then x and 10 to get $10x$. This results in $2x + 10x$. Since both terms have the variable x, they are like terms and should be combined: $2x + 10x = 12x$. (6.EE.A.3)

32. Because both expressions equal 15, when 2 is substituted in for x, then the expressions are equivalent.

$$x = 2$$

$3x + 9$	$3(x + 3)$
$3(2) + 9$	$3(2 + 3)$
$6 + 9$	$3(5)$
15	15

(6.EE.A.4)

33. (B) You can check to see if a value is the solution to an equation by substituting it into the equation and performing the order of operations. When $x = 10$, the equation is true.

$$4x - 10 = 30$$

$$4(10) - 10 = 30$$

$$40 - 10 = 30$$

$$30 = 30$$

(6.EE.B.5)

34. (D) To solve this equation, you must substitute the numbers under the correct variables. You will see that the area is given but that you need to solve for h, which means you need to isolate the variable and use inverse operations.

$$A = \frac{1}{2}bh$$

$$55 = \frac{1}{2}10h$$

$$55 = 5h$$

$$\frac{55}{5} = \frac{5h}{5}$$

$$11 = h$$

(6.EE.B.7 and 6.G.A.1)

35. **Part A. *c* = 10 + 5*h* or another equivalent equation** The $10 for snacks is added onto the cost per hour. The variable *h* is multiplied by 5 because she is paid $5 for every hour of work.

Part B. 8 hours You need to substitute in the number 50 for the *c* variable and then solve the equation using inverse operations.

$$50 = 10 + 5h$$
$$\underline{-10 \quad -10}$$
$$\frac{4x}{4} = \frac{11}{4}$$
$$8 = h$$

(6.EE.C.9 and 6.EE.B.7)

36. **(B)** The symbol means greater than (to the right of the number) or equal to, which is shown as a filled in circle. (6.EE.B.8)

37. **Part A. 4*x* − 2 ≤ 9**

Part B. *x* ≤ 2.75 You should solve the inequality just as you would a two-step equation. You need to isolate the variable by performing inverse operations. The first step is to add 2 to both sides. Then you need to divide both sides by 4.

$$4x - 2 \leq 9$$
$$\underline{+2 \quad +2}$$
$$\frac{4x}{4} \leq \frac{11}{4}$$
$$x \leq 2.75$$

Part C. There should be a filled in circle because it is less than *or* equal to.

(6.EE.B.8, 6.EE.B.5, and 6.NS.C.6)

38. **(C)** You will notice that the *a* values are all multiplied by 3 and then 1 is added to result in the given *b* values. A strategy that can help you is to think about what the closest multiple of the *a* value *b* is near. For example, 50 × 3 = 150, which is one off of 151, 30 × 3 = 60, plus 1 is 61. (6.RP.A.3.A and 6.EE.C.9)

Part B. (B) Letters are substituted into the *a* value and operations are performed resulting in a *b* value; therefore, *b* is dependent upon what you use for *a*. (6.EE.C.9)

39. **44 full cookies** You should divide $5\frac{1}{2}$ by $\frac{1}{8}$.

Dividing fractions can be performed by multiplying the first fraction (dividend) by the reciprocal of the second fraction (divisor). This is shown below. You need to change the mixed numbers into improper fractions.

$$5\frac{1}{2} \div \frac{1}{8}$$
$$\frac{11}{2} \div \frac{1}{8}$$
$$\frac{11}{2} \cdot \frac{8}{1}$$
$$\frac{88}{2} = 44$$

(6.NS.A.1)

40. **(C)** List the multiples of 2, 6, and 9. See which is the first common multiple or LCM. Choice D is a time they will all meet again, but it's not the first time, so it is incorrect.

2: 2, 4, 6, 8, 10, 12, 14, 16, <u>18</u>, 20, 24, . . .
6: 6, 12, <u>18</u>, 24, . . .
9: 9, <u>18</u>, 27, . . .
(6.NS.B.4)

41. **(D)** To rewrite the expression with the distributive property, you need to find the GCF. The GCF goes on the outside of the parentheses. The two numbers are divided by the GCF you chose and the quotients remain inside the parentheses. In this problem, the GCF of 20 and 44 is 4. So 4 goes on the outside of the parentheses. 20*x* divided by 4 is 5*x*, and 44 divided by 4 is 11; (5*x* + 11) is inside the parentheses. (6.NS.B.4)

42. $99\frac{2}{3}$ cm³ Since $\frac{1}{3}$ repeats as a decimal you should keep it as a fraction and then use your fraction skills in the volume formula. You can convert 2.5 to $2\frac{1}{2}$. You also need to convert the mixed numbers to improper fractions. If you can cross reduce ahead of time, it will help make the numbers smaller and more manageable.

$$V = lwh$$
$$V = 2\frac{1}{2} \times 4\frac{1}{3} \times 9\frac{1}{5}$$
$$V = \frac{5}{2} \times \frac{13}{3} \times \frac{46}{5}$$
$$V = \frac{\overset{1}{5}}{\underset{1}{2}} \times \frac{13}{3} \times \frac{\overset{23}{46}}{\underset{1}{5}}$$
$$V = \frac{1}{1} \times \frac{13}{3} \times \frac{23}{1}$$
$$V = \frac{299}{3}$$
$$V = 99\frac{2}{3}$$

(6.NS.A.1 and 6.G.A.2)

219

43. **(A)** Choice A is $V = Bh$ and is used for volume. The capital B stands for the area of the base of the prism, which is lw. When lw is substituted in for B, it results in the lwh formula. Choice B can be used for cubes only since all the sides have the same measure. The formula in choice C is used to find the area of rectangles and parallelograms. Choice D has the equal sign in the wrong spot for it to be lwh. (6.G.A.2)

44. Part A. The coordinates are plotted for you below.

Part B. The perimeter equals 22 units. The distance from point to point can be found by counting the squares in between. The perimeter is then found by adding up the lengths of all the sides: $7 + 7 + 4 + 4 = 22$.

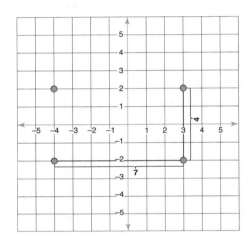

Part C. **The area is 28 square units.**

$$A = bh$$
$$A = 7(4)$$

(6.NS.C.6.C, 6.NS.C.8, and 6.G.A.1)

45. **(B)** A triangular pyramid has to have a triangle for a base and three triangles for sides that meet at a point at the top, as shown.

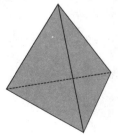

(6.G.A.4)

46. $503\frac{7}{8}$ inches^2 You can sketch a net of the box, label the dimensions, and then find the area of each rectangle. Next, you need to find the total surface area by adding all the rectangles' areas

together. You will notice that there are two of every type of rectangle; therefore, you can find the area of each type and double your answer. (See the chart on page 221.) (6.G.A.4)

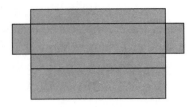

47. **(B)** Variability means that you will receive a lot of different numeric numbers or data. Choices A, C, and D refer to only one person's answer or to a specific time, so there is no variability in the answers. (6.SP.A and 6.SP.B.5)

48. **(A)** You must calculate the 5 statistical summary as shown below. Then check to see which choice matches the 5 statistical summary.

Minimum = 1

Q1 (lower quartile) = 1.5

Median = 4

Q3 (upper quartile) = 10

Maximum = 15

Place the numbers in order from least to greatest to find the minimum and maximum numbers. The median number is the one in the middle.

1, 1, 1, 1, 2, 2, 2, 3, (4,) 6, 7, 8, 9, 11, 13, 14, 15

To find the lower quartiles (Q1), find the middle of the lower numbers, the numbers to the left of the median. To find the upper quartile (Q3), find the middle of the upper numbers, the numbers to the right of the median. If there are two middle numbers, find their average (add them and divide by 2).

1, 1, 1, 1, 2, 2, 2, 3, (4,) 6, 7, 8, 9, 11, 13, 14, 15

Q1 $\frac{1+2}{2} = 1.5$ Q3 $\frac{9+11}{2} = 10$

To create the graph, place dots on a number line for all five pieces of data. The number line should start with at least the minimum number and go to at least the maximum number. Connect a line from the minimum number to the maximum number. The box is from Q1 to Q3 and a line goes in the box at the median. (6.SP.B.4)

(Chart for question 46)

Side	Area Work for One Rectangle	Double the Area of the One Rectangle
Top of the box (same as the bottom)	$A = bh$ $A = 15\frac{1}{2} \cdot 10\frac{3}{4}$ $A = \frac{31}{2} \cdot \frac{43}{4}$ $A = \frac{1{,}333}{8}$	$\frac{1{,}333}{8} \cdot 2$ $\frac{2{,}666}{8}$
Left side of the box (same as the right)	$A = bh$ $A = 10\frac{3}{4} \cdot 3\frac{1}{4}$ $A = \frac{43}{4} \cdot \frac{13}{4}$ $A = \frac{559}{16}$	$\frac{559}{16} \cdot 2$ $\frac{1{,}118}{16}$
Front of the box (same as the back)	$A = bh$ $A = 3\frac{1}{4} \cdot 15\frac{1}{2}$ $A = \frac{13}{4} \cdot \frac{31}{2}$ $A = \frac{403}{8}$	$\frac{403}{8} \cdot 2$ $\frac{806}{8}$
Find the total of all areas calculated:	$\frac{1{,}333}{8} + \frac{1{,}333}{8} + \frac{559}{16} + \frac{559}{16} + \frac{403}{8} + \frac{403}{8}$ This is adding each rectangle separately. Get common denominators.	You can add the doubled areas to make your work quicker. Get common denominators. $\frac{2{,}666}{8} + \frac{1{,}118}{16} + \frac{806}{8}$ $\frac{5{,}332}{16} + \frac{1{,}118}{16} + \frac{1{,}612}{16}$ $\frac{8{,}062}{16}$ $503\frac{14}{16}$ $503\frac{7}{8}$

49. **4.8** First find the mean. To find the mean, add the number of trees and shrubs and divide by the number of categories.

$$\frac{10+23+13+8+3+5+6}{7} = \frac{68}{7} \approx 9.7$$

Then subtract 9.7 from all the values. Use absolute value, meaning any value that is negative needs to drop the negative sign.

Value	Distance from the Mean (9.7)
10	0.3
23	13.3
13	3.3
8	1.7
3	6.7
5	4.7
6	3.7

Now calculate the mean of the deviations (distances from the mean).

$$\frac{0.3 + 13.3 + 3.3 + 1.7 + 6.7 + 4.7 + 3.7}{7} = \frac{33.7}{7} \approx 4.8$$

(6.SP.B.5.C)

50. Part A.

Test Scores	Tally	Frequency
60–69	II	2
70–79	III	3
80–89	IIII	5
90–99	IIII II	7

(6.SP.B.4)

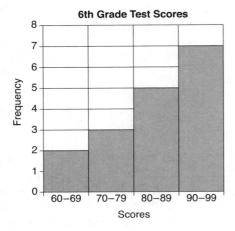

Part B. **The 80–89 score interval is where the median number lays.** You can determine this by first counting the number of scores in the list, which is 17. Half of 17 is 8.5, so the median would fall between the 8th and 9th number. If you start from the lowest score interval, there are only two values. If you go into the next interval, there are three more, totaling five values. The next group is five more, totaling ten from 60–89. You want the value after the 8th one, which falls in the 80–89 interval. Because you do not want to know what the median value is exactly, you can perform the above procedure to find the interval. You could also list all the values in order from least to greatest and from there find the middle value and figure out what interval the middle value would belong in. (6.SP.A.3)

Part C. **The IQR is 15.5.** The interquartile range or IQR is Q3–Q1, which is the difference between the upper and lower quartiles.

Place the numbers in order from least to greatest in order to find the minimum and maximum numbers. The median number is the one in the middle.

60, 65, 73, 76, 78, 81, 84, 87, 88,
89, 90, 90, 94, 95, 96, 97, 99

If there were two middle numbers, you would find their average (add them and divide by 2).

To find the lower quartiles (Q1), find the middle of the lower numbers, the numbers to the left of the median, from 60 to 87. To find the upper quartile (Q3), find the middle of the upper numbers, the numbers to the right of the median, from 89 to 99.

60, 65, 73, 76, 78, 81, 84, 87, 88,
89, 90, 90, 94, 95, 96, 97, 99

Q1 $\frac{76 + 78}{2} = 77$ Q3 $\frac{94 + 95}{2} = 94.5$

Subtract the upper and lower quartiles:

94.5 − 77 = 17.5

(6.SP.A.3)

Part D. The shape of the data is skewed left since the long tail is to the left. Explanations can vary. A suggested response is provided. Because the shape of the data shows that the scores are skewed to the left, it seems that there are more higher scores than there are scores in the 60s range. This can help the teacher understand that her students did very well on the test and scored more toward the 80s and 90s. (6.SP.B.5.D and 6.SP.A.2)

APPENDIX A

ENGLISH LANGUAGE ARTS STANDARDS

Reading: Literature
CCSS RL.6.1 Cite textual evidence to support analysis of what the text says explicitly as well as inferences drawn from the text.
CCSS RL.6.2 Determine a theme or central idea of a text and how it is conveyed through particular details; provide a summary of the text distinct from personal opinions or judgments.
CCSS RL.6.3 Describe how a particular story's or drama's plot unfolds in a series of episodes as well as how the characters respond or change as the plot moves toward a resolution.
CCSS RL.6.4 Determine the meaning of words and phrases as they are used in a text, including figurative and connotative meanings; analyze the impact of a specific word choice on meaning and tone.
CCSS RL.6.5 Analyze how a particular sentence, chapter, scene, or stanza fits into the overall structure of a text and contributes to the development of the theme, setting, or plot.
CCSS RL.6.6 Explain how an author develops the point of view of the narrator or speaker in a text.
CCSS RL.6.7 Compare and contrast the experience of reading a story, drama, or poem to listening to or viewing an audio, video, or live version of the text, including contrasting what they "see" and "hear" when reading the text to what they perceive when they listen or watch.
CCSS RL.6.8 (Not applicable to literature)
CCSS RL.6.9 Compare and contrast texts in different forms or genres (e.g., stories and poems; historical novels and fantasy stories) in terms of their approaches to similar themes and topics.
CCSS RL.6.10 By the end of the year, read and comprehend literature, including stories, dramas, and poems, in the grades 6–8 text complexity band proficiently, with scaffolding as needed at the high end of the range.
Reading: Informational Text
CCSS RI.6.1 Cite textual evidence to support analysis of what the text says explicitly as well as inferences drawn from the text.
CCSS RI.6.2 Determine a central idea of a text and how it is conveyed through particular details; provide a summary of the text distinct from personal opinions or judgments.
CCSS RI.6.3 Analyze in detail how a key individual, event, or idea is introduced, illustrated, and elaborated in a text (e.g., through examples or anecdotes).
CCSS RI.6.4 Determine the meaning of words and phrases as they are used in a text, including figurative, connotative, and technical meanings.
CCSS RI.6.5 Analyze how a particular sentence, paragraph, chapter, or section fits into the overall structure of a text and contributes to the development of the ideas.
CCSS RI.6.6 Determine an author's point of view or purpose in a text and explain how it is conveyed in the text.
CCSS RI.6.7 Integrate information presented in different media or formats (e.g., visually, quantitatively) as well as in words to develop a coherent understanding of a topic or issue.
CCSS RI.6.8 Trace and evaluate the argument and specific claims in a text, distinguishing claims that are supported by reasons and evidence from claims that are not.

CCSS RI.6.9 Compare and contrast one author's presentation of events with that of another (e.g., a memoir written by and a biography on the same person).

CCSS RI.6.10 Compare and contrast one author's presentation of events with that of another (e.g., a memoir written by and a biography on the same person).

Writing

CCSS W.6.1 Write arguments to support claims with clear reasons and relevant evidence.
- A. Introduce claim(s) and organize the reasons and evidence clearly.
- B. Support claim(s) with clear reasons and relevant evidence, using credible sources and demonstrating an understanding of the topic or text.
- C. Use words, phrases, and clauses to clarify the relationships among claim(s) and reasons.
- D. Establish and maintain a formal style.
- E. Provide a concluding statement or section that follows from the argument presented.

CCSS W.6.2 Write informative/explanatory texts to examine a topic and convey ideas, concepts, and information through the selection, organization, and analysis of relevant content.
- A. Introduce a topic; organize ideas, concepts, and information, using strategies such as definition, classification, comparison/contrast, and cause/effect; include formatting (e.g., headings), graphics (e.g., charts, tables), and multimedia when useful to aiding comprehension.
- B. Develop the topic with relevant facts, definitions, concrete details, quotations, or other information and examples.
- C. Use appropriate transitions to clarify the relationships among ideas and concepts.
- D. Use precise language and domain-specific vocabulary to inform about or explain the topic.
- E. Establish and maintain a formal style.
- F. Provide a concluding statement or section that follows from the information or explanation presented.

CCSS W.6.3 Write narratives to develop real or imagined experiences or events using effective technique, relevant descriptive details, and well-structured event sequences.
- A. Engage and orient the reader by establishing a context and introducing a narrator and/or characters; organize an event sequence that unfolds naturally and logically.
- B. Use narrative techniques, such as dialogue, pacing, and description, to develop experiences, events, and/or characters.
- C. Use a variety of transition words, phrases, and clauses to convey sequence and signal shifts from one time frame or setting to another.
- D. Use precise words and phrases, relevant descriptive details, and sensory language to convey experiences and events.
- E. Provide a conclusion that follows from the narrated experiences or events.

CCSS W.6.4 Produce clear and coherent writing in which the development, organization, and style are appropriate to task, purpose, and audience. (Grade-specific expectations for writing types are defined in standards 1–3 above.)

CCSS W.6.5 With some guidance and support from peers and adults, develop and strengthen writing as needed by planning, revising, editing, rewriting, or trying a new approach. (Editing for conventions should demonstrate command of Language standards 1–3 up to and including grade 6.)

CCSS W.6.6 Use technology, including the Internet, to produce and publish writing as well as to interact and collaborate with others; demonstrate sufficient command of keyboarding skills to type a minimum of three pages in a single sitting.

CCSS W.6.7 Conduct short research projects to answer a question, drawing on several sources and refocusing the inquiry when appropriate.

CCSS W.6.8 Gather relevant information from multiple print and digital sources; assess the credibility of each source; and quote or paraphrase the data and conclusions of others while avoiding plagiarism and providing basic bibliographic information for sources.

CCSS W.6.9 Draw evidence from literary or informational texts to support analysis, reflection, and research.
  A. Apply *grade 6 Reading standards* to literature (e.g., "Compare and contrast texts in different forms or genres [e.g., stories and poems; historical novels and fantasy stories] in terms of their approaches to similar themes and topics").
  B. Apply *grade 6 Reading standards* to literary nonfiction (e.g., "Trace and evaluate the argument and specific claims in a text, distinguishing claims that are supported by reasons and evidence from claims that are not").

CCSS W.6.10 Write routinely over extended time frames (time for research, reflection, and revision) and shorter time frames (a single sitting or a day or two) for a range of discipline-specific tasks, purposes, and audiences.

Speaking and Listening

CCSS SL.6.1 Engage effectively in a range of collaborative discussions (one-on-one, in groups, and teacher-led) with diverse partners on *grade 6 topics*, *texts*, *and issues*, building on others' ideas and expressing their own clearly.
  A. Come to discussions prepared, having read or studied required material; explicitly draw on that preparation by referring to evidence on the topic, text, or issue to probe and reflect on ideas under discussion.
  B. Follow rules for collegial discussions, set specific goals and deadlines, and define individual roles as needed.
  C. Pose and respond to specific questions with elaboration and detail by making comments that contribute to the topic, text, or issue under discussion.
  D. Review the key ideas expressed and demonstrate understanding of multiple perspectives through reflection and paraphrasing.

CCSS SL.6.2 Interpret information presented in diverse media and formats (e.g., visually, quantitatively, orally) and explain how it contributes to a topic, text, or issue under study.

CCSS SL.6.3 Delineate a speaker's argument and specific claims, distinguishing claims that are supported by reasons and evidence from claims that are not.

CCSS SL.6.4 Present claims and findings, sequencing ideas logically and using pertinent descriptions, facts, and details to accentuate main ideas or themes; use appropriate eye contact, adequate volume, and clear pronunciation.

CCSS SL.6.5 Include multimedia components (e.g., graphics, images, music, sound) and visual displays in presentations to clarify information.

CCSS SL.6.6 Adapt speech to a variety of contexts and tasks, demonstrating command of formal English when indicated or appropriate. (See grade 6 Language standards 1 and 3 for specific expectations.)

CCSS L.6.1 Demonstrate command of the conventions of standard English grammar and usage when writing or speaking.

    A. Ensure that pronouns are in the proper case (subjective, objective, possessive).

    B. Use intensive pronouns (e.g., myself, ourselves).

    C. Recognize and correct inappropriate shifts in pronoun number and person.

    D. Recognize and correct vague pronouns (i.e., ones with unclear or ambiguous antecedents).

    E. Recognize variations from standard English in their own and others' writing and speaking, and identify and use strategies to improve expression in conventional language.

CCSS L.6.2 Demonstrate command of the conventions of standard English capitalization, punctuation, and spelling when writing.

    A. Use punctuation (commas, parentheses, dashes) to set off nonrestrictive/parenthetical elements.

    B. Spell correctly.

CCSS L.6.3 Use knowledge of language and its conventions when writing, speaking, reading, or listening.

    A. Vary sentence patterns for meaning, reader/listener interest, and style.

    B. Maintain consistency in style and tone.

CCSS L.6.4 Determine or clarify the meaning of unknown and multiple-meaning words and phrases based on *grade 6 reading and content*, choosing flexibly from a range of strategies.

    A. Use context (e.g., the overall meaning of a sentence or paragraph; a word's position or function in a sentence) as a clue to the meaning of a word or phrase.

    B. Use common, grade-appropriate Greek or Latin affixes and roots as clues to the meaning of a word (e.g., *audience*, *auditory*, *audible*).

    C. Consult reference materials (e.g., dictionaries, glossaries, thesauruses), both print and digital, to find the pronunciation of a word or determine or clarify its precise meaning or its part of speech.

    D. Verify the preliminary determination of the meaning of a word or phrase (e.g., by checking the inferred meaning in context or in a dictionary).

CCSS L.6.5 Demonstrate understanding of figurative language, word relationships, and nuances in word meanings.

    A. Interpret figures of speech (e.g., personification) in context.

    B. Use the relationship between particular words (e.g., cause/effect, part/whole, item/category) to better understand each of the words.

    C. Distinguish among the connotations (associations) of words with similar denotations (definitions) (e.g., *stingy*, *scrimping*, *economical*, *unwasteful*, *thrifty*).

CCSS L.6.6 Acquire and use accurately grade-appropriate general academic and domain-specific words and phrases; gather vocabulary knowledge when considering a word or phrase important to comprehension or expression.

APPENDIX B
MATHEMATICS STANDARDS

Ratios and Proportional Relationships

CCSS 6.RP.A.1 Understand the concept of a ratio and use ratio language to describe a ratio relationship between two quantities. For example, "The ratio of wings to beaks in the bird house at the zoo was 2:1, because for every 2 wings there was 1 beak." "For every vote candidate *A* received, candidate *C* received nearly three votes."

CCSS 6.RP.A.2 Understand the concept of a unit rate a/b associated with a ratio $a:b$ with $b \neq 0$, and use rate language in the context of a ratio relationship. For example, "This recipe has a ratio of 3 cups of flour to 4 cups of sugar, so there is 3/4 cup of flour for each cup of sugar." "We paid $75 for 15 hamburgers, which is a rate of $5 per hamburger."

CCSS 6.RP.A.3 Use ratio and rate reasoning to solve real-world and mathematical problems, e.g., by reasoning about tables of equivalent ratios, tape diagrams, double number line diagrams, or equations.
  - **A.** Make tables of equivalent ratios relating quantities with whole-number measurements, find missing values in the tables, and plot the pairs of values on the coordinate plane. Use tables to compare ratios.
  - **B.** Solve unit rate problems including those involving unit pricing and constant speed. For example, if it took 7 hours to mow 4 lawns, then at that rate, how many lawns could be mowed in 35 hours? At what rate were lawns being mowed?
  - **C.** Find a percent of a quantity as a rate per 100 (e.g., 30% of a quantity means 30/100 times the quantity); solve problems involving finding the whole, given a part and the percent.
  - **D.** Use ratio reasoning to convert measurement units; manipulate and transform units appropriately when multiplying or dividing quantities.

Expressions and Equations

CCSS 6.EE.A.1 Write and evaluate numerical expressions involving whole-number exponents.

CCSS 6.EE.A.2 Write, read, and evaluate expressions in which letters stand for numbers.
  - **A.** Write expressions that record operations with numbers and with letters standing for numbers. For example, express the calculation "Subtract *y* from 5" as $5 - y$.
  - **B.** Identify parts of an expression using mathematical terms (sum, term, product, factor, quotient, coefficient); view one or more parts of an expression as a single entity. For example, describe the expression $2(8 + 7)$ as a product of two factors; view $(8 + 7)$ as both a single entity and a sum of two terms.
  - **C.** Evaluate expressions at specific values of their variables. Include expressions that arise from formulas used in real-world problems. Perform arithmetic operations, including those involving whole-number exponents, in the conventional order when there are no parentheses to specify a particular order (Order of Operations). For example, use the formulas $V = s^3$ and $A = 6s^2$ to find the volume and surface area of a cube with sides of length $s = 1/2$.

CCSS 6.EE.A.3 Apply the properties of operations to generate equivalent expressions. For example, apply the distributive property to the expression $3(2 + x)$ to produce the equivalent expression $6 + 3x$; apply the distributive property to the expression $24x + 18y$ to produce the equivalent expression $6(4x + 3y)$; apply properties of operations to $y + y + y$ to produce the equivalent expression $3y$.

CCSS 6.EE.A.4 Identify when two expressions are equivalent (i.e., when the two expressions name the same number regardless of which value is substituted into them). For example, the expressions $y + y + y$ and $3y$ are equivalent because they name the same number regardless of which number *y* stands for.

Reason about and solve one-variable equations and inequalities.

CCSS 6.EE.B.5 Understand solving an equation or inequality as a process of answering a question: which values from a specified set, if any, make the equation or inequality true? Use substitution to determine whether a given number in a specified set makes an equation or inequality true.

CCSS 6.EE.B.6 Use variables to represent numbers and write expressions when solving a real-world or mathematical problem; understand that a variable can represent an unknown number, or, depending on the purpose at hand, any number in a specified set.

CCSS 6.EE.B.7 Solve real-world and mathematical problems by writing and solving equations of the form $x + p = q$ and $px = q$ for cases in which p, q and x are all nonnegative rational numbers.

CCSS 6.EE.B.8 Write an inequality of the form $x > c$ or $x < c$ to represent a constraint or condition in a real-world or mathematical problem. Recognize that inequalities of the form $x > c$ or $x < c$ have infinitely many solutions; represent solutions of such inequalities on number line diagrams.

Represent and analyze quantitative relationships between dependent and independent variables.

CCSS 6.EE.C.9 Use variables to represent two quantities in a real-world problem that change in relationship to one another; write an equation to express one quantity, thought of as the dependent variable, in terms of the other quantity, thought of as the independent variable. Analyze the relationship between the dependent and independent variables using graphs and tables, and relate these to the equation. For example, in a problem involving motion at constant speed, list and graph ordered pairs of distances and times, and write the equation $d = 65t$ to represent the relationship between distance and time.

The Number System

Apply and extend previous understandings of multiplication and division to divide fractions by fractions.

CCSS 6.NS.A.1 Interpret and compute quotients of fractions, and solve word problems involving division of fractions by fractions, e.g., by using visual fraction models and equations to represent the problem. For example, create a story context for $(2/3) \div (3/4)$ and use a visual fraction model to show the quotient; use the relationship between multiplication and division to explain that $(2/3) \div (3/4) = 8/9$ because $3/4$ of $8/9$ is $2/3$. (In general, $(a/b) \div (c/d) = ad/bc$.) How much chocolate will each person get if 3 people share 1/2 lb of chocolate equally? How many 3/4-cup servings are in 2/3 of a cup of yogurt? How wide is a rectangular strip of land with length 3/4 mi and area 1/2 square mi?

Compute fluently with multi-digit numbers and find common factors and multiples.

CCSS 6.NS.B.2 Fluently divide multi-digit numbers using the standard algorithm.

CCSS 6.NS.B.3 Fluently add, subtract, multiply, and divide multi-digit decimals using the standard algorithm for each operation.

CCSS 6.NS.B.4 Find the greatest common factor of two whole numbers less than or equal to 100 and the least common multiple of two whole numbers less than or equal to 12. Use the distributive property to express a sum of two whole numbers 1–100 with a common factor as a multiple of a sum of two whole numbers with no common factor. For example, express 36 + 8 as 4 (9 + 2).

Apply and extend previous understandings of numbers to the system of rational numbers.

CCSS 6.NS.C.5 Understand that positive and negative numbers are used together to describe quantities having opposite directions or values (e.g., temperature above/below zero, elevation above/below sea level, credits/debits, positive/negative electric charge); use positive and negative numbers to represent quantities in real-world contexts, explaining the meaning of 0 in each situation.

CCSS 6.NS.C.6 Understand a rational number as a point on the number line. Extend number line diagrams and coordinate axes familiar from previous grades to represent points on the line and in the plane with negative number coordinates.

- **A.** Recognize opposite signs of numbers as indicating locations on opposite sides of 0 on the number line; recognize that the opposite of the opposite of a number is the number itself, e.g., –(–3) = 3, and that 0 is its own opposite.
- **B.** Understand signs of numbers in ordered pairs as indicating locations in quadrants of the coordinate plane; recognize that when two ordered pairs differ only by signs, the locations of the points are related by reflections across one or both axes.
- **C.** Find and position integers and other rational numbers on a horizontal or vertical number line diagram; find and position pairs of integers and other rational numbers on a coordinate plane.

CCSS 6.NS.C.7 Understand ordering and absolute value of rational numbers.

- **A.** Interpret statements of inequality as statements about the relative position of two numbers on a number line diagram. For example, interpret –3 > –7 as a statement that –3 is located to the right of –7 on a number line oriented from left to right.
- **B.** Write, interpret, and explain statements of order for rational numbers in real-world contexts. For example, write –3°C > –7°C to express the fact that –3°C is warmer than –7°C.
- **C.** Understand the absolute value of a rational number as its distance from 0 on the number line; interpret absolute value as magnitude for a positive or negative quantity in a real-world situation. For example, for an account balance of –30 dollars, write |–30| = 30 to describe the size of the debt in dollars.
- **D.** Distinguish comparisons of absolute value from statements about order. For example, recognize that an account balance less than –30 dollars represents a debt greater than 30 dollars.

CCSS 6.NS.C.8 Solve real-world and mathematical problems by graphing points in all four quadrants of the coordinate plane. Include use of coordinates and absolute value to find distances between points with the same first coordinate or the same second coordinate.

Geometry

Solve real-world and mathematical problems involving area, surface area, and volume.

CCSS 6.G.A.1 Find the area of right triangles, other triangles, special quadrilaterals, and polygons by composing into rectangles or decomposing into triangles and other shapes; apply these techniques in the context of solving real-world and mathematical problems.

CCSS 6.G.A.2 Find the volume of a right rectangular prism with fractional edge lengths by packing it with unit cubes of the appropriate unit fraction edge lengths, and show that the volume is the same as would be found by multiplying the edge lengths of the prism. Apply the formulas $V = lwh$ and $V = Bh$ to find volumes of right rectangular prisms with fractional edge lengths in the context of solving real-world and mathematical problems.

CCSS 6.G.A.3 Draw polygons in the coordinate plane given coordinates for the vertices; use coordinates to find the length of a side joining points with the same first coordinate or the same second coordinate. Apply these techniques in the context of solving real-world and mathematical problems.

CCSS 6.G.A.4 Represent three-dimensional figures using nets made up of rectangles and triangles, and use the nets to find the surface area of these figures. Apply these techniques in the context of solving real-world and mathematical problems.

Statistics and Probability

Develop understanding of statistical variability.

CCSS 6.SP.A.1 Recognize a statistical question as one that anticipates variability in the data related to the question and accounts for it in the answers. For example, "How old am I?" is not a statistical question, but "How old are the students in my school?" is a statistical question because one anticipates variability in students' ages.

CCSS 6.SP.A.2 Understand that a set of data collected to answer a statistical question has a distribution which can be described by its center, spread, and overall shape.

CCSS 6.SP.A.3 Recognize that a measure of center for a numerical data set summarizes all of its values with a single number, while a measure of variation describes how its values vary with a single number.

Summarize and describe distributions.

CCSS 6.SP.B.4 Display numerical data in plots on a number line, including dot plots, histograms, and box plots.

CCSS 6.SP.B.5 Summarize numerical data sets in relation to their context, such as by:
  A. Reporting the number of observations.
  B. Describing the nature of the attribute under investigation, including how it was measured and its units of measurement.
  C. Giving quantitative measures of center (median and/or mean) and variability (interquartile range and/ or mean absolute deviation), as well as describing any overall pattern and any striking deviations from the overall pattern with reference to the context in which the data were gathered.
  D. Relating the choice of measures of center and variability to the shape of the data distribution and the context in which the data were gathered.